Bringing Your Product to Market . . . *In Less Than a Year*

BRINGING YOUR PRODUCT TO MARKET . . . *IN LESS THAN A YEAR*

Fast-Track Approaches to Cashing in on Your Great Idea

DON DEBELAK

WILEY

John Wiley & Sons, Inc.

Published by John Wiley & Sons, Inc., Hoboken, New Jersey.
Published simultaneously in Canada.

For general information on our other products and services please contact our
Customer Care Department within the United States at (800) 762-2974, outside
the United States at (317) 572-3993 or fax (317) 572-4002.

Wiley also publishes its books in a variety of electronic formats. Some content
that appears in print may not be available in electronic books. For more information about Wiley products, visit our web site at www.Wiley.com.

Library of Congress Cataloging-in-Publication Data:

Debelak, Don.
  Bringing your product to market—in less than a year : fast-track approaches
to cashing in on your great idea / Don Debelak.— Rev. and expanded.
      p. cm.
  Rev. and expanded ed. of: Entrepreneur magazine's bringing your product
to market / Don Debelak. 2nd ed. c2001
  ISBN 0-471-71553-0 (pbk.)
 1. New products—Management.   2. New products—Marketing.
3. New business enterprises—United States—Management—Handbooks,
manuals, etc.   I. Debelak, Don. Entrepreneur magazine's bringing your
product to market.   II. Title.
  HF5415.153.D432 2005
  658.5'75—dc22   2005003020

Printed in the United States of America

10 9 8 7 6 5 4 3 2 1

ACKNOWLEDGMENTS

To Emily Conway, my editor, for her support and suggestions during the writing of the book.

To Bill Murphy, for his help with the agreement and contract language throughout the book.

To Jesse Gamble, for his assistance regarding prototypes, engineering documentation, and bill of materials.

To Eric Debelak, for his chapter critiques and reviews that have helped me keep the book straightforward and easy to read.

CONTENTS

PART II   THE FAST TRACK:
LICENSING YOUR IDEA

PART III   THE FAST TRACK:
TURBO-OUTSOURCING

PREFACE
WELCOME TO THE WORLD
OF INVENTING

My first marketing job in 1980 was for a company founded by the inventor of the first reclining dental chair. While he was selling recliners at the Iowa State Fair, a dentist with a bad back said it sure would be nice to have a dental chair that leaned back so that dentists wouldn't have to twist their backs to treat patients. The inventor took that comment and turned it into a $30 million business. By the time I joined the company it had acquired another inventor-based company where a dental serviceman understood that high-speed dental handpieces (also referred to as *dental drills*) that used water coolant would require a new type of vacuum pump. He used that knowledge to create a pump that met the specific needs of dentists, a $5 million business, which he sold for a huge profit.

I've been with inventors and new products ever since, working on more than 100 new products, sometimes as a private consultant, sometimes as a marketing manager of companies, and sometimes working for Small Business Development Centers. I've also written columns about more than 100 inventors for *Entrepreneur* magazine (starting in 2000) and *Business Start-Ups* (1998–2001). The world of inventors has always fascinated me, not because inventors are Einsteins with secret magic formulas, but instead for the opposite reason: Most successful inventors are ordinary people who just took a chance, stepped into the market, and kept working until they succeeded. Their stories do not necessarily reflect sudden flashes of brilliance, but instead consist of simple steps, taken one at a time, and lots of perseverance.

This is my fourth book on inventions since 1990. Every new book has responded to the rapidly changing world, where innovations in the Internet, manufacturing, and research and development (R&D) outsourcing dramatically alter the invention landscape. This book's formula for success has altered dramatically from the previous edition of *Bringing Your Product to Market*. That edition included a 40-step path to market and required a comprehensive knowledge of all product introduction activities. At the time, there was tremendous pressure on the inventor to be able to control all aspects of the new product introduction process. That knowledge was necessary, as the market was not that accepting of inventors. Today is different. Markets look to inventors for new ideas, and the introduction process is simpler, easier, and potentially much faster than even five years ago. This edition has just 10 steps to follow and offers a new fast-track approach, turbo-outsourcing, in addition to the traditional inventor options of licensing and building a company.

The market has changed, but inventors themselves have not. They continue to be ordinary people who believe they can make it big. I receive news clippings and Google alerts about successful inventors, and I have a chance to talk to inventors at invention club meetings and invention conventions as part of my duties as an *Entrepreneur* magazine columnist. I believe, along with many other invention introduction experts I talk to, that more inventors are getting their products to market than ever before. My goal in all my books has been to help inventors win, offering a step-by-step formula for success, with constant cautions that the invention business is not a guaranteed route to profits and that inventors can lose lots of money if they aren't careful. I want you to succeed, and I hope this book helps you profit from your invention. You may contact me at Don Debelak, DSD Marketing, P.O. Box 120861, New Brighton, MN 55112, www.dondebelak.com, or dondebelak@dondebelak.com.

INTRODUCTION
FAST-TRACK INVENTING:
A GAME ANYONE CAN PLAY

A GREAT TIME TO BECOME AN INVENTOR

Today is a wonderful time to try and put your invention on the market. Earlier this year I was at Inpex, an invention convention, and one booth belonged to Dial Corporation, makers of Dial soap, Renuzit air fresheners, and Purex laundry detergents. The company was there looking for products from inventors. And Dial is not alone. The Electronic Retailing Show this year has saved spots for 75 inventors to display their products to direct response TV retailers who are looking for the next hot product. Licensing deals aren't all that is available. Home Depot allows store managers to try out new local products to see whether they will sell. Marketing companies are buying products from one-product inventor companies, and manufacturers are willing to fund start-up costs for inventor products. Inventors are finding their best market reception in years.

What makes today exciting for me is that now the inventing game is spreading out from a small group of serious inventors to include those willing to put in even a little bit of time to promote their ideas—a very big group, since everybody has had at least one new product idea and many people have dozens. Not a week goes by that I don't have several people tell me about an idea they think will sell. Ideas come in all sizes: small potential products for niche markets like the scrapbook industry; big-time consumer product ideas like roll-up silicone bakeware; production aids for manufacturers; presentation folders for business-to-business presentations; and mathematical games for high school educators. Inventors even succeed with products like easy-to-install highway guardrails. I've written stories for *Entrepreneur* and *Business Start-Ups* magazines about more than 100 inventors who have had their product pass the $1 million sales mark. What is amazing to me is the variety of products that sell; there is no single type of product that always succeeds or always fails to succeed. My favorite inventor story is about a retired chemist named Bob Black. His wife nagged him to do something about eliminating mildew in their shower. Black finally succumbed to his wife's requests and developed Clean Shower, a chemical spray to use on your shower once a day. Not only has the product been a success, but within five years Clean Shower hit the coveted $100 million per year sales level. Look at the adjoining box of inventors. Most of those listed are everyday people with ideas that anyone could have thought of. The only thing that makes these inventors different is that they decided to try marketing their idea.

Inventor Success

Here are just a few of the products that might be familiar to you.

Jay Sorenson, Java Jacket—coffee cup sleeve to allow people to comfortably hold a hot cup of coffee

Bob Olodort, Stowaway Keyboard—folding keyboard for personal digital assistants (PDAs) that fits into a suit pocket

Bob Evans, Force Fins—high-performance swimming fins for navy personnel and underwater photographers

Wayne Willert, Gutter-Bolt—an aluminum bolt for attaching gutters that won't bend when hammered

Rod Albert, Bug Button—insect repellent you wear on a shirt so you don't need insect sprays

Dan Grace and Jeff Polke, Everywhere Chair—outdoor chair with adjustable legs for camping and golf tournaments

Brian Glover and Francisco Guerra, Date-Rape Drug Test Kit—drink coasters with test circles that show whether a drink is safe

Mary Ellroy, Great States—board game targeted at middle-school-age children

Jeff Pettit, Floppy Sprinkler—sprinkler that avoids misting to improve water distribution patterns

Marcel Sbrollini, Java-Log—easy-to-ignite, long-lasting fireplace log made from coffee grounds

Scott Androff and Bruce Hilson, Atmosklear Odor Eliminator—spray that attacks and eliminates unwanted odors

William Boyer, digEplayer—personal in-flight entertainment center that replaces current integrated expensive in-flight entertainment centers

Glen and Sheri Hogel, Easy Motion CPM—a keyboard that moves up and down to reduce carpal tunnel syndrome symptoms

Jason Clute, Prop-A-Bye Baby—sleeping aid for babies that keeps them from rolling over on their stomachs while sleeping

Daniel Henry, Wipe-Out—CD repair kit that repairs or replaces the CD's optical layer

---

WHAT HAPPENED TO THE ROADBLOCKS?

Inventors still run into roadblocks: the cost of prototypes, funding manufacturing, patent expenses, creating effective packaging, finding distribution, and reducing manufacturing costs. Ten years ago inventors had to overcome all these roadblocks on their own. Today, however, inventors with strong ideas can find help, including financing, from potential partners, from retailers and distributors in the market, and from willing investors.

Why the change? Market forces that worked against inventors in the past have now changed to the inventor's advantage:

- Outsourcing of engineering, manufacturing, marketing, and almost every other function in many small and midsize companies. Outsourcing pays off for inventors in two ways. First, inventors are now looked upon as outsourced R&D vendors or partners, which is a lot better than in past years, when companies frequently wouldn't talk to inventors with great ideas. Second, because many manufacturers now depend on outsourcing work from marketers, they are more willing than ever to financially support a new product. Outsourcing has companies in the right mind-set to look for alliances and partnerships to penetrate new markets, including alliances with inventors. I've found that outsourcing is involved in nearly 50 percent of the last 15 invention columns I've written, and I expect this trend to continue.

- Products that truly stand out in the market are more important than ever for marketers. The market is saturated with new products, but for the most part they are just a rehash of current products on the market. Marketing Intelligence Service (www.productscan.com)

estimates the percentage of innovative new products each year. I've never seen this figure exceed 10 percent. Companies struggle to obtain products that are simply a rehash of established products and won't require cutting their price to leading retailers. Even if they place a product once, without true innovation, marketers will find their product dropped in favor of another company's that offers better pricing and terms. The only way marketers can avoid eroding profit margins at big retailers is to have innovative new products that consumers want. R&D departments no longer use a not-invented-here mentality to resist products from inventors, because they know their companies' survival depends on imaginative products, no matter where they come from.

- Companies have come to realize that inventors often know more about customers' needs and desires than their own marketing departments do. Inventors understand customers, because often inventors are potential customers; they invent products for their own needs. Six Sigma and other quality programs have drilled home the importance of the "voice of the customer." Many companies have learned that they aren't hearing the voice of the customer. Inventors hear the customer because they *are* the customer, and they often develop products that are just what the market wants.

I don't mean to imply that all people in the market will like and buy all inventor products. I expect more inventors will continue to fail than succeed for a variety of reasons. But I do feel that inventors will succeed if they learn how to recognize winning products and understand how to deliver a product with high value to the end user. That's the knowledge I hope to deliver to you in this book.

FAST TRACK TO SUCCESS

The changes in the market for inventors has opened up another exciting possibility for inventors, a new fast track, called *turbo-outsourcing*, whereby an inventor outsources production to an investing manufacturing partner and sales to an investing marketing partner, while the inventor maintains control. Usually, the fast track forces the inventor to give up some share of his or her invention, but giving up a portion of the invention also reduces the inventor's risk and allows inventors to move on to another product if things don't work out. The fast-track turbo-outsourcing formula isn't for everybody. It calls for strong skills in negotiating and deal-making mentality, and it moves faster than some inventors may like. But the fast-track formula will appeal to many readers, especially those who want to turn inventing into a high-paying career.

Ten Steps to Invention Success

1. Create the great idea.
2. Know the market and the competition.
3. Find key helpers and financing.
4. Obtain patents and prototypes.
5. Choose a path to market, licensing, turbo-outsourcing, or building a company.
6. Demonstrate that the product will sell.
7. Choose your licensing, outsourcing, or distribution targets.
8. Preserve your capital.
9. Develop a winning plan.
10. Sell, sell, sell.

INSPIRATION TO MOVE AHEAD

This book is written for two types of inventors: (1) serious inventors who have already invested in an idea and are looking for ways to maximize their chances for success; (2) people with a potentially winning idea but not a lot of invention knowledge who are sitting on the sidelines. I hope to inspire every reader to at least check out the market potential of his or her invention. The time has never been better, and most people can complete the 10 steps offered in this book without risking their life savings.

If you are still on the fence about moving ahead, visit my web site, www.dondebelak.com, where I've listed more than 100 articles about inventors, no different than the average reader, who have turned an invention idea into a winning product. Read their stories and you'll realize you can do the same. Appendix D in the back of this book lists most of the inventions discussed in the book, their inventors, and a Web page where you can read their stories. When you join the ranks of successful inventors, drop me an e-mail at dondebelak@dondebelak.com and I'll try to feature you in a magazine story.

PART I

PREPARE FOR SUCCESS

1

STEP 1. EVALUATE POTENTIAL IDEAS: RECOGNIZE THE MONEYMAKERS

There are three types of inventions. The first is what I call *technology-enhanced ideas*, which are inventions that use current technology to improve existing products. For example, engineer Lonnie Johnson created the Super Soaker, those superpopular high-powered squirt guns, by borrowing industrial pumping technology to build air pressure and develop more thrust in a squirt gun. The second category, *technology-created products,* arises when a newly discovered technology leads to the development of entirely new products—such as Segway Human Transporters (those balancing two-wheel scooters by Dean Kamen), microwave ovens, and weed whackers. The first two categories are dominated by inventors with a technology background, typically not the everyday person. The third and by far the largest, category—*end-user-dominated inventions*—are new product ideas geared toward satisfying the people using the product. I've found that end-user-dominated inventions represent more than 80 percent, and probably more than 90 percent, of the inventions from individuals. Inventors find ideas in their everyday lives, work, or hobbies. The inventions might meet a functional need in the everyday world, like the Java Jacket, which provides extra insulation for paper coffee cups so people don't burn their fingers; they might come from employees assisting their employers, such as a portable in-flight entertainment system that cuts the cost of in-flight entertainment by $1 million per plane; or they might jump-start people into scrapbooking,

9

like the Scrapbook Genie, which offers almost 30 easy-to-use scrapbook templates. People come up with these kinds of ideas all the time.

I know that most readers already have an idea in mind. You'll be in great shape if your idea scores well in this chapter's product evaluation. Even if your product doesn't score well, don't worry; you will probably create another idea with high potential. You learn in this chapter not only to look in your life for new products ideas but also to follow a scorecard for success that helps you recognize which ideas have a chance to succeed. This chapter covers how to:

- Generate a great idea: Discover "hot" product ideas in your daily life.
- Search for winning characteristics: Use a new product scorecard to forecast success.
- Perform quick and easy market research: Employ tactics that generate quick feedback.
- Know whether your product will make money: Determine perceived value versus manufacturing cost.

Work Irritant Leads to Success

Dan Tribastone was a registered nurse in an orthopedic operating room. Orthopedic surgery requires that the area undergoing surgery be constantly bathed in water. A typical orthopedic surgery requires 75 to 100 liters (20 to 25 gallons) of water per patient. Before Tribastone created the Omni-Jug, disposing of this water was a major problem for the nurses, since they had to use 25 to 35 waste canisters during each procedure. Nurses had to make 150 to 200 new connections to the canisters during every operation. At first Tribastone simply recommended that the hospital purchase larger containers, but a search of available products didn't turn up any containers designed with the proper connections for orthopedic surgery. A major problem for nurses represented major opportunities for an inventor, and Tribastone was poised to cash in.

He failed in his early attempts to find a larger container to modify. The containers all collapsed with the required vacuum pressure, but in time he was able to find a larger, 3.5-gallon container that could withstand the pressure. After adding a couple of ports for input and evacuation, Tribastone introduced the Omni-Jug, which has since had annual sales of more than $5 million per year. Two keys in Tribastone's success were (1) he knew exactly what the product had to do because he used the products himself every day; and (2) he was able to establish quick rapport with his target audience early in his sales effort because he worked in the same environment as they did.

GENERATE A GREAT IDEA: DISCOVER "HOT" PRODUCT IDEAS IN YOUR DAILY LIFE

Everyday inventors glean ideas from everyday life. The best ideas improve product performance, meet a critical customer need, or simply have widespread appeal because of the product's status or technology. Often these ideas are right in front of you, but you have to exercise some creative thinking to identify them. I frequently teach invention classes, and to demonstrate how frequently we overlook the obvious I ask how many people are satisfied with the hot water systems in their shower. Most people raise their hand. When I ask what they do before they get into a shower, people typically respond that they stick a hand in the shower to make sure the water is the right temperature. My next question is, why would people do that? People look at me and reply that they don't want to get burned. Then I ask how the water company knows not to charge you for the water wasted before you hop into the shower. People respond, logically, that the water company simply charges you for all the water. By the time I'm finished, people are starting to wonder about their hot water system. Perhaps it isn't nearly as efficient as they first thought. Some inventors have tried to produce a means for instant hot water in the bathroom, but at $300 to $500 a pop, the solution is too expensive. Someday an inventor will discover an economical solution. The point is that everyone's lives have at least a few problems waiting for solutions. Those problems are all opportunities for the inventors who notice them.

Potential ideas are everywhere, but learning to see them requires a perceptive outlook. You can start by using four criteria to determine where to look for a potentially winning idea:

1. *What is important to you?* At home, important items might be things you use frequently; accessories to your passions, hobbies, or collections; or something your children or your pets need. The Swiffer, a mop with a throwaway dust-accumulating cover, is a good example of a frequently used product. People clean their floors all the time, and they were ready for an easier-to-use product. At work, an important item would be something that produces more profits or better products for your employer. William Boyer, an employee of Alaska Airlines, knew how expensive in-flight entertainment systems were so he created the digEplayer, a much cheaper in-flight personal entertainment player.

2. *What annoys you?* Too-hot coffee cups at the 7-Eleven were the inspiration for the Java Jacket from Jay Sorenson. Mountain bikers Frank Hermansen and Carl Winefordner thought it was too difficult to change a bike tire and came up with a 10-second tire-changing tool for bikes.

3. *What would be nice?* Someone in the late 1990s decided a mulching lawn mower would be nice, and today they are the dominant type of lawn mowers. Brian Glover and Francisco Guerra thought it was dangerous for women to accept drinks in public settings due to the availability of date-rape drugs in today's bar scene, so they created a coaster with test circles that would activate a warning from even one drop of a drink that had been tampered with. Bryon and Melody Swetland thought glow-in-the-dark bubbles would be great fun for students and young adults, and they responded by creating Tekno Bubbles. The same opportunities apply at work. Patrick McNaughton, who worked in a restaurant, thought it would be nice to write dinner specials on a board that people could read in the dark. So he came up with fluorescent chalk that would glow under neon lighting.

4. *What would finish a job more quickly or easily?* People buy one product to provide a total solution to whatever they are trying to accomplish. Look for products that need other products to finish a job. The Scrubber, a dishwashing tool with a handle that drips dishwashing soap into a scrub brush is a good example. It eliminates the need to add soap to your brush each time you do dishes. Brad Young was a diehard outdoor enthusiast who liked music. Rather than struggle to comfortably use his headphones with a hat, he came up with the HeadBANdZ, a headband with built-in headphones.

Now you need to start using these four tactics to come up with ideas for inventions. Your goal is to list ideas that you want to explore, not necessarily whether you've discovered a potential product winner. Don't worry now about how to make the invention, how to get a patent, or how to build a prototype. Your first step is simply to make a list of two to five, maybe more, ideas for which there is potentially enough end-user demand to justify moving ahead.

SEARCH FOR WINNING CHARACTERISTICS: USE A NEW PRODUCT SCORECARD TO FORECAST SUCCESS

Your first evaluation determines whether the product is perceived to be unique, with obvious and important benefits, and whether the product will have the right distribution channels. Use the product scorecard (see Figure 1.1) to rate your product on a 1-to-5 scale, with 1 being *very true* and 5 being *not true*. Your product should rate a 1 or 2 for at least half the responses. Explanations for each item follow the scorecard.

Figure 1.1 New Product Scorecard: Inventor Evaluation

	1	2	3	4	5
The product has the "wow" factor.					
People agree with your premise.					
The product offers a total solution.					
The product targets people with passion.					
The product relates to an emerging market.					
The product targets new trends in existing markets.					
The product offers few technical challenges.					
Targeted customers can easily find the product.					
The product conveys its major benefits quickly.					
The product avoids competition with category-dominating companies.					

1. *The product has the "wow" factor.* When you have a product that does great things or meets important needs it will resonate with people. Later in the chapter I explain how to test the product idea with more people, but here's the first question: When you first thought of the idea, did your eyes open wide and did you say, "Yes, this is it. I've got a great idea."

2. *People agree with your premise.* Many times you have a premise, or a reason for your idea. Brad Young's premise for his Head-BANdZ was that it is annoying to deal with both a hat or headband and headphones during outdoor fall and winter activities. For the Swetlands and their Tekno Bubbles, the premise was that people love to buy gimmicks to liven up a party.

3. *The product offers a total solution.* Cutting the number of products required for an activity from three to two isn't all that impressive in the market, but you hit pay dirt when you cut the products needed to just one. Consider Christmas tree lights. When people

string lights across the eaves of their house or in front-yard trees they are forced to deal with lots of extension cords. One solution has been to have a cord with an eight- or ten-cord receptacle box on the end. That reduces the difficulty in connecting the cords, but you still need many extension cords. Kevin O'Rourke created a total solution with the ElectraTrac, an extension cord that has a plug-in every eight feet. Within two years his product sales exceeded $3 million during the Christmas season. The Electra-Trac is a total solution because customers need only one cord.

4. *The invention targets people with passion.* Everyone is passionate about something, and you want people you are targeting to be passionate about your type of product. When people care about a product they evaluate it closely, read magazines, attend trade shows, and are generally easy to contact. They also buy products for their passion and are willing to spend more money to get a better-quality product. Passionate people will also replace a perfectly good product if they see something better on the market. Gourmet cooks have passion and are an ideal market for cooking supplies. If people aren't passionate, they may buy the same product previously purchased, without even considering other options.

   In the case of business purchases, products that have importance to or impact on a company produce similar results: A product that improves fit and finish of a consumer product would be valuable to a company that had a perceived quality problem.

5. *The product relates to an emerging market.* During 2003, inventors introduced many new products to the scrapbook market. Scrapbooking had just started to take off, and products were first sold in small scrapbook stores. As scrapbooking caught on, large chains such as Michaels started adding scrapbook sections to their stores. Individuals and inventors who understood what scrapbookers wanted supplied many of the market's initial products. Sales were relatively easy because stores need products to fill their shelves. This same situation existed when kitchen-organizing shops such as Lechters first opened and when personal digital assistants (PDAs) became popular. The first cell phone accessories, such as belt holders and earphones, also came primarily from inventors.

   For businesses, new trends are often the result of new processes, systems, or equipment that becomes popular. Inventors are the ones who typically come up with auxiliary products to make new innovative equipment or to make manufacturing and office systems work better. Supporting tools, such as sliding keyboard shelves for computers, shelving for office cubicles, and sharpening devices for new cutting tools, are examples of products introduced by inventors to support new technology or products.

6. *The product targets new trends in existing markets.* Stay up-to-date in areas where you have a passion and take advantage of the latest trends. If you love dirt-bike racing, that's where you look for trends. You can also check with your family, friends, and acquaintances. When you talk to people, ask what they are passionate about, what their hobbies are, and what other interests they might have. Ask how that area is changing, what new things are occurring, and in what directions the market is going. I've found that at least 4 out of 10 people have some area that they are passionate about, and about half of those people are involved in an area where major market changes are developing. That means 2 out of 10 people might know a developing trend that you could act on.

7. *The product offers few technical challenges.* Inventors can and do introduce technically difficult products (the Apple computer was invented by two individuals), but this type of invention requires more money and more time than you are likely to have. You don't need to invent a technical product to be successful. Rollerblades, invented by Scott Olson, are not technically complicated at all, but they became an enormous success. Products with few technical challenges take less time and money to introduce, and they present far fewer challenges to the average inventor.

8. *Targeted customers can easily find the product.* Products are easy to find if you can buy them at a specialty store, from a catalog or mass merchandiser, and/or on a variety of Internet web sites. One of the nice features of a scrapbook product is that your target customers frequently go to scrapbook stores and will see your product several times during a six-month period. George Gruber's GeoMask, a tool for quickly applying masking tape to woodwork when painting, is sold in paint stores, in hardware stores, and by mass merchandisers. People painting can see the product every time they look at paint colors to buy. This exposure to target customers, which is not difficult to achieve for the right type of product, helps inventors build sales momentum.

Other products don't fit easily into a buying category. Where do people looking for a Date-Rape Drug Test Kit go if they want to buy it? For that matter, how do they even know it exists unless the inventors can afford a promotional campaign? Bars aren't places in which people will look to buy it, and the product has a negative connotation for a bar, implying that customers are at risk of receiving a doctored drink. Inventors can run into many problems when there is not a logical place to sell the product to end users. The inventors, Brian Glover and Francisco Guerra, finally found a successful outlet in convenience stores, where young women stopped to buy last-minute supplies. Before that success, their efforts to sell the product to bars, liquor stores, liquor companies, and drugstores all failed.

Finding Distribution

Kelly Greene liked swimming laps for recreation and fitness, but when she moved into an apartment complex the pool was too small to provide a meaningful workout. She decided that the solution was to find a way to swim in place. Greene tried several ways to hold her ankle so would swim in place, but everything she tried caused rubbing and abrasions. Greene found her solution when she saw surfboarders using plastic leashes to attach the board to their ankle. With some minor modifications, Greene had a product that wouldn't rub her ankle, and her product was ready to go. But sporting goods stores, the logical sales location, wouldn't take it. They had never sold a similar product and didn't think there was much demand for a product that allowed people to swim in place.

Greene's next step was to generate support for her product. She started talking to swim teams and showing them how her product could increase the number of places swimmers could train. After several years of persistence, the UCLA swim team started using Greene's product, and that started the ball rolling, as other teams adopted her training method. Sporting goods stores still wouldn't handle the product, because Greene's store display took up too much room. Greene finally achieved success when her displays started to sell products in pool supply stores. It was a long road for Greene because her product didn't fit in an established category.

9. *The product conveys its major benefits quickly.* Complex packaging and promotion are expensive, and since most inventors can't afford that expense their products need to sell themselves. Conveying benefits quickly means that 50 percent of the prospects can look at your product for about two to five seconds and know what it is and what its benefits are. A paint-can collar that keeps paint from dripping down the side conveys its benefits in one second. You'll know you have a winner when someone sees your product and says, "Hey, I know what that's for." Retail stores and distributors are heavily influenced by how quickly a product's benefits are grasped by customers; only when consumers have

this immediate understanding will products move off the shelf. Most inventors will find that the distribution network won't take a product if its benefits are unclear.

10. *The product avoids competition with category-dominating companies.* Rubbermaid dominates rubber-based housewares products. The company controls shelf space with a broad product line in supermarkets, at mass merchandisers, in hardware stores, and just about everywhere else this type of product line is sold. Breaking in a new product against Rubbermaid is tough, mostly because retailers like the convenience of buying the entire line from one supplier. Inventors have a much easier time selling into a fragmented market, where stores fill their shelves with products from a variety of manufacturers.

The 10 criteria on the product scorecard help you choose the best ideas to pursue. You need to be flexible in choosing an idea to pursue, because a product is rarely an ideal fit with each and every criterion. Selecting an idea calls for the inventor to weigh all the factors and choose the ideas with the best potential. I believe the most important consideration in any idea's potential is how innovative the idea is and the strength of its "wow" factor. The market wants and needs products with a high "wow" factor, and those products can overcome all sorts of obstacles to make it to market.

PERFORM QUICK AND EASY MARKET RESEARCH: EMPLOY TACTICS THAT GENERATE QUICK FEEDBACK

Defining Your Idea

Clarifying the features and benefits of your product will help you communicate your product idea with a brochure or handout, which you will need for initial market testing. Sometimes a product looks much better in your mind than it does on paper. This process helps you flesh out your idea a little more so you can better judge its potential. Start by laying out a simple one- or two-page document labeled "Preliminary Product Specifications—Product Name" and include the following nine points.

1. *Brief product description.* Try to limit this to one or two sentences. If the description takes more than that, your idea is too complicated.
2. *Target customer.* List those you think will buy your product. If several groups of target customers might buy it, list the primary group (those who will want the product most) first.

3. *Why the product is needed.* Explain why you feel a new product is needed in the market.

4. *Main product benefits.* List no more than three benefits. List only the ones that will make a difference in the buyer's purchasing decision.

5. *Product features.* Here you should list every product feature, even ones that you won't promote and those that don't make any difference in the purchasing decision. This list helps prevent you from omitting something during the design process.

6. *Product components.* Include every major piece that goes into the product. Listing the components helps you realize just how simple or complicated a product will be.

7. *How the product works.* A brief description of three to four lines should be sufficient.

8. *Process product assists.* This is needed only for an invention that is an accessory or aid to a process. For example, if you have a new type of dispensing tip for cake frosting that makes it possible to create better cake decorations, your invention is part of the process of decorating a cake. You then want to list which decorating tubes your invention will fit. This is often a key item for industrial inventions or auto repair tools and other service-related items that facilitate an already existing process.

9. *Preliminary drawing.* A drawing, even a simple line drawing of your product, is essential to show placement of the features and how they will look on the product. If you are unable to produce a rough drawing yourself, ask at art stores or art schools for the names of people who would do a drawing inexpensively.

Conducting an Early Screening with Friends, Family, and Acquaintances

Family and friends can help you determine whether you have a great idea and whether they'd be users of the product. But you can't just ask people if they like your idea. You will get the best feedback if you set up a test. Here are a few simple guidelines to prevent overly friendly advice.

- *Have evaluators sign a confidential statement.* Appendix C has a sample Statement of Confidentiality and Nonuse. You receive two benefits from having people sign a statement of confidentiality: (1) It provides a written record that you are keeping your idea secret, which will help provide documentation about the date you first had your idea. (2) It will provide evidence that you

Preliminary Product Specification

Portable Workstation for Bikes

1. *Brief product description:* A holding device for bicycle repair that can be mounted on a post, tree, or two-by-four. Allows repair in the field or at home.

2. *Target customer:* Serious bike enthusiasts, racers, and mountain bike riders who fine-tune their own bikes between uses and make their own repairs.

3. *Why the product is needed:* Bikes need to be lifted off the ground and held stationary for best results during tune-ups and repairs. Currently, bulky and costly bike repair stations are required, and bikers aren't able to take them to a race for between-heat tune-ups and/or repairs. Bike races and events have several heats, and, especially on mountain bike events, riders would like to make bike adjustments between heats.

4. *Main product benefits:* Field-repair bike station that is easily transported and assembled. Less bulky and less expensive for home repairs.

5. *Product features*
   a. Strap can be adjusted to mount on poles or on a tree up to 12 inches in circumference.
   b. Clamping mechanism holds up to 125 pounds.
   c. System folds up into a 6- by 6- by 18-inch package.
   d. Bike holding system will adjust to handle most bikes on the market.

6. *Product components*
   a. Adjustable strap
   b. Clamping mechanism to attach to tree or pole
   c. Holder (positioned on strap) for frame, front- and rear-wheel stabilizing bars
   d. Adjusting mechanism in holder to accommodate different bike sizes
   e. Locking device to hold bars stationary in the holding device
   f. Front- and rear-wheel clamping device
   g. Frame clamping device
   h. Bar from holder on strap to frame holder

7. *How product works:* The bike stand is quickly mounted on a pole or tree, and the strapping mechanism has built-in ribs to hold the strap firmly. Three rods, which can be rotated, attach to the front and back wheel and center frame. Once locked in place the bars hold the bike rigid.

haven't publicly disclosed your idea in case of a patent dispute. Signing a confidentiality statement will also help put your participants in a more serious frame of mind; they will realize that you are about to spend money to introduce your idea, and as a result they will be more careful in their evaluations.

- *Collect a range of products.* People are buying your product for a reason: Maybe they need a good party favor or a tool for surfacing a driveway. You want to find other products that people buy for the same reason they will buy yours. The products do not have to mirror existing products; they need only to serve a similar purpose.

  In some cases, especially for a brand-new product type, find similarly priced products in the same category, even though they may not be used for the same purpose. For example, once I was doing a test on Dishnet, a net that keeps plastic glasses and baby products from flying around the dishwasher. There was only one product for the same use on the market and it was more of a rack than a net. Therefore I couldn't test five or six other products that keep plastic glasses and baby products in the dishwasher rack. Instead I found other plastic kitchen-related devices, including one that prevents milk from spilling when a container is full, a different style of Tupperware-type container, an apple-coring device, a banana holder, and similar items (see Figure 1.2).

- *Make a sales flyer for your product idea.* If you have a prototype, show that along with the other products; if you don't, create a brochure or an Internet page that shows a picture of the product and list its features and benefits clearly and concisely. Then do the same for the other products you plan to have people evaluate at the same time. If your flyer is just a rough draft, cut out pictures of similarly priced products and make a rough flyer for each of them.

  Your goal is to have people evaluate all products with similar information. Pasting Internet photos on a sheet of paper with a little bit of copy about features and benefits works just fine. You don't want people comparing a nice product they can feel and touch to just a sales flyer for your product. The ideal situation is when people don't even know which product idea is yours.

- *Ask people to rate the products they are most likely to buy.* Have the people rank each product based on how likely they are to buy it, with 1 being the product they are most likely to buy. You don't need to have every customer rate your product as a 1 or 2. However, you do want at least 25 percent of the people to rate your product highly. Otherwise, the product just doesn't have enough appeal to sell well.

Figure 1.2 New Product Scorecard for Dishnet and Similar Products

Product	*Likely to Buy**	*Value†*	*Reason for "Likely to Buy" Rating*	*Reason for "Value" Rating*
Dishnet				
Easy-pour milk spout				
New style of Tupperware-type container				
Apple-coring device				
Banana holder				
Sponge Glove				

* Rate the products from 1 to 6, with 1 being the product you are most likely to buy.

† Rate the products from 1 to 6, with 1 being the product perceived to have the most value.

- *Ask people to rate products by value, with the highest value first.* The actual perceived value of a product is one of the toughest points for inventors to determine. This step helps clarify perceived value because every product you use for testing has a known price. If people consistently place your product between those costing $8 to $12 you will know your product has a perceived value of $9 to $11.

- *Ask people why they rated products highly or poorly.* Asking people this question helps you in two ways. First it helps you understand features people want or don't want in their product. This helps you decide on your own final feature mix. More important, I like to use lots of follow-up questions to better understand what potential buyers want in a product. For example, on a stationary bike rack some might say they rated the product poorly because they didn't like the way the front wheel was locked. You can then ask why they didn't like that feature. A respondent may state that the stand will make one or more repairs difficult. You can finish by asking what design might work better for that person.

Evaluating How Others Score Your Product

After the initial screening, adjust your product to include the features people want and exclude the features that bothered people. After incorporating your test group's input you should be able to answer yes to the following questions. (If you can't, you may want to make some additional adjustments to your idea).

- Did at least 25 to 35 percent of the people rate your product among the top three products they would most likely buy?
- Did people grasp your product's benefit quickly?
- Was the product perceived to be clearly different?
- Was your benefit perceived to be significantly better?
- Does your product have a strong perceived value?

If your idea didn't do well in the test, don't immediately drop your idea. If you asked your participants lots of follow-up questions you may have gathered information needed to move forward. Look over your responses from your survey and consider these three points.

1. *Did people have a strong positive or negative reaction to the products?* Strong reactions about a product indicate either that the product is important to prospects or that people find current products inadequate. You should work a little harder on the idea if people

---

Hit Cost Targets for Success

Ross Youngs first invented the Safety-sleeve, a sleeve using a clear plastic that allowed CDs to be stored in three-ring, fabric, and clear plastic binders. The Safety-sleeve was a big success, and 1.5 billion sleeves are sold per year. One thing Youngs learned from his first product was that the right manufacturing costs are key in determining profitability. Youngs was looking for another idea to introduce when he noticed that three-ring binders didn't stack well and looked old-fashioned for sales presentations. He decided to use his knowledge of plastics to create the UniKeep, a stackable, flat three-ring binder that provides a great-looking presentation tool for salespeople. To be sure he would make money, Youngs started by figuring out what the product could sell for in the stores. His binder was more deluxe than the traditional three-ring binder but still had to compete with it. After doing market research, Youngs set his retail target price at $3.00. He then set his manufacturing target cost at 60 cents and his packaging costs at 10 percent of the manufacturing costs, or 6 cents. To meet those cost targets, Youngs had to figure out a way to make the binder, including the plastic rings in the plastic mold, in one step and how to put product information inside the UniKeep to keep packaging costs down. At the right price, the UniKeep was a good value. Shortly after its introduction, sales exceeded $2.5 million per year.

---

are looking for something better. If people are satisfied or ambivalent toward most products, you should pursue another product area that people feel passionate about.

2. *Was there a consistency about an unmet need in the product category that you may have overlooked in your product?* If so, could you meet this need with new product features or some modifications to your idea? Just because people don't see your premise as being true or important doesn't mean that another need or premise won't work for them.

3. *Did the people understand and appreciate the benefits of your idea?* Inventors see and understand the benefit of an idea clearly, and often they just assume that other people see their idea as clearly as they do. That is almost never the case. You might have the benefit that will really sell, but on your first pass people don't see it. You may need to rework your idea or brochure so people grasp its benefit. If people don't see your benefit, ask them what would help them see it better. You may be able to make some simple changes to clarify your benefits for customers.

KNOW WHETHER YOUR PRODUCT WILL MAKE MONEY: DETERMINING PERCEIVED VALUE VERSUS MANUFACTURING COST

Determining the Price/Value Relationship

You had some indication of the price you can charge in your earlier research with family and friends. Your next best step is to do a similar focus group survey with people you *don't* know to determine what they might be willing to pay for your product. You might find, though, that it is difficult to get people to spend that much time with you. In that case, you can use a product questionnaire as a substitute to determine the price point people feel comfortable with. Figure 1.3 is a product comparison for a new style of window awning (to keep out the sun on hot days) that can be easily taken down in the winter to prevent winter damage. The inventor thinks the easily detachable awning will create a buzz in northern climes and wants to know whether the market will support the product and its price despite its shorter life compared to competitive awnings. Be sure to notice the questions at the end of the questionnaire comparing this purchase to other potential home purchases. What you do to gauge the price/value relationship is vary the pricing of your product in several different versions of your questionnaire. For example, for the knockdown awning you might show a price range in one questionnaire of $400 to $550 and in another of $1,000 to $1,200. The questionnaires should show a

Figure 1.3 Knockdown Awning System Product Questionnaire

Product description: A new, less expensive, lightweight canvas awning alternative. The product has permanently attached top and side holding bars, but the rest of the awning can be quickly detached and stored. The awning would have a life of 5 to 6 years versus a life of 7 to 10 years for a standard heavy-canvas awning and 10 to 15 years for an aluminum or metal awning. This lightweight awning requires less maintenance, especially in the colder climates, where it could be removed in the winter.

Yes _____ No _____ Do you have windows in your home that receive too
much sun on hot days?

Yes _____ No _____ Do you have any awnings on your home now, or have
you had them in the past?

Consider the following options for the next questions:

A. Vertical, insulating window blinds; cost for a double window, $650.00
B. Standard heavy canvas awning; price for a double window, $850 to $1,200
C. Knockdown lightweight awning; price for a double window, $600 to $750
D. Aluminum or steel permanent awning; price for a double window, $1,200
   to $1,500

   [If possible, attach drawings or pictures for people to review.]

Rate the four options in the order you would buy them, with the product you would buy first rated 1.

_____ A. _____ B. _____ C. _____ D.

List the top reasons for choosing this model.

_____ Appearance
_____ Ability to remove in winter
_____ Ability to open in winter
_____ Ease of maintenance
_____ Ease of installations
_____ Ability to open on cloudy days
_____ Product life
_____ Familiarity with product
_____ Price
_____ Blocks out the most sun

Rate the models below 1, 2, and 3, with 1 placed next to the option you like best.

1. _____ A. _____ B. _____ C.
   A. Lightweight, easily removed aluminum awnings, $1,400
   B. Standard canvas awning that snaps onto an aluminum frame; awning
      can be removed but frame stays on the house, $1,100
   C. Steel, permanently attached awning, $1,400
2. _____ A. _____ B. _____ C.
   A. New knockdown lightweight canvas awning, $650
   B. Heavy canvas awning with removable sidebars so the awning can be
      rolled up (rather than just folded in half), $1,000

(Continued)

Figure 1.3 *Continued*

C. Heavy canvas awning that stays down all year long,
$800

3. _____ A. _____ B. _____ C.

A. New knockdown lightweight canvas awning, $650

B. Heavy canvas awning on same frame as the knockdown awning,
$875.00

C. Lightweight, easily removable aluminum awning, $1,400

4. _____ A. _____ B. _____ C.

A. Heavy canvas awning that stays up all year long, $800

B. Heavy canvas awning that can be easily rolled up on cloudy days,
$1,000

C. Heavy canvas awning on the same frame as the new knockdown
awning, $875

5. _____ A. _____ B. _____ C.

A. Knockdown lightweight canvas awning, $650

B. Knockdown lightweight canvas awning that can be rolled up on cloudy
days, $800

C. Knockdown lightweight canvas awning with an extra layer of material
underneath to better block out the sun, $750

Rate the following features 1 through 12 in order of how important they are to
you.

_____ Appearance

_____ Ability to block out the sun

_____ Can be rolled up on cloudy days

_____ Can be removed in winter

_____ Durability

_____ Price

_____ Ease of maintenance

_____ Ease of installation

_____ Weight of fabric (preference: _____ heavy _____ light)

_____ Metal or aluminum versus canvas

_____ Past performance history

_____ Recommendation of friends

Rate the following prospective purchases from 1 to 6 based on the possibility
of your buying each product. Rate your most likely purchase 1.

_____ Storage shed for the backyard, $800–$1,000

_____ Insulating, high-security steel front door, $750–$850

_____ Low-maintenance aluminum gutters, one side of the house, $600

_____ New knockdown lightweight awnings, one double window, $650

_____ New curtains for the living room, $900

_____ Storm doors for sliding double doors to patio, $600

sharp drop in your product's acceptance at some price point—the point at which the market assigns its top dollar value for your product. If it's easy to find people to take the survey, give everyone only one survey. If you have a limited number of people to choose from, you may give them surveys with different price points and still receive valid input.

Determining Preliminary Manufacturing Costs

The two major cost components are the actual manufacturing costs and the packaging costs. About 7 to 10 percent of a product's total costs are smaller items, including scrap rework, warranty returns, and product liability. For this preliminary stage you need only worry about manufacturing and packaging costs. Unfortunately, there isn't an easy way to estimate manufacturing costs with just the product specification drawings you did earlier in the chapter. You also may have a tough time estimating your manufacturing costs for low-volume production. You can approximate costs by using comparable products when obtaining quotes. Here are seven guidelines that will help.

1. Find a product that is about the same size, is made of the same materials, and has about the same complexity as your product that is already being sold on the market. Anything at all similar to your product helps. For example, if your product holds garden tools such as rakes, is made of high-impact plastic, is 24 inches high by 24 inches wide by 18 inches deep, and has 12 slots for tools, you would look for another product made of similar high-impact plastic parts with similar complexity. That could be a laundry-sorting holder, a basement shelf system, a stereo rack, or an office supply product.

2. Estimate the actual production costs of the similar product. Since most products sell at a retail price that is three to four times their manufacturing costs, you should take the comparable product's retail price and multiply it by 25 percent (or 0.25). For example, if the similar product's retail price is $19.99, you would estimate its production costs as follows: $19.99 × 0.25, or approximately $5.00.

3. Find manufacturers who have the equipment to produce products similar to your product and the comparable product. There are several ways you can find these manufacturers:
   - Ask contacts in the industry.
   - Look in the Yellow Pages or in a business-to-business telephone book.
   - Look in your state and surrounding states' industrial directories.
   - Use the *Thomas Register of American Manufacturers* to find local companies that manufacture products made similarly to yours.

- Get assistance from your local Small Business Development Center (SBDC), at www.sbaonline.gov, or Service Corps of Retired Executives (SCORE), at www.sba.gov/gopher/Local-Information/Service-Corps-Of-Retired-Executives/.
- Check out the web site of *Job Shop Technology* magazine (www.jobshoptechnology.com), which lists manufacturers by type of manufacturing capability.

4. Get a quote for producing 1,000 units of your product and the similar product and for producing 5,000 units of each. You can adjust the numbers, but the lower number should be what you expect for a first production run, and the larger number should be for what you might order in a year.

5. Determine the ratio of your production costs to the established product's production costs. Say the quote to produce 1,000 units of your product is $6.00 and that for the established product is $5.50; then the ratio is 1.09, with your product costing more.

6. Take your estimated cost for the established product (from step 2) and multiply it by your ratio from step 5. Your projected cost would be $5.00 × 1.09, or $5.45. This is not 100 percent accurate, but it gives you an idea of whether your product will make money.

7. Understand the cost differences. Sometimes the costs won't make sense. In the preceding example, a $5.45 price versus $5.00 price might reflect a slightly larger or more complex product. But if the price difference is $15.00 versus $5.00, ask *why*. You may have one or two features that raise the product's price substantially. You might be able to reconfigure those features to cut the cost.

Estimating Packaging Costs

Packing costs can be critical for some products, especially those in the lower price ranges. Packaging can total 20 to 25 percent of the total costs. A small consumer product in a *blister pack* (a clear-plastic molded piece glued to a cardboard backing) might cost 8 cents per piece at high volume or cost 25 cents per piece at low volume. Estimating costs is much simpler for packaging, as you can typically get quotes from packaging suppliers in your town. Follow these three steps to determine your packaging costs.

1. Decide on a type or types of packaging. Look at the products in the marketplace and see which ones have packaging that you like. Don't select just one type, though, as there could be considerable cost differences in packaging types.

2. Visit packaging suppliers in your town and get quotes for your product, or if your product isn't developed ask for a rough quote for packaging just like one you found on the market. You can also

find packaging suppliers, both local and nationwide, in the *Thomas Register of American Manufacturers* (check your library).

3. Ask for quotes that separate the up-front costs. Packaging requires an up-front investment for plates, tooling, and setup. But those are one-time expenses, so your first 1,000 units (which include up-front costs) will cost more than subsequent units. Get quotes that separate the up-front and setup costs from the per-unit price, and just use the per-unit price for the packaging estimate.

Comparing Manufacturing Cost Pricing to Perceived Value

Marketers can compute selling prices in two ways: based on (1) costs or (2) the value that customers place on your product. Cost-based pricing typically prices a product four to five times the cost of its manufacture and is used because that's a price point at which the manufacturer can make money. If a product costs $6.25 to make, the manufacturer knows it must sell the product for $25.00 or there will be no profit. Value-based pricing is determined by what people are willing to pay for your product. Customers don't care if inventors need to sell a product for $25.00; they only care about what the product is worth to them. You want to sell your product at its consumer value, but you don't want to sell the product at a price below what's needed to make money. Your last step is to multiply your manufacturing cost by 4 to get a projected cost-based sales price, then compare it to the value given to the product by the focus groups and production questionnaires you did earlier. You have a great chance to make money if the price based on manufacturing cost is lower than the value-based price. If the value-based price is lower than the cost-based price, you probably won't be successful.

Manufacture cost pricing (4 × cost estimate)   ____
    + packaging costs
Value from focus group sessions   ____
Value from product questionnaire   ____

THE EDGE COUNTS

I believe a product that performs 10 percent better might have 100 percent more sales in the market, which might mean that developing a product with just a 10 percent edge might make the difference between your success and failure. Choosing the right idea is the most crucial decision an inventor makes in the entire process. Take your time to choose the best idea, and then dedicate enough energy and time to perfecting that idea. Inventing is a risky business, so you want to do all you can to improve your odds.

STEP 2. LOOK LIKE A WINNER: DEMONSTRATE BUSINESS SAVVY AND CUSTOMER KNOWLEDGE

Product entrepreneurs have to realize that, before they can sell an idea, they have to first sell themselves. They have to convince people that they understand customers, the competition, and the market. Inventors need to show they will be easy to work with and will be reliable business partners. Inventors also need to have a great attitude with their industry helpers, which includes being confident, appreciative, open to suggestions, and able to cope when things go wrong. This chapter covers the key points you need to learn in order to project a winning image.

- Drop your paranoia: Talk about your product idea.
- Cope with problems: Learn that every situation has a solution.
- Get savvy: Create the right impression with contacts by doing your homework.
- Know your customers: Understand who they are and what they're like.
- Check out the competition: Discover what customers think.
- Create a sizzling difference: Ensure that your product stands out.

DROP YOUR PARANOIA: TALK ABOUT YOUR PRODUCT IDEA

One overwhelming common characteristic of new inventors is paranoia—concern that their great product idea will be stolen and they will end up with nothing for their trouble. That *has* happened to some inventors in the past, but if inventors don't show their idea and get feedback to verify they have a potential winner they could spend thousands, if not tens of thousands, of dollars on an idea that won't go anywhere in the market. There are several reasons why inventors don't need to be paranoid and instead can feel free to get the input they need to (1) know whether their product has a chance of selling profitably and (2) perfect their product for the needs of both the distribution channel and end users.

- *People typically don't steal unproven ideas.* Certainly less than 10 percent and probably less than 5 percent of all new product ideas don't make it to market, and this includes product concepts from major companies. Nobody knows for sure which products will sell. Someone who wants to steal an idea can just copy or modify one that already has some success in market. That is less expensive and risky than taking on an unproven product concept that will require an investment with no assurance the product will sell. As an example, Mr. Coffee, which has several patents, was the first drip coffeemaker on the market, but before long it had at least 10 competitors. Did those other companies steal the idea? Maybe, but most people consider it normal competition.

- *Plenty of ideas are available.* Marketers and companies that know how to promote products have plenty to choose from. They don't have to steal ideas. A marketer looking for products to promote can easily find 50 to 60 each year, and many of those can be bought cheaply from down-and-out product creators.

- *Purchasing an idea doesn't require a large up-front investment.* Ideas are typically not bought outright. Instead, they are usually purchased under a royalty arrangement that pays the inventor anywhere from 1 to 15 percent of the net sales of a product. An inventor with a 5 percent royalty agreement would receive $5,000 for every $100,000 of product sales. The only up-front investment is to the licensee (perhaps a manufacturer or a marketer), in the form of a royalty advance, which could range from $1,000 to $20,000, with the higher amounts only rarely paid. If a company likes your proposal, it can offer you a license rather than stealing the idea.

- *The United States awards patents on a first-to-invent basis.* This offers some protection against thieves, as inventors can receive a patent by showing that they developed the idea first. Inventors can make a strong case for patent rights if they have documentation from a properly witnessed inventor's notebook or other proof of idea conception, including the U.S. Patent and Trademark Office's (USPTO) document disclosure program (go to www.uspto.gov for more information). An inventor's book is a bound book that has numbered pages. You simply write down everything you do while creating your idea, dating the pages and every week or so having someone read the pages, write "I have read and understood this page," and sign and date the page. Here are two web sites with laboratory notebooks: www.eurekalabbook.com/standard_scientific_notebooks.htm and www.snco.com. The document disclosure program allows you to mail a copy of your invention documents to the patent office. The patent office holds the documents for only two years. The date the patent office acknowledges receipt of your idea establishes that you've invented the idea.

COPE WITH PROBLEMS: LEARN THAT EVERY SITUATION HAS A SOLUTION

Things go very wrong all the time in the invention development business. Inventors need to learn early how to cope with these problems—and to do so in a way that inspires confidence in their investors, partners, and helpers. Here are just a few of the problems that inventors run into regularly:

- An investor backs out at the last minute, leaving you $3,000 short for an important purchase.
- Your prototype supplier delivers a unit with the wrong clearance for a key feature.
- Your key distribution contact suddenly quits and moves to California.
- Your product is moved from a store's checkout register to the back of the store.
- The packaging supplier demands $2,000 before releasing any packaging.
- Your patent claims are denied and you have to settle for minor patent claims.
- The licensing deal you are negotiating is canceled at the last minute by the potential licensee's president.
- A new competitive product is introduced at a much lower price than yours.

- The marketing message that people were drawn to in focus groups doesn't work on the product's package.

Don't get upset when things go wrong; it won't produce any results, and your partners, helpers, and contacts will lose faith in you. Instead go through these five steps to find another solution.

1. Determine whether the setback calls for action on your part. Some events, such as a store asking you to take back the product, don't call for immediate action.
2. What action can you take to rectify the problem? You may be able to reverse the situation. You can demand, for instance, that the prototype builder correct an error.
3. Determine two or three options to follow if your first solution doesn't work. For example, if you lose an investor at the last minute, you might (1) contact three other potential investors, (2) request 30-day terms from the supplier, or (3) ask the supplier to accept part ownership in your product.
4. Take action: First try your action to rectify the situation, and then follow your options.
5. Create a timetable for taking action. Set a date by which you hope to rectify the situation first and then allow time to pursue your options.

The worst thing you can do is to hide the problems from your partners or helpers. Tell them what has happened and what you plan to do about it. That is the only way to cope in a positive way with all the problems you'll eventually face with your product.

Looking Good in Every Way

Dan and Russell Schlueter were in the pet business selling the dog treat Harvest Chews when they stumbled across silica sand, a sand with enormous absorbing power. They immediately grasped that silica sand could be a great new kitty litter. At first glance, kitty litter might look like a pretty tough category for inventors. They would need to compete against plenty of competition from big companies while selling into giant pet store chains and supermarkets that typically avoid small-inventor-based firms. But the brothers researched the market and competing products and built a case for their potential success. Four pounds of their product, Crystal Clear Litter Pearls, lasted as long as 28 pounds of traditional kitty litter. That was great for stores, since they would handle less inventory, but the Schlueters knew they

needed an extra edge to break into the market. They decided to set their prod-
uct price high enough to offer supermarkets a bigger margin than they could
get for traditional kitty litter. This meant that a 4-pound bag of Crystal Clear
kitty litter would sell for $14 compared to a 14-pound bag of traditional kitty
litter for $6 to $7. The Schlueters promoted the fact that one package of Crys-
tal Clear Litter Pearls would last as long as 28 pounds of traditional kitty lit-
ter. This meant supermarkets could make more money with less shelf space.
The Schlueters used their knowledge of their competition and their markets to
deliver a winning message and a winning product to their key contacts.

GET SAVVY: CREATE THE RIGHT IMPRESSION WITH CONTACTS BY DOING YOUR HOMEWORK

Contacts won't talk freely with you unless you project a professional image and know the details of introducing your product. Understanding your market is the most important aspect of creating a good impression, and this section covers a wide range of topics you need to comprehend and that can be further elucidated by market research and library inquiry.

Sources for Market Research

You will be able to find some information on your own by observing the market or by talking to people who know the market. Excellent information is also available from trade magazines and associations. *Trade magazines* (as opposed to consumer magazines) target companies, manufacturers, distributors, and/or retailers in a given market. *Air Conditioning, Heating & Refrigeration*, for example, is a trade magazine directed at distributors and manufacturers of residential air-conditioning and heating equipment. Trade magazines publish articles on how their readers can sell their products, which is a great source of market information for inventors. Trade magazines also have large new-product sections. You can always phone people listed as offering new products, especially from smaller companies, and ask questions about market channels. Trade associations are another potential source of market statistics. If you are considering entering a big market, the association may even have local chapters. Those chapters typically have meetings and exhibitions where you can pick up valuable market intelligence. (See resources at the end of the book to locate trade shows and associations.)

Know Your Market

You must know your market if you want to project a professional image. Here are some of the key questions that you'll need answers to: What distribution channels exist in your market? How does your chosen distribution channel work? What pricing and discounts are common in your distribution channel? Which distribution channels are inventor-friendly, and what type of packing does each distribution channel in your market require.

Distribution Channels

Your first step to know a market is to list its *distribution channels,* a term that indicates how a product is sold to end users. There are dozens of potential distribution channels. Distribution channels have two components. One is the final sales outlet to consumers, such as mass merchandisers, convenience stores, Internet stores, direct mail, TV sales, and catalogs. The second component is how you sell to those final outlets, which could be through manufacturers' representatives, independent representatives at trade shows, another marketing company, distributors or brokers, and/or your own sales force (also called *direct sales*). Start by listing all the final sales outlets where end users buy your product; then list ways you could sell the product to each outlet. Each combination of components is a separate channel. For example, a channel selling to drugstores might consist of manufacturer's sales representatives who sell to *rack-jobber distributors* (distributors who rent space in a store and are paid only when a product is sold). Another channel would be selling to that same rack-jobber distributor through your own sales force. Figure 2.1 is a chart for a microwave buddy, a rack that lets you heat up to three plates in a microwave oven at the same time. In some cases, you have two levels of sales to the same outlet. You might sell to distributors who sell to outlets, which would be your first level; then your second level is how you sell to the distributors, which could be manufacturer's representatives or direct sale or some other avenue. When you finish your own chart, talk with someone you know in the market who can verify the chart or suggest how it should be changed.

How the Chosen Distribution Channel Works

List all of your potential distribution channels in a chart similar to Figure 2.1. Then select the sales outlets and distribution channels you want to target. Start with just two channels so you have enough focus to succeed. Inventors may know some of this information already.

List who your channels buy from, who they sell to, and the responsibilities and actions of each party in the channel. For example, rack jobbers buy from distributors, from manufacturer's representatives, or

Figure 2.1   Distribution Chart for Microwave Oven

Sales Outlets	How Outlets Are Sold: First-Level Distribution	How First Level Is Sold: Second-Level Distribution
Mass merchandisers	Manufacturer's representatives	N/A
	Direct sales	N/A
	Distributors	Manufacturer's representatives
		Direct sales
Kitchen stores	Manufacturer's representatives	N/A
	Distributors—traditional	Manufacturer's representatives
		Direct sales
	Distributors—rack jobbers	Manufacturer's representatives
		Direct sales
Hardware stores	Buying groups	Manufacturer's representatives
		Direct sales
	Distributors—traditional	Manufacturer's representatives
		Direct sales
	Distributors—rack jobbers	Manufacturer's representatives
		Direct sales
	Sales through another company	Direct sales
Catalogs	Direct sales	N/A
	Manufacturer's representatives	Direct sales
TV marketing	Through another company	Direct sales
	Through brokers	Direct sales
	Direct sales	N/A

directly from companies. They don't really sell to a store, as they own the merchandise they stock in the store. They collect from the store 65 to 70 percent of the selling price after the merchandise is sold. Their responsibilities include stocking the store frequently, paying rent or leasing shelf space if required, and absorbing the cost of damaged or stolen merchandise. Rack jobbers are common in many markets, including drugstores, supermarkets, and convenience stores, but they are also found in major retailers like Home Depot. Another example is manufacturer's representatives; they don't buy products, but instead receive a commission of from 10 to 15 percent on the products they sell. Stocking distributors buy and stock products and then sell to stores or industrial customers with immediate delivery. Dealers are similar to distributors except that they also typically offer manufacturer-authorized service, installation, and technical support for the products they carry.

List key players. These vary from market to market, but they typically include retailers, distributors, manufacturers, and end users. Key players deciding whether to buy or represent a new product might dictate which products succeed in the market. Key players may or may not be receptive to small-inventor companies for any number of reasons, including bad past experiences, poor financing structure of inventors' firms, loyalty to current suppliers, or just an unwillingness to change. Understanding key players in a market is especially important if you are licensing your idea.

Margins and Discounts

For inventors to make money, they need to sell their product for at least double their manufacturing cost. Every channel has different markups, and the relationship between end-user price and manufacturer's price varies. An inventor selling through wholesalers and rack jobbers might receive only 30 to 35 percent of the final retail price. Figure 2.2 shows a typical cost flow-through chart for a hardware product with a retail price of $100. You want to work out these charts in advance so you understand what your margins need to be when you consider how to price your product to different distribution channels. Additional resources are listed in the back of the book if you can't find this information in trade magazines or association data.

Inventor-Friendly Channels

Distribution channels often distinguish themselves from their competitors by buying from a different set of suppliers than their competition. For example, toy catalogs and specialty toy retailers don't want to carry the same merchandise as mass merchandisers because they can't compete on price, so they buy from smaller companies with innovative lines, which allows them to carry unique products at a higher price. As a rule, each chan-

Figure 2.2   Typical Cost Flow-Through Chart for a Hardware Product

Manufacturer's Share of the Retail Price

Item	Cost	Comments
Retail price	$100	
Less: Retailer discount	40	Can go as high as 50 to 55% in some markets
Distributor discounts	9	10–20% discounts to distributors or manufacturer's sales agents are common
Net to manufacturer	51	Manufacturer's net sales price

Manufacturer's Profit from Its Share of the Retail Price

Item	Cost	Comments
Net to manufacture	51	
Less: Manufacturing cost	25	Includes packaging and shipping
Sales Cost	6	Salespeople, customer service, and order entry
Product support	3	Warranty returns, regulatory approvals, and technical service
Marketing cost	6	Advertising, literature, promotional materials, trade show attendance
Administrative cost	6	Interest charges, accounting, executive salaries, insurance, and legal fees
Equals: Profit	5	$5 of $51 is 10% profit per sales dollar; many manufacturing companies make less than 10% return on sales dollars

nel tends to have a different set of suppliers, with large suppliers favoring the big sales channels and smaller suppliers favoring the smaller specialty market channels.

Inventors do best when they choose a channel that favors smaller suppliers if they want to sell their product on their own, but any channel will work if you plan to license your product or sell through turbo-outsourcing.

Packaging

Distribution channels you use will determine the type of packaging your product requires. A plain box with a product information sheet may be all you need to sell to catalogs or home-shopping TV networks. Drugstores might want products to hang from hooks, and convenience stores might want a high-impulse box placed near the cash register. Packaging can be a major cost, so you want to have only as much packaging as you absolutely need for the distribution channel.

Know Manufacturing Basics

The main reason inventors need to know a little about manufacturing is that people, especially those already in the market, will ask you how the product will be produced or offer you suggestions about how it can be produced. You may also get questions about outsourcing or manufacturing overseas, but those can be deferred simply by answering that you aren't going to worry about overseas manufacturing until you have the final design completed. Your goal in the beginning of the product introduction process is to understand enough about the manufacturing techniques common in your chosen market so that you appear professional to your contacts. Later, this knowledge will help save you money when you pay for prototypes and initial production runs. You can find out about your industry by following these three steps. Check out the resources listed at the back of the book if you want more comprehensive information.

1. Collect data on competitive products. Collect ads, brochures, product packages, or the actual product itself.
2. Collect data on products that are made somewhat similarly. For comparative products it doesn't matter which market they are sold in, only that they appear to be manufactured by a process similar to that used for your product. You can get pictures of these products from consumer or trade magazines, or you can obtain brochures, the products themselves, or product packing information.
3. Find local resources to help explain the manufacturing process used to make each competitive or similar product. Ask your resources how each product is probably made, but also how the product *could* be made and the advantages and costs of each process. Here are some sources you can use:
   - Consult engineers you know.
   - Use local Service Corps of Retired Executives (SCORE) chapters, which typically have several people with extensive

manufacturing experience who will assist you at no (or a nominal) charge (www.sba.gov/gopher/Local-Information/Service-Corps-Of-Retired-Executives).

- Local Small Business Development Centers (SBDCs) can help you, or if they can't, they'll know local contacts you can approach. Check out www.sba.online.gov for additional information on SBDCs.
- Local inventors' clubs often have people with prototyping and manufacturing experience. To find a club near you, go to www.uiausa.com or www.inventorsdigest.com.

KNOW YOUR CUSTOMERS: UNDERSTAND WHO THEY ARE AND WHAT THEY'RE LIKE

Prepare a Target Customer Profile

An ideal invention serves a customer with unmet needs. When you are preparing a target customer profile, you hope to discover a segment of targeted customers without access to a product that meets their needs. If that is not the case, you will have to prove that your product has features and benefits superior to other products serving those customers. Your goal is to categorize groups of targets and then to describe which product serves which group.

Figure 2.3 examines the market for *faux painting sponges*, patterned sponges that are dipped in either glazed or normal paint and then used to create a wallpaper-like appearance. The figure illustrates that there is a big market segment of new users who desire this look but who are underserved by current products.

Feedback from Real Customers

Stephanie Kellar curled her eyelashes and was highly annoyed that on occasion she pinched her face with the casing (the part that holds the metal piece that curls the lashes). She decided there must be a better way to make this product. Rather than just plunge in and make the product the way she would like it, Kellar took steps to ensure her final design would include all the features other people want. Kellar used the Internet Usenet, alt.fashion (www.usenet-replayer.com/groups/alt.fashion.html) to pose questions (e.g., "Has anyone had problems pinching their face with an eyelash curler?"). Kellar received input from more than 100 people using this strategy. She also applied Usenet to finding people who would be willing to test out her initial prototypes. Through this research she developed her product, which included moving the casing away from the face (Kellar's original idea) and also, as a

Figure 2.3   Target Market Profile—Faux Painting Supplies

Market Segment	Needs	How Needs Are Met	Products Purchased
High-end wallpaper and paint contractors	Patterned look	Make their own designs out of sponges	Sea sponges
Midrange paint contractors	Patterned and standard look	Have trouble doing patterns, sea sponges for standard look	Sea sponges
New users wanting sponge look	Standard sponge look with a simple pattern	Sea sponges	Sea sponges
New users wanting patterned wallpaper-type look	Advanced patterns	Products not available	None available

result of her research, designing a larger and rounder curling surface to min-imize the chances of overcurling eyelashes.

To find a Usenet for your product, go to www.google.com and click on Groups to access Google's Usenet directory.

Determining Users' Needs and Desires

The next step to understanding customers is to determine what features they want (or will want) and what features (product drawbacks) they *don't* want. In Chapter 1 you did some preliminary customer evaluation to determine whether people saw a need for your product. The step here is more comprehensive, letting you understand your customers' motivations and buying behavior. I use three primary tactics to focus on what a new product should be like: (1) asking people why they buy or don't buy products; (2) laying out all the steps to a customer solution; (3) observing how people actually use the product.

1. *Ask people what products they purchase, why they purchase those prod-ucts, and why they don't purchase other products.* When you question

Figure 2.4   Needs/Features Chart—Mole Removal from Lawns

Product	*Easy to Use?*	*Effective on Site?*	*Nonrecurring*	*Quick Action*	*Not Gory*
Insecticide to kill grubs	Yes	Sometimes, grubs may move	No, moles may move to another part of yard	Two weeks	Yes
Loop traps	Requires precise location	If moles are caught	New moles may arrive	Yes, if moles are caught	No, moles are killed
Cage traps	Somewhat, requires digging	Only occasionally	New moles may arrive	Can take weeks to catch mole	Yes, moles caught and released
Chemical sprays, castor-oil-based	Yes, sprayed on with hose attachment	70% of the time	Moles may move to new part of lawn	Two to three days	Yes

people about the need for your product idea you always run the risk that they will simply respond "everything is okay; the current products work fine." That could be true, or it might be that people are trying to brush you off. You increase your chances of getting significant input by preparing a need or feature chart that people can look at and respond to, as shown in Figure 2.4.

For some products it might be easier to show people brochures of existing products and ask which one they purchased and why they preferred it to the others. Start by researching products that people might buy for a certain purpose. For example, if you are considering an improved lawn chair that slips into a bag, you would get flyers or information on four or five different makes of similar products. Then ask people what type of outdoor "chair in a bag" they have purchased and why. Perhaps they saw it in a store, or preferred a chair that tilted back, or wanted a drink holder in the armrest. Then pull out your flyers of the other products and ask whether they like their purchase better than the one on the flyer. For best results, show only one flyer at a time. Soon you will start to understand what features people like or don't like about that product category.

2. *Lay out the entire solution.* People buy products either for emotional reasons or to perform a task. It is helpful to understand

every step in the solution process if your product is purchased to do a task. Your product might be able to combine some steps of the task, or it might be able to better coordinate the steps before and after the task. Crock-Pots, or slow cookers (you throw everything in the pot in the morning and have dinner ready at night), are an example of a product that provides a total solution. So are lawn sprinklers that move across the lawn on their own so a person doesn't need to keep moving the garden hose.

3. *Observe people using the product.* People become accustomed to compensating for a product's shortcomings and often don't even realize that they would prefer certain product improvements. For instance, a company I once worked for was introducing a vibratory root canal cleaner. At first, dentists told us that they didn't have any problems cleaning root canals. However, when we watched them during procedures we saw that they always took an X-ray before starting and studied it closely. When asked why, they responded that they wanted to check whether the patient had a curved root canal. Curved root canals are a problem because they can cause the old rotary root canal cleaners to break, causing a major disaster. It could take a dentist two hours to remove the broken-off section. Our vibratory root canal cleaner solved that problem by vibrating rather than turning. The product was a big success primarily because of that single benefit, even though dentists weren't aware of the benefit until we showed it to them. Watch people in action with a product and ask the purpose of each step. It helps to do this several times; people will reveal much more about the product if you observe them over time.

Prepare a Key Needs and Desires Chart

After you complete your three steps you can prepare a key needs and desires chart, like the one in Figure 2.5, for your product based on market input. This chart helps you finalize your own product design, but it is especially useful when you are preparing a licensing, turbo-outsourcing, or funding-request presentation. The chart shows why your product is needed and that you have carefully researched the market. The data will impress industry contacts and encourage them to help you with your product introduction.

CHECK OUT THE COMPETITION: DISCOVER WHAT CUSTOMERS THINK

A product's indirect and direct competition plays a key role in determining an inventor's successful new product strategy. More important than an

Figure 2.5   Key Needs and Desires Chart

Key Needs and Desires	How Well Met in the Market*	What Changes Are Desired?	Market Opening†

* Rate 1 to 5, with 1 representing a desire the market strongly meets, and 5 being an unmet need.

† Rate 1 to 5, with 1 being a strong market opportunity (unmet need) your product can meet and 5 being either a need that's already being met or a need your product doesn't meet.

actual feature or benefit comparison is how competition is perceived by both the sales channel and end users. If current customers are happy, it will be difficult to get them to switch to a new product unless there is a big price difference. Other key considerations that contribute to your product's potential success are how much competition there is, what type of companies are competitors, and the strength of competitors' brand name recognition.

Find All Competitors

These sources typically will list all your competitors.

- *Trade show programs with lists of exhibitors.* I like using trade show programs because the companies who exhibit are typically the strongest firms in the market. Contact the relevant trade show and they will usually send you the most recent program if you express an interest in exhibiting or attending the next show. You can find trade shows for your market in directories at the local library or on the web site www.tsnn.com. You can sometimes locate a list of exhibitors on the show's web site, but I have found that an actual show program, either this year's or last year's, offers the most complete information.

- *Trade magazine directories.* Trade magazines frequently have an annual or a biannual directory. This is especially true in industrial and business-to-business markets. These directories list products by category and also list contact information for each company, including most companies' web sites.

- *Association membership directories.* These directories typically don't list companies by product categories, but they will provide member companies' web sites and contact information. Most associations have their membership lists on their web sites. Some major companies don't join associations, which is why I prefer trade show programs.

- *Internet searches.* You can also search by using any of the major search engines on the Internet. Pay attention to products that are listed on many Internet store sites rather than on just their own site. I don't completely trust an Internet search because some companies sell only through retail stores or another distribution channel. They avoid extensive Internet sales efforts because they believe it competes with their current distribution channel. Use the Internet only as a supplement to trade show, trade magazine, and trade association directories.

- *Patent searches.* You can do a search at www.uspto.gov, the web site of the U.S. Patent and Trademark Office. Patent searches reveal some additional products, but you won't know whether the company is on the market. Patents list the name and address of the patent holder for patents granted to individuals. You can call patent holders and inquire what happened with their idea.

Determining the Market Leaders

Underfinanced inventors probably won't be selling right away to the largest distribution channel. But you'll find that people in the market will still compare you to the overall market leaders, as well as to the market leaders in their distribution channel. So you need to be ready to talk about why your product is head and shoulders above market leaders. For large product categories, you can usually get statistics about market leaders from trade magazines or associations. For smaller product categories, you can talk to the following people, who will often share this information.

- *Sales representatives.* Once you start to receive trade magazines, look in the back for what are called *bingo cards*, which have numbers that relate to ads and press releases in the magazine. Each ad or press release in the magazine will include a number that corresponds to one on the bingo card. By circling the desired numbers on the card and sending it in, you will receive free literature—and usually the name of your local sales representative. Call and ask that person market-related questions; explain that you are trying to identify the major players in the market. You can also go to the company's web site and request literature and the name of your local salesperson.

- *People in the distribution channel.* You might know someone in the distribution channel. If not, you can check in the Yellow Pages, call companies, and ask for a salesperson. Then ask what products they carry that would fall into your product's category. The distributor might also have a catalog to send you. Typically, the person you talk to will know which products are the market leaders and give you that information.

- *Editors at trade magazines.* Editors and writers at trade magazines can be helpful, and they are always worth a call. If they don't know the information themselves, they might know some sources where you can get the data.

- *Marketing people at trade associations.* Bigger associations will have a market development committee whose job it is to promote the industry. Typically, the people on that committee are marketing people from industry companies. The association staff person assigned to that committee generally knows much of the industry scuttlebutt and market share data, and he or she will often share that data with you. To find this person, call the association and ask whether there's a market development committee and, if so, request the name of the staff person assigned to that committee. A second choice is to contact the association member who runs the association's annual meeting or trade show.

Prepare a Features/Benefits Chart

Once you know who the market leaders are you should use a chart similar to the one in Figure 2.6 to compare your product to the market leaders' products.

Figure 2.6   Feature/Benefit Chart for Dryers

Feature	Brand A	Brand B	Brand C	Brand D
Extra-large drying capacity	Yes	Yes	No	No
Electronic touch-pad controls	Yes	No	No	Yes
5-year warranty	Yes	1-year	3-year	3-year
Signals when lint cleaner is full	Yes	No	No	No
Lighted display	Yes	Yes	Yes	No
Exterior drying rack	Yes	Yes	No	No
Moisture sensor	Yes	No	No	No
Drum light	Yes	Yes	Yes	Yes
Gas dryer	Yes	Yes	Yes	Yes
Extra temperature settings	Yes	Yes	No	No
Price	$675.00	$625.00	$475.00	$395.00

Discover How the Market Views Competitors' Performance

Inventors have the best luck when the market, including end users and distributors, thinks competitive products are inadequate. They could be too expensive, inadequate for certain jobs, or not suited to meet key market needs. For example, there are hundreds of pillboxes on the market to help people, especially the elderly, take the right pills every day. But the pillbox system breaks down if a person forgets to take his or her pills, which is something doctors and families worry about. The market would be receptive to a product with an audio and visual alarm system to remind people to take their pills at a certain time of the day. The alarm might also be set to go off if they forget to refill the pillbox by a certain time in the week. Paint rollers, on the other hand, are products that people are satisfied with. An inventor with a new paint roller will have trouble introducing the product unless people can immediately grasp why the new one will perform better.

Determining the market's perception of current products is different than the early market evaluation that you did in Chapter 1, which was a preliminary screening of family and friends to see whether your product would be perceived as different or better than other products. The research you will do now is with people you don't know, including people who work in the market and end users. The goal is to have research that appears more professional and impartial than research with your family and friends so that you can make a better presentation regarding the benefits of your idea to the industry.

- *End users.* Approach end users first, as you may need that information later when you approach retailers and people in the distribution channel. Start with open-ended questions about products in the market:

  Do you ever have a use for this type of product?

  Have you ever purchased this type of product?

  Why didn't you buy the product?

  Were you happy with the product?

  Would you buy this product again?

  Were there areas about the product that need improving?

  You can follow up with more specific questions about a product that relates to your invention. Here are some sample questions about paint rollers.

  Would you like a roller to hold more paint without dripping?

  Are you satisfied with how a roller does the corner between the wall and the ceiling?

  Do you think rollers splatter too much paint?

  Do you think rollers are effective in getting all the paint out of a roller pan?

- *Retailers.* Retailers are interested in higher margins, higher inventory turnover, less shelf space, and few if any returns. You need to ask them questions similar to the ones that follow, which are geared to a hardware store about the Earth Bud-Eze product line.

  Have you ever carried easier-to-use or more ergonomically designed garden hand tools?

  What were the results of those sales efforts?

  Do any gardeners ever express interest in easier-to-use tools?

  The product line you carry is similar or the same as ones carried by other chains. Do you need to sell the tools at a lower margin to compete?

  Is the garden hand tool line you sell similar to what you've sold for many years?

With little change in the line, are sales and inventory turns slow?

Is this a product category where you look for new products to stimulate more buying?

- *People in the distribution channel.* You can ask the same questions of the people in the distribution channel, which would include distributor personnel or manufacturers' representatives. Distribution channels, which typically look a little harder at new products than do retailers, are the best source for information about products with benefits similar to yours that others have tried to market. Past product introductions affect you because distributors and retailers will be cautious about introducing similar products that have failed repeatedly.

After you finish your research on market perception, make a chart similar to the one shown in Figure 2.7 that can be used later in your presentations and industry contacts.

CREATE A SIZZLING DIFFERENCE: ENSURE THAT YOUR PRODUCT STANDS OUT

Inventors start out in a big hole compared to most companies, as they have few resources and less market recognition. Inventors need to create special product appeal that generates at least a 30 percent advantage to have a realistic chance of success. With something special, product line inventors can get major retailers to carry their product, pick up top sales agents, and receive extensive publicity, all working to push the inventor's product to success. Inventors' products can stand out in many ways, including product design, features, and application-specific benefits. Looking at your product is not how you find product sizzle. You find it by looking at your *customers*, finding out what they are like and what they want, and then giving it to them.

Figure 2.7   Market Perceptions

Market Group	Perceptions of Competitor A	Perceptions of Competitor B	Perceptions of Competitor C	Perceptions of Competitor D
End users				
Retailers				
Distribution channel				

Not Good—*Great*

Bob Olodort was an inventor looking for a product at about the time everyone in Silicon Valley was talking about creating handheld computers. Olodort wondered what peripherals would be useful. His choice was a folding keyboard that he thought would be needed. These handheld computers became personal digital assistants (PDAs). Olodort didn't think a tiny keyboard that worked with a pen or pencil was the ticket to success. People didn't want to adjust to a smaller keyboard. They wanted a full-size keyboard. Olodort decided that his special ingredient had to be a keyboard that could fold up and fit in a shirt pocket. Unless he could achieve such a small size, the product just wouldn't be exceptional. Olodort started early, before PDAs were available on the market, and came out with his product, the Stowaway Keyboard, which he sells on a private-label basis to major PDA suppliers. His success came because he insisted on developing a product with that one exceptional "wow" feature.

Figure 2.8 illustrates a tool that will help you decide if you have a winning product. The horizontal axis is a scale of the importance of a feature or benefit to the target customer. The more important the feature, the

Figure 2.8   Target Customers' Desired Features or Benefits

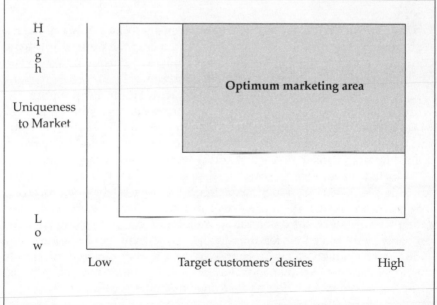

Figure 2.9   Target Customers' Desired Features or Benefits—
Suddenly Salad

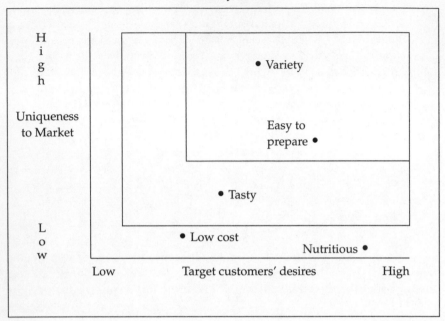

farther to the right it is placed. The vertical axis indicates how unique the feature is to your product or company. Products in the upper-right-hand corner are unique to the market and important to the customer. When you are in the right-hand corner, your product sizzles.

You should be able to fill out the chart in Figure 2.8 preliminarily with the input you received from your earlier surveys with end users. Make a list of all your features and then put them on the chart where you think they belong. Figure 2.9 shows targeted features for Suddenly Salad, a line of pasta salads that you just add water to for an instant dinner dish.

Include in your feature list items like aesthetics and emotional appeal; for example, if your product has a trendy look, a celebrity endorser, or upscale materials such as stainless steel, put that in. Try to be objective when rating your product, since overrating it will hurt you in the long run. You probably don't have any features in the upper-right-hand corner if you didn't receive a high "wow" response in your testing. If you don't fit into the upper-right-hand corner, look at changing your target market, reconfiguring your features/benefits, and adding emotional appeal.

Changing the Target Market

In this step you reduce your target market until you hit a market where your product is important. Then the only question is whether that market is big enough to support your product. Take, for example, an ice cube tray that makes cubes small enough to slip into a water bottle or other drink container. To the general public that feature might not mean much. People just put ice in a glass along with their drink. But this could be an important feature to runners, bicyclists, Frisbee players, or campers. If you reduce the market to these core customers and develop features for your product that will appeal to them, you could have the right ingredients for success.

Reconfiguring and Restating Your Features

Inventors, as well as many companies, have a tendency to focus on their product features instead of on customer-driven benefits to sell their product. The result is that a perfectly marketable product won't sell. Products sell well when customers realize the product meets their wishes or needs.

As an example, someone invented a mobile truck-washing unit for cleaning truck trailers. The unit sold for $40,000, and its primary customers were bus and trucking companies. This was a great product for the market because it was easy to use, cleaned a truck in eight minutes, and recycled all the wastewater. The company's competition consisted of bay washing systems, which cost $200,000, and mobile truck-washing businesses, which visit truck terminals once a week to wash trucks. This inventor company promoted the following product features:

- Self-contained unit
- Lower cost
- Ease of maintenance
- Airbrushing
- EPA compliance
- Mobility
- Ease of use
- Four-wheel steering
- Hot water
- Indoor or outdoor washing

These product-oriented features are nice, but they don't directly address what the customers wanted: trucks and trailers with a clean, high-class image. The inventor sold his product as a maintenance item, whereas the customer was interested in attracting more business.

The inventor simply needed to present the features of his product as meeting the customer's needs. The product could be marketed with the tagline "Never send out a dirty truck again." The product's benefits were that a truck could be cleaned in just eight minutes, by anyone in the yard, without any setup time, inside a bay or out in the parking lot, and that it could clean up to 15 trucks in a row. That message would sell the concept that every trucking company could have a top-of-the line image.

This inventor didn't have to add features to sell his product effectively. However, that is not always the case: You may need to add features or modify features to give customers what they want. Don't try to skimp and offer features that just meet the customers' needs. You need a product that sizzles, and it will only do that if it meets as many customer needs and desires as possible.

Adding Emotional Appeal

People typically buy a product for many more reasons than its features and benefits. They also buy products because those products reinforce their image. Many high-tech inventions drop rapidly in price in the first two years after introduction, and many of those high-tech products have quality problems during their first six months of operation. Why, then, do people buy them? In part because those products support a buyer's desired image of being on the cutting edge, being a technology buff, or being a high-class consumer with money to burn.

Your product has emotional appeal when you match a customer's desired image—whether by the features you offer, the product's name and construction, or the product's visual appeal. Almost every customer group has a desired image. Here is a sampling of some images your prospects might desire to have.

- High achiever
- Unconventional
- Progressive
- Financially savvy
- Dedicated volunteer
- Intelligent
- Hardworking
- Party animal
- Romantic
- Outdoorsperson
- Family-oriented

- Fast climber
- Adventuresome
- Cutting-edge
- Technology-savvy
- Low-profile
- Conservative
- Frugal

Looking at other products your target customer buys and determining how those products support that image will help you figure out how to configure your product to match. People might like garish colors, a sporty look, or extremely rugged construction. Woodworkers, for example, might desire an image of having all the tools and only the best tools. They may want products that look expensive and have every possible feature, products that will make visitors say: "Now that is really fancy."

Does *Your* Product Sizzle?

Once you have finished considering ways to upgrade your product, go back to Figure 2.8 and see whether you've been able to discover a way to move your product into the upper-right-hand corner — that is, whether you have features unique to the market that are important to the customer. If not, consider going back and starting with a new idea, as you might not have enough product advantages to move forward. Inventors need products that are clearly different, with benefits that are understood quickly. The most important criteria is that the product needs to have a *significantly* better benefit. Product creators are often confused over this issue because *companies* repeatedly introduce products that offer only minimal improvements, but companies are in a much different position than inventors. Companies often replace their own product on the shelf; they have established distributors; they are already set up as vendors; they have financial strength; they often have brand-name recognition. Only a truly novel product with better benefits lets inventors overcome these challenges. Being in the upper-right-hand corner of Figure 2.8 is crucial for inventor products.

3

STEP 3. BUILD A BUSINESS FOUNDATION: LINE UP KEY HELPERS AND FINANCING

There are many minor and major obstacles for an inventor to overcome. The two biggest obstacles are inexperience in the inventor's target market and finding the money to introduce your product. In my view, helpers (i.e., people with industry and market experience in your targeted market) are even more important than financing. Unless an inventor has considerable experience in the market, he or she will need to find at the very least a mentor to rely on for advice—or, better yet, an involved partner who will help take the product to market. Key helpers can provide contacts, open doors, offer insights about how a product should be packaged or priced, suggest timing for a product to hit the market during a key buying season, identify appropriate trade shows, and share cost-effective marketing activities.

You also want to consider your financing before you start spending money. You especially need to plan in advance if you have few resources. The invention business is one in which you can spend money in a big hurry, but money is available if you tap into those resources right away rather than relying on your own funds. I've found that underfinanced inventors are sometimes are better off than inventors with money because they seek financing help from the beginning. Inventors with money too often end up spending it all before they realize they need help. Spending your life savings simply isn't necessary. This chapter shows you how to get the help you need before launching your product. Inventors, anxious to take their product to market, often don't want to take the time to find helpers and financing. But the small delay time required to do so pays off dramatically by increasing your odds for success. This chapter shows inventors how to get the help they need:

- Find advisors and helpers: Strengthen your team with experts.
- Strike a deal that works: Get the most from your helpers.
- Prepare a financing plan: Grow without giving up control.
- Find funding: Look beyond traditional investors.
- Prepare an investor presentation: Create a can't-miss scenario.

Accelerating Sales with Market Savvy

Rod Sprules was a young engineer working on cold-weather suits when he discovered the high heating value of coffee grounds. Gathering coffee grounds was a problem until, in the late 1990s, coffee shops became popular, and that made it easy to collect used coffee grounds. At that point, Sprules reinitiated his Java-Log product concept—fireplace logs similar to Duralogs but made of coffee grounds—and went to work to develop a smooth manufacturing process. Sprules solved his production problems, but then faced something completely unfamiliar to him: selling the product. Sprules put out feelers to his friends for a top-notch marketing person with plenty of consumer product experience. Through a contact, Sprules met Marcel Sbrollini, a former marketing staffer at Procter & Gamble Canada. Sbrollini was not only able to offer advice, he became a partner in the firm and quickly produced sales all across Canada.

FIND ADVISORS AND HELPERS: STRENGTHEN YOUR TEAM WITH EXPERTS

Understanding What Assistance Key Helpers Provide

Key helpers are people experienced in the industry who know how the market works, which products have succeeded and failed, and what the best marketing strategies are. In addition they provide so much more useful advice that I don't think any inventor should proceed without help from these key people. Here is just a partial list of some of the more important assistance they can offer.

- *History.* What similar products have been successfully introduced? What percentage of users will buy a new product in its first years? What mistakes caused other products to fail? What is a typical first year's sales volume? Which products will yours likely be compared to? Answers to these questions give you insights into how you should introduce your product.

- *Product review.* Most product categories have nuances or required product features that might not be apparent to the inventor. For example, a hedge clipper might need a grease fitting to lubricate the gear case. A new hedge clipper won't sell without a grease fitting. Typically, helpers will immediately spot these mistakes. In addition, product review helpers can offer a fairly accurate view of how the market will perceive the value of your product's features and benefits, including people's notions of how well it works and what price they might be willing to pay.

- *Manufacturing help.* Helpers can typically give you names of companies that might make a product on a contract basis and tell you what manufacturing process the market likes for your type of product. You'll also probably receive more financial help and engineering assistance from a manufacturer if you can show that you've received input from one or more people in the industry.

- *Distribution hints.* Helpers from the industry will know which distribution networks are easiest to enter; which networks are most likely to take on a product from a small, one-product company; the best price point for a product; how much marketing a product needs; and what payment terms you should expect.

- *Connections.* People in the industry will also know many people and companies in the market. The names of these contacts will help you expand your potential sales base, and you'll have much better luck in approaching those contacts when you can state that your industry helper suggested the call.

Finding the Right Industry Helpers

I've mentioned using salespeople as a resource. Their help is valuable, but they really aren't the ideal key industry helpers. They may know only how a portion of the market works and often don't have enough clout to help get sales off to a fast start. If possible, you want to find someone who has a significant presence in your local market. A buyer for a chain of hardware stores, the president or sales manager of a large distributor, a key executive in an association, or the marketing manager of a manufacturer selling products into your target market are all better choices. These key people are more difficult to find than manufacturer's representatives or salespeople, but you should make an effort to enlist some of them to support your product launch. Here are four ways you can meet insiders:

1. *Use your initial contacts.* The people you meet in the market initially, either through inventors' clubs or contacts with sales representatives, probably know several people with more industry knowledge. I prefer to meet the contacts more casually at an event. If your initial contact knows someone who could help, ask about conventions, meetings, or conferences that both your contact and the potential helper attend; arrange to go to that meeting and meet your contact. If there are no convenient upcoming events, ask your initial contact to set up a lunch or meeting to discuss a potential new product. Your initial contact will typically do this for you if he or she likes your product idea.

2. *Join trade associations.* I mentioned this in Chapter 2, but it bears repeating because people who attend trade association meetings are interested in promoting the industry and are the most likely people to help you. They will be even more likely to help you if you volunteer to be on committees or do other work for the association.

3. *Use chambers of commerce.* Chambers exist to promote business growth. They do this primarily by lobbying legislatures and city governments for business, but they also are supportive of new business ventures. You may meet people who can help you at their meetings, or you might meet people who can direct you to key contacts. Tell people you talk to at a meeting that you are introducing a product into a specific market and explain that you'd like to meet people who are already in that market. They may be able to give you helpful names.

4. *Read magazine articles.* One time I needed key helpers to evaluate equipment for surface-mounted electronic assembly equipment. I found them by looking through a year's back issues of trade magazines. Two of the people had written lengthy articles regarding equipment similar to the new product I was researching. About half the magazine authors I've called over the years have been willing to at least talk to me, and many have helped with product evaluations or marketing advice.

Why would the key helpers be willing to help you? One reason is that even though not every inventor succeeds, many do, and every industry has stories like Microsoft: One or two people start a company on a shoestring and then go on to dominate an industry. A second reason is that almost everyone likes to be involved in a start-up success story. Many people, no matter what their experience or background, are intrigued by a new start-up with a great new product. Your product, if the industry person likes it, will provide a fun, exciting experience. People will try to make time for you, even when they have a very busy schedule.

STRIKE A DEAL THAT WORKS: GET THE MOST FROM YOUR HELPERS

Offer Rewards That Depend on the Product's Success

The ideal scenario for an inventor is to have a key person in the industry as a participant in the company. That strengthens the inventor's position with distribution networks, potential investors, and future manufacturing partners (who might also become investors). That participation could be as an advisor, an investor, or a working partner. The more involved your industry contact is, the better off your are. The advice that follows shows you how to make it easy for the key helper to become involved in your company. As you go through this process, keep in mind that you really can't afford to pay the key helper what he or she is worth for their time. Offering compensation in either small payments or stock shows that you respect their time.

- *Initial input.* A two- to three-hour session with a key helper, reviewing and suggesting changes for your product, your distribution, and your manufacturing plans, is extremely valuable. I recommend you ask the helper if you could spend two hours discussing your product and introduction plans. Tell the contact that you could pay them $200 to $300 for their time. Most industry helpers will turn down the money, but offering it is a sign of good faith on your part.

- *Further development.* Once you get initial input from your helper you should make at least some of the changes suggested, then request a follow-up meeting to review those changes. Sometimes inventors don't really need more input from their helpers right away, but remember, your goal is to get the industry helper on your team, and you can only do that by keeping that person involved. Ask the insider to help you during the next six months. Be up front that you cannot pay for the advice because you need to save your money for the product introduction, but make it clear that when you can afford the expense of incorporating and issuing stock, you'll give your mentor 5 to 10 percent of your shares.

Ownership Plan Strategy

Inventors often end up giving away too much of their companies to investors because they don't have an ownership plan that continues to give them control. You need to have a plan in mind and explain it to key helpers and other potential shareholders when they agree to give you help or money. Before offering any shares consult with an attorney to make sure you are meeting any applicable state and federal laws. Though you may not initially be incorporated, here are six concepts you should explain to investors.

1. You are going to authorize 5 million shares for the corporation. This doesn't mean you own 5 million shares, just that the company can offer 5 million shares to potential shareholders over time.

2. You award yourself 100,000 shares for initiating the first steps of a product introduction. Offering your industry helper 5 percent of your current ownership position will amount to 5,000 shares.

3. You will receive an additional 100,000 shares for every three months you work on the project for at least 40 hours per month without pay. By granting additional shares for your effort, you can keep taking on investors or giving away shares without diluting your ownership position. You can also keep increasing the shares you offer industry helpers without diluting your ownership.

4. Additional shares, valued at somewhere between $0.10 and $2.00 per share, will be offered for investors in the initial production process. You may take investments early, when there is more uncertainty, at $0.05 or $0.25 cents per share and then raise the price as your chances of success go up. People will judge your 50,000 shares for every three months against the share price. At $0.25 per share, 50,000 shares of stock is worth $12,500, which is a good starting point. Your helper(s) and subsequent investors may press you to take fewer shares if they think you are getting too much control of the company. You should respond to this by explaining that $4,000 a month is reasonable, that you are not taking a salary, and that you deserve to be compensated. You can also offer to sell the investors additional shares every three months so that they can retain their relative ownership position in the company. You must explain that you will be increasing your shares over time, so shareholders understand that they will not own 5 percent of the company forever in exchange for their initial investment. They should also understand that their ownership percentage will decline when you sell shares to other investors in the future.

5. Have helpers share in prototype and model costs. Your most likely investors at any point in time are those who invested with you earlier. Even if you don't need the money, it is wise to ask industry helpers to assist with model or prototype costs. It doesn't need to be a big investment—even a $1,000 will do—but it keeps your helpers involved in offering you tips and suggestions to protect their investment. It will also encourage them to invest again later. You can offer a simple stock agreement to the investor, which you can get from an attorney, or you can consider using stock sale agreements from some of the web sites listed in the resources section at the back of the book.

6. Secure investors for introduction production runs. Your major investors in a project may end up being a manufacturer, a distributor, or an individual. I've found that having an investment from an industry insider is the most powerful tool you can have in convincing any type of investor to say yes to your funding request. You can show that an industry person has been helping you for several months, and, again, you don't need a big investment. In most cases, $5,000 is enough to show that the industry person believes in your idea. If your industry helper can't invest, you can still enlist his or her support as a regular advisor or a board member.

Creating a Strategy to Effectively Use the Helper

Industry helpers like to be kept abreast of what's going on with a project, and their input is key to your success, so I recommend meetings at least monthly for updates. To maximize the value of helpers use them for these specific projects:

- *When you select a manufacturer to make a prototype.* Your helper may be able to help you choose a manufacturer, and might even know some personally, which can help you get a better deal. Building a prototype is an area where costs can escalate, especially if you need several before the product is right. You want the manufacturer to work with you to control costs. Manufacturers will be more willing to make some sacrifices on costs if they think your product has a good chance of success. Having a worthy industry helper is a strong indicator to the manufacturer that you might succeed.

- *Deciding your alliance strategy.* You might be able to fast-track your product through a marketing alliance, a private label strategy, or an outright distribution deal. Your industry helper will understand who might be good partners and who would be the key contacts.

- *Setting up your list of early sale prospects.* An invention success is often a matter of building momentum with early sales outlets. Often, inventors have limited inventory at first and can sell only to a limited distribution. Helpers can use connections to give you a list of initial sales prospects. They may even be able to assist in making those sales if they have a strong group of contacts.
- *Determining a licensing plan.* You can use your industry helper's expertise in deciding how far to advance your idea before you try to introduce it. In some markets, companies will license a product that has never been sold, but in others they will only license a product that has had some sales success. Once you determine the right time for licensing, your helper should be able to assist you in targeting the companies where you have the best chance of success.

Small Town—No Problem

Marlene Carlson noticed that children ages three to seven often have trouble putting the right shoe on the right foot. She created Puzzle Toes, children's shoes with a picture of a dinosaur on the toes, with half the picture on the left foot and half on the right. Children could look at their toes to see whether their shoes were on the correct foot. Carlson did not know what type of licensing arrangement to make, how far to develop her product, or which companies to approach. She found an industry contact, David Cousins, who had been in product development at LA Gear, to help her. Cousins negotiated to get Carlson's samples made, talked about her product at trade shows, and looked for companies who might license the idea. Cousins eventually located Carlson's licensor, Quest Products. Carlson located Cousins when she made an initial presentation on her own to LA Gear. LA Gear turned her down, but Cousins, who liked the idea, was willing to help Carlson launch her product.

PREPARE A FINANCING PLAN: GROW WITHOUT GIVING UP CONTROL

Understanding All the Different Financing Options

Money from Individuals

- *Self-funding.* You can obtain funding from savings, credit cards, or personal loans, or from the sale of personal property, homes, or stocks. Though you may be able to fund the process for a while, try to get investments from others. It cuts your risks, and inventions typically cost far more than people expect. It's easier to offer people a small investment earlier in the product life cycle. It is more difficult to convince them if you've invested $20,000 to $30,000 without any results.

- *Family and friends.* Try not to take investments that represent more than 10 percent of a friend or relative's total investment money. New products are a high-risk venture, and you don't want to have a friend lose too high a percentage of their assets.

- *Industry helpers.* As explained earlier, these are your best investment option.

- *Angel investors.* There are people who are looking to invest in start-up companies. You might be able to find them at your local inventor's club (see www.uiausa.com) or by contacting your local Small Business Development Center (SBDC) (www.sbaonline.org lists centers for each state). Your local SBDC can tell you if there are any entrepreneurs' clubs or investment conferences in your area. You might also get investments from neighbors or professionals you know if you can convince them you have a great idea. Explain your stock plan to family and friends and offer a letter or agreement documenting investments by family and friends in the same way you would for an industry helper.

Money from Manufacturers

- *In-kind investments.* This is a concept whereby a manufacturer will have its employees do work for you at no charge. It could be machining a part or doing engineering drawings. Manufacturers will do this if they aren't busy, because they will be paying the employee anyway, so working on your project doesn't cost any extra money. Many times the manufacturer will offer the in-kind investment for the opportunity to produce your product. Other times you might have to offer some of your shares in return for the investment.

- *Extended terms.* Normal payment terms are 30 days after the receipt of a service or finished product. The manufacturer *could* let you pay in 60 days or 90 days to stretch out your cash flow. If you are producing the product yourself, you can ask for extended terms from your suppliers.

- *Amortized tooling.* Tooling consists of molds and other equipment accessories needed to make your product. Fixtures are items that manufacturers put into the manufacturing process to improve production rates and quality. Typically, inventors have to pay for the tooling and fixtures up front. When tooling is amortized, the manufacturer instead charges an extra fee (say, 10 cents) on every part manufactured until the initial costs are covered.

- *Prototypes and product development.* If you agree to have the manufacturer make your product for at least a year or two, a manufacturer with in-house prototype capabilities might offer to build prototypes and complete your product's development without charging you.
- *Outright investments.* Manufacturers who have excess manufacturing capacity might also buy stock in your company or lend you money to launch your product if you have strong orders when your product is introduced. The manufacturer might also offer to invest and become 50 percent owner of the product.

Money from Distribution

- *Cash deposits.* Many inventor companies require a down payment from customers of anywhere from 25 to 50 percent on orders, especially for custom-made or industrial products. This funding can then help produce the products you've sold.
- *Payment for an exclusive sales agreement.* Companies might be willing to pay up front to help you get started, either with a straight payment or in return for a discount in the future. You might, for instance, get a $15,000 up-front payment in return receiving a 10 percent discount on their purchases for 12 months.

Raising Big Money

- *Professional investors.* These are investors who can put $50,000 to $1 million into a project. They are more similar to venture capitalists than to angel investors. You typically learn of them from other start-up companies or by attending new-venture conferences in your area.
- *Venture capitalists.* These are people who invest $1 million and up in companies with high growth potential, experienced management, and a sound business plan. They don't usually invest in companies without a sales history unless the company has a dramatic new technology. Check out *Pratt's Guide to Venture Capital Sources* (published by Venture Economics) in larger libraries for the names of firms and the types of deals they invest in.
- *Private placements.* These allow you to sell stock through a broker before you are large enough to list on an exchange. Legal fees and broker fees for a $1 to $2 million private placement can run up to $250,000. Most investors in a private placement must be accredited, which means they either earn $200,000 per year or have a net worth in excess of $1 million.
- *IPOs.* An initial public offering (IPO) refers to the time at which you launch sales of stock that can be freely traded by the general

public, typically when a company has tens of millions in sales or more.

- *Community funding.* Many rural communities offer low- or no-interest loans from the city or county, tax-increment financing, and outright grants. You can access some of this money if you start your company in a rural area, but you can also access it if you work with a rural manufacturer who may pass those benefits on to you by building prototypes and absorbing tooling and fixture costs.

Other Types of Funding

- *Options.* If a potential partner wants you to hold off negotiations with other parties, you can offer a three- to six-month option, during which time the other party has exclusive rights to your idea in return for a dollar value. You might sell an option to a distribution partner, a private label purchaser, or a potential licensee.
- *Factoring.* This is also called *receivables financing.* Factoring companies will buy your receivables for anywhere from 4 to 8 percent off their face value.
- *Bank loans.* Banks do give out loans, but they are not typically a good source of financing for new companies because they want collateral for their loans, and they want personal collateral if you don't have business collateral.
- *SBA loans.* Small Business Administration (SBA) loans are similar to bank loans, except that they are backed by a government guarantee.
- *Borrowing money against orders.* If you have a big order from a reputable company, you may be able to get a short-term loan from a bank or private investor to build the product.

STRUCTURING A FUNDING PLAN

Inventors can follow one of two paths to the market. One is to do everything on their own, keep things close to the vest, and ask for help only when they are desperate. These inventors typically have a hard time getting help because they don't appear to be handling their introduction well. Smart inventors take the other path, enlisting helpers, both industry experts and finance help, from the beginning and involving them all along the introduction path so they are ready to pitch in when they are really needed. If you want to nurture your supporters, you should understand when you will need money and who you plan to ask for it. Get people involved with small investments, or simply ask for advice before you ask for funding. Figure 3.1 shows a typical funding process and likely investors. You probably won't know at the start who your investors will be, but it should be clear whether you will need many outside investors and whether you will require a manufacturer or distribution partner to put up funds. This knowledge should help you dedicate the time required to find partners and investors to fund your project.

- *Initial seed money.* You'll need $100 to $1,000. Some funds are required for a patent search, initial market analysis, verification of the inventor's premise, and possibly attending a trade show to see competitive products. This stage is typically self-funded or funded by a family member or friend.

- *Initial market research.* Costs can be anywhere from $200 to $2,000. In this stage you'll attend association meetings, do informal market research and product evaluations, make up simple product brochures, and possibly produce a mockup. You should be networking and meeting salespeople, potential industry helpers, and possible candidates for future investment. This stage is also self-funded or funded by family or friends.

- *Patents and intellectual property protection.* Costs range from $500 to $10,000, depending on your patent strategy. In addition to a patent, you should prepare a product brochure and advertising package to help promote your idea to others. Patents provide an ideal moment to obtain initial investments from individuals. You have done some preliminary market testing, which hopefully has gone well. Now is the time to ask your family, friends, or industry acquaintances what you should do next. My experience is that more than 50 percent of the people will encourage you to get a patent. You can explain that you can't pay all the patent costs and still afford to introduce your product, and ask if the person would be willing to invest $1,000 to $2,000 in exchange for part ownership of the business. There's a good chance that people will invest, because you are asking for a small amount and because they think the patent is a good investment. This stage can be self-funded if you can afford it, but you are better off having two or three industry helpers, family, or friends invest a small amount so they become more involved with your introduction. When you accept money for patent costs, be sure to have an agreement regarding what percentage of ownership an investor receives. For example, you can offer the investor 10 percent ownership for a $5,000 investment. Otherwise, you could run into a dispute later on. For example, the investor may state that he or she owns 50 percent of your product or its patent if the patent fees totaled $10,000.

Figure 3.1   The Financing Process for Underfinanced
Product Entrepreneurs

---

1. Pull together as much money as you can to pay for a rough ad, prototype, or model.
2. Find potential investors among family, friends, industry helpers, or fellow workers.
3. Ask several people for small amounts of money to help pay for a model for market research.
4. Find a manufacturer willing to help with prototypes and small production runs.
5. Work out a low-cost arrangement for further prototype work.
6. Ask investors for another small sum of money for a market sales test.
7. Based on the results of that test, either move to license the product or ask a manufacturer to pay tooling costs as an investment or to amortize them over time.
8. Ask all suppliers for 60- to 90-day terms.
9. Request that investors cosign for a loan or invest additional money to help fund an initial sales period.
10. Use creative cash flow strategies (e.g., borrow money against orders for product, sell receivables, or get down payments to defray cash requirements during the initial sales period).
11. Request additional investments from investors and the manufacturer for a large-scale production launch.
12. Raise additional money from traditional sources such as private investors, banks, venture capitalists, or public stock offerings.

- *Prototypes.* Costs range from $500 to $20,000. Prototypes are a very dangerous investment because you might end up needing three or four before the product is right. If you have a low-cost prototype of less than $3,000 to $4,000, you can invite investments at the same time you invite investments for patents. Or you can strike a deal with a manufacturer who might pick up at least part of the prototype costs if you agree to have that company make your product. If you have an expensive product to build, you almost always need to enlist the aid of a manufacturer.
- *Market test results.* Costs may be from $500 to $10,000. Once you have a prototype, you can produce a simple brochure, and then you need to interview people, both end users and people in the distribution channel, to see whether they would buy your product. If

it is inexpensive to manufacture, you might produce a small volume of your product for sale. This stage can be self-funded, or it can be supported by friends, family, individual investors, manufacturers, or distribution partners.

- *Product introduction.* Manufacturing costs can range from $5,000 to $1 million, including tooling, fixtures, inventory, packaging, working capital, and all other materials and equipment. This stage typically calls for the inventor and/or families to put up lots of money or for the inventor to convince the manufacturer or investors to fund the product.

- *Marketing introduction.* Marketing costs may run $5,000 to $500,000. If you introduce the product on your own, expenses include brochures, trade shows, advertising, promotions, distribution programs, hiring and training manufacturers, sales representatives, and inside salespeople, and creating a web site. Expenses will be much lower, probably at least 50 to 75 percent lower, if you use a distribution partner. This stage is funded by lots of your own money or by partners, investors, and/or manufacturers.

Factory Help Seals the Deal

Michael Karyo was aware that silicone bakeware used by commercial kitchens had superior heat transfer properties as well nonstick and odor-resistant features that would be ideal for the high-end consumer market. The problem was that Karyo was a marketing expert and not a manufacturing person. Karyo couldn't afford the entire engineering, prototype, and production costs and still have money left to introduce his product. So he started a search for a manufacturing company that would cover the start-up costs in return for a share of the profits. Karyo approached companies that made silicone products to see whether they would be willing to invest in developing a new line of products. Karyo found a company in Hong Kong that made silicone products for the electronics industry and was anxious to expand into new markets. That company funded all the engineering and production activities, and Karyo was able to successfully place his SiliconeZone USA product line into Bed Bath & Beyond, Crate & Barrel, Macy's, and other stores with high-end kitchen departments.

FIND FUNDING: LOOK BEYOND TRADITIONAL INVESTORS

Funding Support from Manufacturers and Marketers

You may not know many people with money to invest in your product. That is not necessarily a problem, because there are many incentives for manufacturers and companies in your distribution channel to invest in your product. You just need to have an idea they believe in, offer an impressive presentation (see the section on presentations later in the chapter), and convince the partners that you have the business acumen to launch your product. Obtaining an investment from manufacturers and distribution companies helps you fund the company and, in addition, assures you that they will do everything they can to help your product succeed. Plus, investments from partner companies make it that much easier to attract the interest of individual investors. I can almost guarantee that inventors of products of even average complexity will eventually need help from a manufacturer or distributor. Your partner companies might be willing to invest because it is a much better deal for them than for an individual investor. Here are three reasons why:

1. *Win two ways.* The distribution channel and the manufacturer you work through will both make money if your product is successful. The distribution channel will receive a profit on every sale and the manufacturer will make money on every unit produced. If your product does well, your partners gain twice: once from selling or making your product and once by owning a piece of the product.

2. *Lock up the rights.* Inventors without partner investors can move their product from one manufacturer to another and to a lesser degree from one distributor to another. Bidding for a product from manufacturers and distributors often heats up as the product becomes more successful. With an investment, the manufacturer and distribution companies can typically be assured that their relationships will continue.

3. *Offer more input.* Everyone involved in a product has ideas about how the product's profits can be improved, either by cutting costs or offering more benefits to the market. Without an investment, the partners' input may or may not be followed. With an investment, the chances increase substantially that the changes suggested by the partners will be made.

Not every manufacturer or distributor is going to be able to invest. They may not have enough money; they may have other obligations; they may be too busy promoting other products or ideas. Don't assume that potential partners don't like your idea just because they won't invest in it. If you are relying on investments, you need to discuss the distributor's or manufacturer's willingness to invest before you make any firm agreement.

There are many ways to get funding from your partner company other than investment. The advantage of other forms of financing is that you don't have to give up equity in your company. I discussed earlier in the chapter how manufacturers might give extended terms, offer in-kind resources for prototypes and product engineering, and use an amortization schedule to pay for tooling in return for a two- to three-year manufacturing contract. Here are some options for obtaining money from companies in the distribution channel.

- *Up-front money in return for an exclusive sales agreement.* You might have a straight-up fee or you might offer a 10 percent discount on purchases until the money is paid off.
- *Down payments with orders.* Ask your sales partners to give you a 25 or 50 percent down payment with each order so that you can produce the product. Cash flow is an enormous investment; typically you need cash flow to equal 20 to 25 percent of your annual sales. Down payments accelerate your cash flow and might save you 30 to 50 percent in your working capital requirements.
- *Short payment terms.* Negotiating for 15-day payment terms rather than the standard 30-day terms means the distributor will pay invoices 15 days sooner, thus improving your cash flow.
- *Joint promotion programs.* The manufacturer could display your product in its trade show booth, feature you in sales flyers and promotional programs, and/or provide sales literature and training for salespeople. All these programs cut your promotion costs.
- *Installation or technical service support.* You could have high expenses in these areas if you have a complex or technical product. The distribution company can probably add these to its existing services at a minimal cost, whereas your costs to add those same services will be very high.

PREPARE AN INVESTOR PRESENTATION: CREATE A CAN'T-MISS SCENARIO

What's a Product Worth?

There's no firm formula for determining a product or company's value. A product is worth only what someone will pay for it or, in the case of inventors, what people are willing to pay for shares. As a starting point, you can value your product at three times the profit it will make per year or at its annual sales volume. If your product sales are growing rapidly, it might be worth four to five times its profits or up to double its annual sales. This is just a starting point, and high margins, explosive growth potential, lack of competition, or secure contracts with distribution channels can all alter the product's value.

Investors will look at the number of shares you have outstanding and your share price to determine your *capitalization,* which is the amount of money your company or product is worth. For example, if you have issue 100,000 shares to yourself and are selling 25,000 shares at 25 cents each, your company is capitalized at, or worth, $31,000 (125,000 shares × $0.25 per share). If investors think that $31,000 is about right for your product or company, they might invest. But savvy investors won't invest if they think your capitalization is too high. For example, investors will think a stock purchase is a bad option if they believe your product is worth $50,000 and you've sold 50,000 shares at 50 cents per share, with 400,000 shares issued, for a total capitalization of $225,000 (450,000 shares × $0.50 per share). If investors turn you down, you want to know whether it is because the price is too high or because you are overvaluing your product. Always ask why an investor doesn't want to invest, and adjust your stock pricing if it's perceived to be too high.

Inventors don't always have sales or profits to define a product. In these cases, you need to *estimate* sales. Here are three methods you can use:

1. Average the sales estimates you receive from industry insiders or sales representatives.
2. Analyze the sales of one or two similar products in the target market.
3. Use the actual sales per outlet or per salesperson achieved in the test or initial sales period.

As an example of the third method, suppose you approached 50 convenience stores in your initial sales period and were able to convince 10 of them to carry your product. After four months, each store averaged 10 units sold per month. If your next marketing program targets 800 stores and you can count on the same success rate (20 percent), you could expect to place product in 160 stores (800 × 0.20). Each store would sell an average of 120 units per year (10 per month × 12 months), for an estimated annual volume of 19,200 units.

Creating a Presentation for Investors

Investor's presentations change as you develop more information about your product and create more market success. I've listed here all the elements in a presentation for investors. You won't have some of the data for early investors, but in most cases you can substitute other data. For example, you won't have sales data for your initial investors, but you will have end-user research results and possibly industry expert research results you can put into this section. The following list offers 14 suggestions for information you can substitute in your initial presentations. Don't make your presentation too long or people will lose interest. Shoot for a 15-minute presentation.

1. *Give a high-impact statement.* You need to catch people's attention immediately, and the best way to do this is by showing why there is a big opportunity for your product. You can create this impact in several ways:
   - Offer fact(s) that the market is unhappy with current products. "More than 75 percent of homeowners don't think mulching mowers eliminate raking."
   - Include news about a new developing trend. "There is a 350 percent annual growth rate in the number of people buying scrapbook supplies."
   - Feature a strong benefit. "New PC board assembly methods cut production cost 34 percent."
   - Present research results from your distribution channel. "Four out of five retailers stated they were highly likely to buy [your product name]."
   - State your market's unmet needs. "None of the pie pans on the market prevent piecrust from blackening. More than half of the pie makers interviewed list dark crusts as a frequent or annoying problem."

2. *Show your product and list its two main benefits.* A picture of your product is best, a drawing is next, and a description alone is third. Make sure that whatever you show is professional-looking.

3. *Define your target market.* Give an overview of the industry with statistics. State where products are sold, and, ideally, offer examples of other recently introduced products and their sales statistics.

4. *State how you plan to position your product in the market and explain your distribution strategy.* *Positioning* is a term that relates to how you differentiate your product in the market. For example, when Michael Karyo invented SiliconeZone products, he pitched his positioning strategy as the first commercial-quality silicone bakeware available to consumers. His distribution strategy was to sell to high-end department stores and kitchen stores.

5. *Offer a brief history.* Provide a short summary of why you came up with the idea, what made you think of it, and why you think it will sell. Include a list of industry helpers you have been working with.

6. *Show a competitive product's chart.* Analyze the competitive product's weak points, what they cost, their market share, and where they are sold. Conclude with a statement that supports your positioning and distribution strategy as laid out in point 3. For example, Michael Karyo could say that no competitor is providing commercial-grade bakeware to the high-end consumer market.

7. *Discuss current status and what you plan to do next.* Explain where you are in the development process and what you need to do next. For example, you have completed initial research and validated the market opportunity and your next step is to obtain a high-quality prototype for further market testing.

8. *Summarize current sales efforts.* Provide a listing of where the product has been sold and a summary of the sales results at each location. If you don't yet have sales results, give a brief summary of your market research to date, including the evaluation by family and friends. Also include research with people in the industry, since this has the highest impact on investors.

9. *Present a distribution channel report.* Disclose your sales distribution channel, explain what it's like, and mention other inventor successes. Include a short synopsis of the interviews you've had with people in the channel, any promised orders, and a brief plan for who you will approach first. Add information about any key helpers you may have in the distribution channel.

10. *State the product's price.* If you've sold the product successfully, you will have a price set by the market. If you haven't sold it yet, use the results from your research panels that rated the product by value (see Chapter 1, pages 23 to 26), or use the projected price determined from interviews with people in the market.

11. *Reveal the product's costs.* To make money, your product's manufacturing cost must be less than 25 percent of its retail price. You need to demonstrate this cost-value relationship in your presentation. Use product costs that reflect the costs of the larger production volume you'll have once the product is established in the market. Your cost for a small production run will be too high. Your manufacturer, if you have one, should be able to give you a cost estimate. You can also get a cost of overseas production by using some of the sourcing agents listed in the resources section at the back of the book. If you are very early in the introduction process, you can still demonstrate that your product will have low costs by finding products with similar manufacturing complexity and showing that their price is in line with yours. For example, if you have a plastic rack organizer for closets, show

the selling price of other plastic racks in the market for other applications. You can state that if those products can be profitably sold at a certain price, your product should sell profitably at a comparable price.

12. *Exhibit an orderly funding plan.* Showing a funding plan helps you in two ways. First, it tells investors that there will be other investors coming on board, which means that their percentage of ownership will decline in the future. This is especially important for family or friends who may have never made this type of investment before. Second, it show investors that you have thought things through and are managing the project responsibly. You can show them the funding plan you prepared earlier in the chapter (page 64).

13. *Unveil your list of current and promised investors.* You can also list yourself here. You don't have to name family or friends—simply state that, for example, four family members invested. You do want to call attention to any investments, in-kind or in cash, from people in the industry, including your industry helpers, distributor channel people, or companies and manufacturers.

14. *Discuss the size investment you are looking for and how it will be spent.* List both the total amount of money you are looking for and the specific amount you are requesting from the investor you are talking to. Try to make the entire investment for a specific purpose: to pay for a patent, to design and build a prototype, to attend a trade show, to pay for a product brochure. People are much more willing to invest for specific items than for company operations, paying the phone bill, or providing you with a salary. Some investors might balk at giving you a portion of the money you need until the entire amount is raised. For example, if your prototype will cost $20,000, an investor might not want to give $5,000 to you right away in case you aren't able to raise the rest of the money. Rather than wait (as all your investors will have the same concern), ask them for a letter of intent to give you $5,000 when you have raised the rest of the money. Then you can collect the investment when you line up other funding.

Experience Counts

From the time she was a little girl, Kristin Penta loved mixing up her own cosmetics. She routinely sent letters to Estée Lauder discussing her latest formulas. So it was no surprise that when she graduated from college her one goal was to start her own cosmetic company and use her own formulas. First she decided to build up her resume by going to work for a company that private-labeled cosmetic pencils. She not only learned the ropes of the cosmetic business but started several new lines. After a few years, Penta decided she was ready to go out on her own. She found several investors willing to support an experienced pro, and she launched her company, Fun Cosmetics, which creates cosmetics for teenage girls. The investors were confident Penta would succeed with her product line because she had already proven she could create winners.

Key Points for Quick Success

You will have the best chance for quick funding if you pick a project that has the following characteristics.

- *Someone with success.* The ideal situation is when you have had market success similar to that of Kristin Penta in the inventor story. If not, try to involve an initial investor with a track record of success, people with industry or market expertise as advisors to you or as board members, or successful people who will endorse your products. Someone with success involved with your project inspires confidence in investors and potential partners and accelerates their decision process about whether to help you.

- *Moderately priced investment.* The higher your product introduction costs, the more time you will need to spend raising money from investors. Large investments slow down the invention process, and high costs also force you into a classic what-comes-first scenario. You need invention progress to land investors and you need investors to push your product ahead. If you have a product you can introduce for less than $20,000, people will see the risk as low, you won't need as many investors, and you can move fast. Once the investment rises above $100,000, everyone will slow down their decision-making process because the risk is much higher.

- *Quick-start market opportunity.* For many products you need only one small or medium-size store chain to take on your product to create immediate sales momentum. In Penta's case, she targeted Claire's Boutique, a chain of mall stores catering to teenage girls. A deal with Claire's is enough to launch a cosmetic company. Having a chain to sell to is one level of support. You are in a much better position if you or one of your advisors has had success selling to that chain. If you have a chain you are targeting, try to involve some advisors with success in selling to that chain. Go through the store and make a list of the manufacturers that are selling there, then contact them. Some might be inventor-started companies that might help you; other products might be sold through distributors that you can approach for advice.

- *High-margin products.* Inventors taking on distributors and manufacturers as investors sometimes have to pay a premium for products or offer additional distributor discounts. Typical manufacturing costs for successful products are about 25 percent of the retail price of the product. If your cost ratios are in that range, you won't have much room to absorb any contingency costs, and investors and potential partners will want to carefully investigate the agreements to ensure the product will be profitable. You need to have a better cost ratio than 20 percent of retail price so that your investors know you can absorb unexpected costs and still be profitable. Investors and partners will move quickly only when they are comfortable that the product can absorb extra costs and still make money.
- *Small penalty for low-volume production.* Cosmetics are a great quick-start product because they are produced in batches, with small batches costing only 10 to 20 percent more than large batches. That allows inventors to produce smaller quantities for testing without taking on too much financial risk. Other people's decision process will be much slower for riskier ventures—those requiring expensive tooling, large production runs, and large inventory buys.

4

STEP 4. PREPARE FOR KICKOFF: DECIDE ON PATENTS AND PROTOTYPES

The next step in the invention process is to decide on and implement your intellectual property and prototype strategy. There is not one strategy that works for all products, since the strength of a patent varies for each product, as does the difficulty of making a prototype. This is a difficult time for inventors because the expense of this step can be high, yet at the same time inventors may not succeed without either the right patents or prototypes. Fortunately, as explained in Chapter 3, inventors can frequently get funding from investors for both patents and prototypes. This chapter offers insights on both.

- Understand what patents offer: Get the most mileage out of a patent investment.
- Implement a patent strategy: Protect everyone's investments.
- Build a prototype that demonstrates the concept: Show that your product delivers.
- Create a "looks like, acts like" prototype and package: Leave nothing to the imagination.

Preventing Competition

James Tiscione didn't like carrying a bulging wallet, fat with credit cards, that he had to dig through to find the card he wanted. He thought people would prefer a way to conveniently carry cards in their pocket. He responded by creating the Auto Card Manager (ACM), a thin metal case that holds a driver's license and up to six credit cards. With the push of a button, the ACM slides out the desired card. To add appeal, the ACM doubles as a money clip. Tiscione's first concern was his patent strategy. He worried that potential competitors would be able to easily copy his idea, and he wanted patent protection. He started with a thorough patent search to make sure that no one had tried to patent a similar idea. Tiscione might still have been able to introduce and even patent his idea if a patent on a similar product existed, but previous patent claims might limit the scope of Tiscione's eventual patent claims. Tiscione's search turned up only two remotely similar product ideas, neither of which had claims that affected the ACM. Tiscione proceeded first with a provisional patent, which offered him one year of patent-pending status while he did market research and testing. Once he was confident his product was worth an investment, he applied for a utility patent before introducing the ACM, which is now sold through catalogs, promotional products companies, and high-end specialty retail stores.

UNDERSTAND WHAT PATENTS OFFER: GET THE MOST MILEAGE OUT OF A PATENT INVESTMENT

Patents' Perceived Value

As a columnist for *Entrepreneur* magazine, I see new books every year that debate the value of patents. Some claim you must have a patent to introduce a product, while others say potential competitors can easily get around a patent claim and still introduce their own product. Still others claim it is too expensive to enforce a patent, so why bother? I hear the same remarks at inventors' clubs and from small-business owners. The most common question I get while visiting inventor shows is "What is a patent worth?" The answer I give is that the value of a patent is in the eye of the beholder. If your investors or potential partners or licensees want you to have a patent, then it is valuable; if they don't care whether you have a patent, then the patent isn't very valuable.

A second issue brought up frequently is the strength of a patent, how much competition it will prevent. People will mention narrow claims and broad claims, with narrow claims preventing only products almost exactly like yours and broad claims preventing many competitive products, even those not very similar to yours. The final arbiter of competition-preventing patents is the court system, though patent attorneys can give you a fairly accurate reading. But competition goes beyond products just like yours. A drain can be cleared by a blast of air from a hand pump, and your patent could give protection from that. But drains can also be cleared by pressure from an aerosol can, by a gel that expands when wet, by a chemical cleaner, or by a drain-cleaning auger. A patent on drain cleaning with a hand pump won't protect against those competitors.

The question, though, isn't about how strong a patent is. It's about whether the patent helps you advance your product. I can't say unequivocally that a patent helps you in the introduction process, but I can say that in the vast majority of cases, *not* having one hurts you, because patents are perceived to be valuable and important by the vast majority of people, including investors and potential partners. Patents are a tangible item that investors might be willing to help fund, and I believe you should always indicate an interest in getting a patent at some point, delaying that process only for lack of finances or because you are waiting to finalize your product design. Otherwise, possible supporters may shy away from helping you. Don't worry that you might be wasting money on a patent because you could introduce a product without one or because the patent won't offer meaningful protection. What counts is that without the patent you will face resistance from potential partners and/or investors. Easing the path of production alone typically makes a patent a wise investment.

Key Facts about Patents

There are many fine points of patent law that you should understand to ensure you keep your patent rights intact and to maximize the benefits you get from a patent. Consider the following six points.

1. The patent law contains an on-sale bar that restricts you from getting a patent if you submit your patent application more than one year after you have started to sell a product. Your one-year clock starts ticking if you offer to sell your invention to a neighbor or store, offer your product through a web site or a direct mail campaign, or even offer your product at a flea market or garage sale. An offer to license or sell the future intellectual property rights for your invention does *not* start the one-year clock. Only sale of the product itself counts against the on-sale bar. Pursuing a private-label sales agreement would start the one-year clock ticking, as it is a sale of product rather than a sale of intellectual property rights. A signed confidentiality agreement won't protect you from the on-sale bar.

2. The patent law contains a similar one-year restriction for public disclosure. Public disclosure would include a newspaper, Internet, or TV stories about your product, press releases you send to any organization, demonstrations of your product at conferences or trade shows, or any other activity that discloses your product to the public. This would not cover focus group tests or other market research activities for which you have signed confidential statements. The patent office won't know whether you have violated these first two restrictions, but if you accuse someone of infringement, violations of these restrictions could void your patents.

3. The U.S. patent law is a first-to-invent system, which means the broadest claims will be granted to the inventor who can prove he or she came up with the idea first. This means that you can contest someone else's patent if you can show you had the idea first. Documenting your idea from the moment you start on a product is crucial for your intellectual property rights. The best way to prove your invention date is by keeping an inventor's notebook. Check out www.eurekalabbook.com/standard_scientific_notebooks.htm or www.snco.com. Both Internet sites have good laboratory notebooks that include instructions on properly documenting your idea. You can also use the U.S. Patent and Trademark Office Document Disclosure Program, which you can find at www.USPTO.gov, to establish a date for your invention creation. Patent law changes regarding the first-to-invent concept have been discussed, so be sure to check the patent office's web site at www.uspto.gov for updates. You can also get updates on current regulations at www.inventorsdigest.com, the web site of *Inventors' Digest* magazine.

4. Patents that are pending are not public documents. Placing "patent pending" on a product can offer more protection when a product is in start-up mode because competitors cannot review your potential patent to see whether their product will infringe on it. Once a patent is issued, it becomes a public document, and your competition may see a way to avoid infringing. However, you don't have intellectual protection when your patent is pending, and you can't stop someone else from selling the same idea until a patent is issued.

5. Receiving a patent is not a guarantee that it will be considered valid by a court. You might lose a patent because someone can prove you violated the on-sale or public disclosure bars or because others can prove they had the idea before you did, even though they didn't patent it.

6. An existing patent won't necessarily stop you from introducing and possibly even patenting your idea. Don't be afraid of existing patents on what seem like similar ideas. Figure 4.1 lists the steps you can take to evaluate the strength of someone else's patent (you can find competitive patents on USPTO's web site, www.uspto.gov) to determine whether you might be able to get around that patent and introduce your idea.

Types of Intellectual Property Protection

Trademarks

Names, slogans, phrases, and images can be trademarked. For example, in the fast-food world, McDonald's Fish Filet® is an example of a word trademark, while its golden arches are a trademarked symbol. Burger King has trademarked its phrase "Have it your way." You need a word, phrase, symbol, design, or some combination of those that is distinctive and/or different. For instance, you can't trademark common words like "sky," but you can trademark unusual spellings, like "Skyy" vodka. A trademark lasts for as long as you provide the product or service.

Resources: The Trademark Office is part of the U.S. Patent and Trademark Office (USPTO) and is located in Washington, D.C. You can obtain information about trademarks, as well as the forms for filing, by calling 800-PTO-9199 or 703-308-9000; or log on to the Internet site at www.uspto.gov. The site has a frequently asked questions (FAQ) section that can usually answer your questions.

Copyrights

Writings and other visual works can be copyrighted. Those works include instructions, sales literature, drawings, catalogs, directories, computer programs, books, pamphlets, photographs, and so on. You can also copyright the works that you create to sell your product or service, such as brochures or ads. You should copyright your works as soon as the final version has been decided on. The following format should be used if you have not registered your copyright: "Copyright 2000 by Joe Jones. All rights reserved." You are not required to register your copyright with the Copyright Office, so simply printing these words on your material gives you a valid copyright.

Resources: The Copyright Office is part of the Library of Congress and is located in Washington, D.C. You can obtain information and filing forms by calling 202-707-3000 or 202-707-9100 (forms only), or log on to www.loc.gov/copyright. Another copyright web site is www.lcweb.loc.gov/copyright.

Figure 4.1 Evaluating a Patent's Strength

The strength of a patent depends only on its claims. Follow these initial steps to gauge whether a competitive patent will limit your ability to introduce a product or to obtain your own patent. Check with a patent attorney for a final opinion about whether you can introduce a product, but I think it helps to assess competitive patents before seeing an attorney.

Step 1. Don't worry about the legalese in a patent's description. The claims are the only part of a patent that you need to read, and claims are typically fairly short. Claims are the only part of a patent that offers protection.

Step 2. Follow the patent until you come to the line that states: "What is claimed is," "We claim," or some similar statement. This statement will be in the "Detailed Description" of the invention, but it won't be called out by a major heading.

Step 3. Write down the key words in the first (i.e., the main) product claim. For instance, the key words and phrases in the patent claim shown here are "end wall," "hook," "support plate," "strap," "loop on trap and aperture," and "individually spaced apart ribs." The number of key product phrases in a claim is important because, to violate a patent, your invention must include *every one of the features* represented by the key words. Typically, patents with a large number of key words are weak, and patents with a simple claim containing only one or two key words are strong. For example, a claim stating "the use of subzero temperatures to improve the compressive strength of metal products" has just one key product phrase— "subzero temperatures"—and is consequently a broad, strong claim.

Step 4. Decide whether there is any way to make the product by substituting an alternative feature for any of the features listed in the claim. For instance, one of the key words in the patent claim here is "strap." Could you substitute another feature for the strap, such as a snap-on holder? If so, you can probably get around the patent claim. At one seminar I conducted people came up with 20 ways to get around the following patent claim (emphasis and comments are mine).

(Continued)

Figure 4.1   *Continued*

Patent Claims—Patent #4,969,580

What is claimed is:

1. A hanger support apparatus in a shower with a bottle having a neck on one end thereof. Said one end having an *end wall* that extends laterally of the next to a side wall of such bottle [so far this just a hanging device for a shampoo bottle], said hanger comprising a frame, said frame being elongated along a longitudinal axis and having a *hook* [anything other than a hook may not infringe on this patent] means for supporting the frame at one end thereof, said *support plate* extending generally at right angles to the longitudinal axis of the frame [the invention calls for a plate at a right angle to the frame, and there are dozens of other ways to hold a shampoo bottle] . . . the means for retaining a bottle on said frame comprising a *strap* that surrounds the frame with a method of adjustably securing said strap comprising a *loop at one end* of said strap having an aperture there through that is a selected dimension measure in direction along the length of such strap and the opposite end portion of said strap having a *plurality of individual raised ribs . . .*

This is a patent for a shampoo holder. Now go into your closet and get a hanger. Push the sides of the hanger together so you have the hook on top and the rest of it hanging straight down. Put your hand on the bottom of the hanger and bend it upward. You now have a shampoo holder. You have a hook, but none of the other features of this claim, and therefore you would be in a position to introduce your new shampoo holder without infringing on the original patent.

Utility Patents

Utility patents cover new methods of doing something, new devices for doing something, and new chemical compositions. A method of advertising, a method of washing clothes, and a method of making a product can be patented (new *processes* for doing something)—as can a device that holds advertising, a device that washes clothes, a machine for making a product, and equipment for producing paint remover (new *devices* for doing something). Specific formulas can also be patented, such as a soft cookie mix or a headache medicine. An invention must be novel (new) and nonobvious (a new combination that a person skilled in the field would not have thought of). *Nonobvious* is a subjective term and one that the patent office appears to interpret narrowly; in my experience, they rarely rule that an idea is obvious. Once you have applied for a patent, you can place the words *patent pending* on your product and all your literature. When you receive a patent, you should list the patent number on your product.

Resources: The Patent Office is part of the USPTO and is located in Washington, D.C. You can obtain information and filing forms by calling 800-PTO-9199 or 703-308-HELP (a 24-hour help line), or log on to www.uspto.gov. The FAQ section at the site will answer many of your questions.

Patents are expensive, typically costing more than $5,000, including attorney fees. You should do a patent search before proceeding. You can do an initial patent search yourself on the web site www.uspto.gov, but before applying for a patent you should still have your attorney do a search, as patent classifications can be tricky. *Patent It Yourself*, a book by David Pressman (Nolo Press, 2004), offers in-depth information on patent searches if you want to do a more extensive search yourself.

Design Patents

The design of an object—its shape or ornamental look—can be patented. Some examples are a car fender, a soap holder, and a computer monitor housing (e.g., the design of a new thin-screen computer monitor). Design patents protect only your exact design and rarely offer protection against future competition. The main advantage is that you can place "patent pending" on your product when you apply for the patent and people won't know whether you have applied for a utility or design patent.

Provisional Patents

A *provisional application* is a new tool that has been provided to protect inventions. It was originally created because of differences in U.S. and foreign patent rules. The United States allows inventors one year to file for a patent after the product is offered for sale or given public disclosure. Most foreign patent rules require the product to have a patent applied for *prior to* any public disclosure or sale. The provisional patent is a simplified patent process that doesn't give you the right to sue anyone; you still need a formal patent application within 12 months of filing for a provisional patent, but it does protect an inventor's foreign patent rights and also allows products to be marketed with patent pending. The major drawback to a provisional patent is that you need to apply for U.S. and foreign patent rights within 12 months or you will lose your patent rights.

The application must explain in words and drawings everything about your invention. Photographs can be photocopied and included; however, a drawing of what is shown in the photograph should be provided.

Resources: See previously discussed "Utility Patents" for a list of resources. Pressman's book, *Patent It Yourself,* is very helpful if you want to prepare your own application. See especially the section on "Drafting the Specification."

Foreign Patents

Filing for a U.S. patent protects you only in the United States. To protect yourself elsewhere, you have to file foreign patent applications. The Patent Cooperation Treaty (PCT) application can be used to file your invention in foreign countries that have signed the treaty. The costs typically exceed $10,000 for each foreign patent application.

Confidentiality and Nondisclosure Statements

This agreement goes by many names, but it is an agreement between you and another party (or person) not to disclose to a third party what you have shared concerning your invention. The main advantage is that a confidentiality agreement makes the information you share with the other party a nonpublic disclosure under U.S. patent law, which in many cases protects your patent rights. The biggest disadvantage is that the agreement can't be enforced against a third party who learns of your idea from your cosigner. Enforcement of the agreement against the signing party requires the filing of a lawsuit. You may also find that many companies won't sign confidentiality agreements, so you have to decide between getting a patent first or risking revealing your idea without one.

Resources: There is a Statement of Confidentiality and Nonuse in Appendix E. You can also get copies of confidentiality agreement forms in many of the books listed in the resources section at the back of this book. Most books of legal forms include a sample confidentiality statement.

IMPLEMENT A PATENT STRATEGY: PROTECT EVERYONE'S INVESTMENTS

Deciding on a Patent Strategy

There are several patent strategies to choose from depending on your product and introduction strategy. I've listed six major strategies along with their pros and cons. Choose the one that best fits your financial situation and type of product.

1. *Don't get a patent.* You don't need a patent to sell a product. If you have a product with a short life or you are going to sell it yourself within a very small market, you might want to save your money. This strategy normally won't work if you are trying to raise

money or sign a license agreement, as people won't feel a product has much value without a patent. Even if you don't get a patent, still keep an inventor's notebook documenting your idea to establish your date of invention in case someone else creates and applies for a patent on a similar concept.

2. *Follow a patent-pending strategy.* It can take two to three years to receive a patent after you apply. During that time your product is "patent pending," and you are allowed to put that term on your product and literature. People following this strategy typically don't use an attorney. They apply for their own patents, as they don't worry about the quality of their patent—or even whether it is awarded. The patent-pending notice will scare away most competitors. You can apply for a low-cost design patent or a provisional patent without any intention of filing a final patent, and this allows you to place "patent pending" on your product. This strategy is effective for short-term promotional items or fad items with a short life span. Again, this is not a good strategy if you are licensing your product, as the people you are approaching will ask to see your patent documents before signing an agreement.

3. *File for a provisional patent first.* Provisional patents have lower costs than a utility patent. With a provisional patent you can mark your product "patent pending." You then have one year to test your product in the market before applying for a standard patent. The provisional patent is most useful if you might get foreign patents, because it protects your ability to file in both U.S. and foreign markets.

4. *Apply for a low-quality patent.* In some instances, inventors may not be able to get a broad patent because of patents previously filed by other inventors. Inventors can still typically proceed to get a patent with narrow claims. Utility patents with narrow claims (explained in "Key Facts about Patents" earlier in this chapter) and design patents don't offer significant protection against competitors. They nonetheless have value, as they will stop some competitors, offer a selling advantage in the market, and help inventors license their ideas. A patent attorney can explain to you after a patent search the types of claims you will be able to obtain. In most cases, a patent attorney should be able to find at least one or two narrow claims to allow you to obtain a patent.

5. *Look for broad patent with few specifics or limitations.* This is what an inventor wants, but it is not always possible to obtain due to prior art, which could be either patents previously issued or products previously introduced into the market. You should use a patent

agent or attorney to file this application, since a broad utility patent can be very valuable. This type of patent will help prevent competition and put you in a strong position in licensing negotiations. The main drawback to a broad patent is that there is usually a negotiation process between the patent office and your patent attorney to determine just how broad a claim you will finally have. That means you can expect to pay extra money for your attorney's time during this negotiation process.

6. *Support patents with trademarks.* Or you can use trademarks as your only intellectual property protection. Java Jacket inventor Bob Sorenson feels his trademark name, Java Jacket, is more important to his competitive advantage than his patents are. Devee Govrik's Junk Drawer Organizer doesn't have a patent, but the trademark name has kept competitors at bay for more than five years. Trademarks are also cheaper, averaging $175, as opposed to the $5,000 a patent often costs. A trademark can also take less than six months to obtain versus two to three years for a patent. A trademark strategy can be used to complement any of the patent strategies, and together they offer stronger intellectual property protection.

Trademarks Are Great for Short-Lived Opportunities

Vic Pella was trying to decide how to cure his entrepreneurial urge as the year 2000 approached. He thought, "Why not capitalize on the millennium?" Fortunately he got rolling early in 1999, as all the orders had to placed by July 1999. He created a variety of products, including a baseball hat that flashed 2000 on an LCD panel, a teddy bear that shouted "Happy 2000" when squeezed, and a Countdown Candle that when burned for seven days revealed a Big 2000. Pella didn't have any patents on his products, but instead relied solely on trademarks. Pella decided that patents would be too expensive: $5,000 and up for each patent versus $175 for each trademark. A trademark can take less than six months to obtain versus two to three years for a patent. Pella's entire marketing effort consisted of attending trade shows that catered to retailers, distributors, and manufacturers' sales agents looking for products for the millennium. Shows Pella attended included the Premium Incentive Show in New York, the Advertising Specialties Show in Las Vegas, and the Variety Merchandise show in Chicago. Competitors that saw Pella's products at the show could have stolen his idea and introduced their own version if Pella had obtained patent-pending status. The trademarks that were in effect offered stronger protection. Attending just a few shows was all Pella needed to sell virtually everything he could afford to produce.

Follow a Step-by-Step Process

While patents are important to obtain, they are also expensive, and you don't want to apply for one until you are confident your idea is worth pursuing. You also want to be in a position to generate funding for the patent from investors or key helpers. Follow these steps to help ensure that you invest in the patent at the right time.

Step 1. Do your own patent search on the Internet using the patent office's web site at www.uspto.gov. The site will walk you through a process to help you see what other product ideas have been patented. This is not a definitive search, but it will help you see if ideas just like yours have been patented. If so, you may want to move on to the next idea.

Step 2. Keep a notebook. You should keep a notebook on every idea you work on to any extent. A notebook, besides establishing an invention record, allows you to answer the question "Do you have a patent?" with the answer "I don't have a patent *yet* but I'm keeping an inventor's notebook and will apply for a patent when the product design is finalized."

Step 3. Keep your idea confidential. You probably won't be able to enforce a confidentiality form, but getting one signed helps show that you haven't publicly disclosed your idea, which would start the one-year in-sale clock ticking, and it also shows contacts you are being careful to protect your patent rights. Some people won't sign the agreement primarily because it is against company policy. You still might want to discuss the idea with them, after you ask them to keep the information confidential.

Step 4. Evaluate your product with the scorecards provided in Chapters 1 and 2. Make sure your product appears to have the potential to sell well in the market.

Step 5. Ask your key helpers and other contacts whether they feel you should get a patent. If they do, explain that you will order a patent search first from a patent attorney to ensure a worthwhile patent can be obtained. Ask whether they would be willing to help fund the patent if the search indicates that your product is patentable. Expect to pay $600 to $1,000 for a patent search. If you are short of money, you can try to get two or three people to help pay for the patent search.

Step 6. Order the patent search. Patent search services may be less expensive, but I think you are better off using a patent attorney because you can take your potential investors with you when the attorney explains the results of the patent search.

Step 7.   Understand the protection a potential patent will offer you. Ask your attorney the following questions.
- Is your product eligible for a broad claim?
- Will you be able to have a single-feature claim?
- To what degree would a competitor have to change your product to avoid your potential patent?
- Which of your features would a patent protect?
- Will any of the patents uncovered in the search prevent you from selling your product?
- What parts of your product shouldn't be changed once you apply for a patent?

Step 8.   Decide on a patent strategy you want to pursue and whether you want to ask investors for financial help to obtain one.

Step 9.   Implement the patent strategy. If you decide to hold off on getting a patent, continue to keep your notebook and continue to ask people to sign a statement of confidentiality. Keep your patent rights alive, as you may decide later to apply for a patent.

BUILD A PROTOTYPE THAT DEMONSTRATES THE CONCEPT: SHOW THAT YOUR PRODUCT DELIVERS

Understanding the Importance of Prototypes

Inventors know what they expect their product to be like. That's a result of spending hours reflecting on their idea, how it will be used, and how it will be sold. Unfortunately, other people can't catch that same vision without seeing a model or prototype. In addition to sharing your ideas with others, prototypes are needed to confirm that product works as you thought, to ensure that there are no unanticipated deficiencies, and to enable you to more accurately estimate your manufacturing costs.

If at all possible, inventors should first make a rough prototype themselves to confirm that their concept will work as initially designed. This allows inventors to find and correct any deficiencies in the product, and it lets potential engineers and manufacturers know exactly what you want in the product. This prototype, unless it looks very professional, shouldn't be shown to others for market research. Most people will respond negatively to a rough prototype. They won't be able to get beyond the product's unfinished look.

This section covers many ways to make a rough prototype. You can often simulate production parts fairly easily. You can also have prototypes made for you by prototype specialists, but this can be expensive. Many inventors who aren't engineers or mechanically minded automatically assume they can't make a prototype and immediately seek prototype specialists. However, you might be able to save a lot of money if you first try to make the prototype yourself. Stop at your local inventors' club, where typically there are many people who understand the rough prototype concept and can provide extensive support, including helping you make the parts. Inventors' clubs are among the few places in the invention business where people are willing to help you for little or no expense on your part. Check out the web sites www.inventorsdigest.com and www.uiausa.com for a list of inventors' clubs. Another great resource for instructions on making prototypes is www.inventorhelp.com, which offers an inventors' bookstore with a large list of pamphlets on prototyping. Use a prototype builder only if your product has just too many challenges for your mechanical ability, but at least investigate your other options first.

Prototype Proves the Concept

Jack Panzarella was repossessing cars in Florida when he saw a car with a neon light underneath. He wasn't sure why people would do that, but he learned that it was a show car and that the lights highlighted the car at shows. Being a fan of muscle cars, Panzarella thought that this idea would be great for car buffs. But a plug-in light under a car at a show was a much different proposition than a neon light glowing under a moving car. The first obstacle was figuring out how to get a neon light to run off a car battery without drawing too much power. After many attempts, Panzarella found a solution that worked. But Panzarella still wasn't sure whether his idea would sell, so he started driving his car, equipped with neon lights, around at night. People would stop him on the road to ask him where they could buy such a device. Panzarella got a few auto stereo dealers to carry his product, and within a few years he had 200 employees and $16 million in sales. None of that success would have happened if Panzarella hadn't made his initial prototype.

Producing a Prototype

Producing a first model or prototype often intimidates inventors. You can take away some of the mystique of building a prototype if you break it down into four main steps.

1. Create your parts list and find out which ones are available. Chapter 1, page 19, discussed doing a preliminary product specification, part of which was to create a list of product components.

Once you have the list you should figure out which components you can acquire without any special effort. They might be items that are commonly available, or they might be parts you can take off of existing products (referred to as *cannibalizing*).

2. Figure out what other parts you can produce yourself, either as it will be produced in the final product or by using an item that simulates the final part. Here are some ways you can produce parts:

   • *Wood models.* You can use balsa wood for parts that need to be bent or curved. Your local hobby shop will have balsa wood and instructions. You can also shape wood to your needs with standard woodworking tools.

   • *Plastic parts from stock plastics.* Most towns have a plastics supplier such as Cadillac Plastic that have all types of plastic sheets, rods, rectangles, and blocks. You can buy these parts and carve or machine them for your prototype. If you aren't handy with a home machine center or other tools, perhaps you have a friend who is, or you can get help from an inventors' club. You can often find a local person to help you at a hobby shop or woodworking store. Another easy-to-do task is bending plastic pieces. Wrap the plastic in aluminum foil and, using insulated gloves, hold it over an electric stove until it softens (An electric stove's heating area is more even than that of a gas stove). Then bend the plastic around a block, can, or other surface to form the desired shape.

   • *Homemade plastic models.* You can make a plastic model yourself by making a plastic mold (from a wood, or steel, or clay model). Place mold-making plastic over the model, and after the mold is made, use a plastic compound that can be baked hard in an oven. Both Polytek Development Corp. (www.polytek.com) and Hysol Electronic Chemicals (www.hysol.com) have polymers for both mold making and plastic casting. You often obtain a much more polished prototype when you take a piece of metal or wood and cast a plastic mold.

   • *Fiberglass layup.* Fiberglass makes very strong parts that can be substituted for metal parts. You start by making a form, even out of cardboard, that looks like the inside of the part. Then use polyester resin that you lay down on the form and then cover with a sheet of fiberglass. When done the form is removed and you have a finished part.

3. Use a low-cost process to produce parts. Even when you need to have parts produced, several strategies can keep your costs down.

   • *Temporary tooling.* If you need injection-molded parts, molders can often take old molds of parts bigger than yours and the manufacturer can make an aluminum insert to produce your part. The tooling won't make many parts, but it will give you a good prototype. You may need to visit several molders before you find one that has the right size of old mold in stock.

- *Vacuum-formed parts.* Vacuum-formed parts are typically larger and simpler than injection-molded parts. For example, the front and back panels of a vacuum cleaner could be vacuum-formed. This type of molding takes a sheet of plastic, heats it, and then pulls it over a form, which could be made of wood. You can get a vacuum-formed part made inexpensively if you make your own wooden form and then have a vacuum-forming shop make one or two parts.

4. Look for low-cost processes for the final parts. Prototype and model-building shops can be found on the Internet or in your phone book, but often the best prices can be found on the web site www.jobshoptechnology.com. Try to get quotes from at least three or four prototype shops. Many processes can be used to make prototypes, and you want to find a shop with processes that will hold down your costs.

Prove Your Concept Works

Back in Chapter 1 (pages 19 to 20) you created a product specification that included details about how your product works and its features and benefits. The prototype will ensure that your product concept meets the product specification. The last step on the initial model is to test the product against your product specification. Go through your product specification and check carefully that the prototype works as you had originally envisioned. If it doesn't, make a list of all the deficiencies and then rework your prototype till you come close to or exceed the performance you had in mind when you conceived your idea. You should have one other person, preferably a key helper, also check your product against the product specification and concur that the prototype meets the specification.

CREATE A "LOOKS LIKE, ACTS LIKE" PROTOTYPE AND PACKAGE: LEAVE NOTHING TO THE IMAGINATION

After your initial and hopefully low-cost model proves your concept works and you are satisfied with your product design, you need to create a professional-looking prototype, do end-user research, and estimate manufacturing costs. I used to believe that inventors could get by with a homemade prototype to save money, but I've learned that end users, distributors, manufacturers, and investors just don't respond well to a homemade prototype. Too often, inventors lose out not because the idea is wrong, but because people just can't see past the rough prototype.

Product Design

I believe in the motto "look like success" for new products, which means that your new product needs to be well designed, up-to-date, and pleasing to look at. But you can go one step further and actually have your product design sizzle.

Design Propelled Success

Bob Evans was an underwater photographer who, while waiting for a photographic moment, noticed that fish generate extra propulsion by sending water through their V-shaped rear fins. Evans went to work on his own V-shape design for human swimmers, convinced that he could develop more force with the fins if he could add extra thrust by channeling water during a swimmer's downstroke. Evans succeeded not only in building up extra force, but also in eliminating a swimmer's work in lifting the leg during the upstroke. After the rush of water from the downstroke, the water coming in to fill the void raises the fin. Evans's fins provide more power and forward thrust than any other fin in the world and are used by both the military and top divers. For the average diver, the product's buzz comes from the design. The bright yellow fins are flashy, but it is the sweeping scoop shape, along with the V, that gives them a space age look. The design has a high-performance look, even to those divers who don't understand the aerodynamics of Evans's designs. No other fin on the market even comes close to the high-performance look of Evans's Force Fins.

If you want your product design to sizzle, don't look at products that exist in your market for help. Those products may already have a dated look. Look instead to other products introduced in your industry, even if they don't compete with your product. For example, many blenders and toaster ovens have a very dated look compared to bread machines and food processors.

Industrial designers create many of the modern-looking designs that capture the market's eyes. Larger towns have at least a few industrial design firms you can consult for an advanced product look. The bigger firms tend to be expensive, but your local inventors' club probably will know some firms willing to work for inventors inexpensively or for a percentage of eventual sales. You can also check out the industrial designers web page at www.idsa.com.

Improving Your Prototype Reception with Packaging

Inventors want a positive response to their prototype, and often you can improve on or at least equal the positive response to your product on a store shelf by including packaging prototypes with your product prototypes. That combination is most representative of what you will actually sell. Inventors occasionally look at packaging last, almost as an afterthought. I've seen companies that spend more time on the package than they do on the product; although that may be excessive, time spent on packaging typically has a big payback. The reality is that for many products packaging needs to do all the work in selling the product including:

- Catching people's attention
- Describing what the product is
- Suggesting why you should buy the product
- Explaining how it works

Packaging prototypes help an inventor sell his or her product to evaluators and potential partners in just the same way that they help marketers sell to consumers. Your local inventors' club is again a good place to start for help with what type of packaging you should use and how you can make an inexpensive prototype of it. You can also do a Google search for packaging designers whom you can consult for an effective package.

Packaging Sells

Devee Govrik got tired of her kitchen junk drawer being a big mess. She decided that she wanted something to help organize the drawer. She created a plastic tray that did the job, with each compartment in the tray sized for items like scissors, adhesive tape, paper clips, and batteries typically found in a kitchen junk drawer. The product was all white, and Govrik's challenge was how to package it so it would jump off store shelves. She started by having an attention-grabbing red-and-black color splash on only the top left and bottom right corners of the product with the word kitchen *on the top left corner and* Junk Drawer Organizer *on the bottom. Then she added decals with pictures of the items belonging in each compartment of the junk drawer. The product was shrink-wrapped so people could see the product and decals. The result was that people noticed the product because of the color, immediately understood what it was by its name, and could see exactly how it worked from the*

> *decals. One or two seconds is all it took for people to understand why they wanted Govrik's product, which has been a big success in mass merchandise stores and organizational stores.*

————————

Have your packaging prototype follow these three simple rules to add sizzle to your product.

1. *Match the value range of the product.* A high-end product should have a high-end package. Buyers are influenced by all the clues you offer, which includes the packaging image.
2. *Show the customers' desired result.* Customers buy products not for features, but to achieve some end result. Pictures of a neat junk drawer, a happy, well-fed family, or a winning bike race create desire for your product.
3. *Have your package colors stand out.* For some reason, most product categories have certain color schemes that blend well with the products. Walk down the cereal aisle in a grocery store and you'll notice how all the packages have a similar look. Don't clash with the color scheme of other products, but do have a color scheme that will set you apart. In the case of the junk drawer organizer, most organizing products had beige packaging, so Govrik chose red and black to stand out.

Creating the Polished Look without Spending a Fortune

You can, of course, just pay for "looks like, acts like" product and packaging prototypes designed at a prototype shop, manufacturer, or packaging house if you don't think you have the mechanical aptitude to produce the models yourself. But there are tactics that keep the costs down even if you need professional help.

- Find an industrial designer to be your partner. The industrial designer might make your prototype at cost in return for a small share of your invention. New graduates often do this to help build a portfolio. Inventors' clubs are the best spot to find designers willing to participate in your invention.
- Find a prototype builder who will build your product at cost or just for materials costs in return for a share of the invention. You can save a great deal of money (their rates are typically $60 to $100 per hour). In most cases you need to offer 10 to 20 percent of your idea in exchange for low-cost help with prototypes.

- Offer to have your product eventually produced by a manufacturer who helps you develop a prototype for below-market cost. You can also offer to do work for the manufacturer for free to offset part of the prototype cost. This is the best tactic to try first, and you don't need to give away a part of your invention or idea.

Note: For these tactics to work you need to find designers, prototype builders, or manufacturers who have spare time and who would be willing to use that time to earn a share of what they hope will be a successful product.

- If you or your investors want to pay for an initial prototype, check out the web sites at www.uiausa.com (United Inventors Association), www.inventorsdigest.com (*Inventors' Digest* magazine), and www.dondebelak.com (yours truly!).

Ready to Go?

I don't feel inventors are really ready to pursue their product introduction options until they have a product in a package that leaves nothing to a contact's imagination. I've found that having that professional-quality prototype generates at least double the inventor's chances of success with each meeting or presentation. At the same time, I realize that obtaining a "looks like, acts like" prototype can be prohibitively expensive for some products. My caution to readers is that you drastically reduce your odds for success by going with a less-than-ideal prototype. I encourage you to look extra hard for a partner—an investor, an engineer, an industrial designer, or a manufacturer—to help you develop the prototype you need to launch your product.

5

STEP 5. CHOOSE THE RIGHT FAST-TRACK STRATEGY: UNDERSTAND WHAT WORKS BEST FOR YOUR PRODUCT

How inventors decide to proceed with their product introduction isn't based solely on their preferences. It is based more on the characteristics and relationships of the product, the market, and the end user. While many inventors prefer licensing since it leaves them free to invent (not bogged down in developing companies), only a certain percentage of marketable ideas, I believe at most 25 percent, are good candidates for licensing. And a healthy percentage of products that can be licensed will succeed only after the inventor has had some initial sales success. The other 75 percent of the products have to succeed either through turbo-outsourcing or through the traditional route of starting a company to promote the new product. This chapter discusses the different routes inventors can take to market and how you can determine which route offers the best chance of success. The chapter explains how to make the choice that works for you and your product:

- Three strategies for market introduction: Explore multiple options to increase your chances of success.
- Key factors in determining your strategy: Choose what works for you, your product, and your market.
- License to a market player: Lower your risk and collect a royalty.

- Capitalize on turbo-outsourcing: Keep control while minimizing risk.
- Build a company: Maximize your profit and wealth potential.

THREE STRATEGIES FOR MARKET INTRODUCTION: EXPLORE MULTIPLE OPTIONS TO INCREASE YOUR CHANCES OF SUCCESS

Outsourcing has produced an age of specialization—of defining core competencies in companies. Companies no longer view themselves as all-in-one production-to-sales organizations, but often instead as specialized service providers. Their specialty could be producing high-temperature ceramics, marketing innovative consumer products to drugstores, selling through home shopping networks, producing baby-safe fabric products, or marketing innovative promotional ideas to executives. This tilt toward specialization has helped inventors, since companies look outwardly for products that fit their specialty. Smaller research and development (R&D) departments encourage companies to look to inventors for ideas. Unfortunately, companies with small R&D departments can't finish product development on their own and often need inventors to complete the process before they will consider a license. Inventors might be requested to finish a product's development, they might be faced with a request to produce the initial production run, or they might be asked to find a U.S. or overseas manufacturer before licensing an idea.

Rather than just license the product, a company might purchase it in a private-label agreement, whereby the company sells the inventor's product under its own brand name. The inventor would still need to arrange for production, either through another partner or through his or her own resources, which results in a turbo-outsourcing agreement. *Turbo-outsourcing* is a new introduction strategy that meets two goals for inventors. One is that it allows inventors to address requests by companies looking to license their idea and gives them tools to set up other types of agreements when a licensing won't work. These agreements allow partner companies to participate in parts of a new product introduction without taking on all of the product launch responsibilities. These new partnerships reduce the investment of each partner, including the inventor, and leave inventors with much more control over their ideas than they would have with a licensing agreement.

Turbo-outsourcing also helps inventors meet a second goal: introducing their own product without having to put up a major investment. Inventors can easily find production sources to make their products, and many of those sources will fund at least a part of the production start-up. In partnerships, there are more marketing companies to help sell products, and many retailers have programs that search for new ideas with the goal of becoming the only place where consumers can buy the product.

Despite the advantages of licensing and turbo-outsourcing, many inventors still prefer to start their own company, because it is still the best way to build long-term, sustained wealth with a major company. Bill Gates, after all, started out with a product concept and turned it into Microsoft. Only starting your own company can lead to this type of wealth.

This new market environment spawns new strategies. Even the traditional concepts like licensing and starting your own company have new wrinkles that improve inventors' chances of success. The three main routes to introduction—licensing, turbo-outsourcing, and starting your own business—are not mutually exclusive. Many times your best chance of success comes from a combination of the three.

Checking Out the Options

Karen Alvarez, a mother of three, was worried about her baby falling out of a shopping cart after a near disaster at the local supermarket. As a result, she created the Baby Comfort Strap, a soft strap that pulls over the seat and holds the baby firmly in place. Alvarez's aim was to license her idea, but she wasn't sure how to go about it. She started selling her product at a few baby products stores, including the KaZoo's consignment shop in San Ramon, California. Alvarez continued to try to license her product, even as she added retail stores (100 in all before she got her final license agreement) with the help of KaZoo's owner, but she wasn't able to generate interest at the big baby products companies.

While making licensing contacts she ran into Mark Bettker, president of Koala Corporation, manufacturer of the baby changing stations you see in public restrooms. He wasn't interested in a license agreement as the product didn't fit with his corporate goals, but he encouraged Alvarez to start her own publicity campaign, providing articles to local media outlets about her new product and the fact that 16,000 toddlers per year are injured by falling out of shopping carts. Those articles, published in numerous California newspapers, generated buzz and business for the Baby Comfort Strap. But Alvarez still wasn't able to attract interest in a license agreement because the potential licensees she approached, which were baby accessory companies, didn't have the right manufacturing equipment.

Then Alvarez started looking for a company with the fabric-oriented manufacturing process that could make her product. One of her retail customers told her about a manufacturer of a similar item, the Safety Strap, which was sold directly to supermarkets to install in their carts (versus being sold to retailers and thence to consumers). The Safety Strap manufacturer wasn't willing to license Alvarez's idea, but it was willing to manufacture the product. With sales at over 100 stores and a manufacturing contract, Alvarez was finally able to license the Baby Comfort Strap to Dex products, which was able to sell her product in a big way. Alvarez realized that the market *dictated the direction she needed to take, and in the end she obtained the deal she wanted by following that path.*

Often, as shown in Alvarez's story, you need to use licensing, turbo-outsourcing, and start-up strategies to successfully place your product in the market. The following list provides a brief explanation of each approach. (Later in the chapter there is an in-depth analysis of the positive and negative aspects of each strategy.) Remember as you read the chapter that the market might require you to use pieces of each strategy to pull off your introduction. Flexibility is the key, and you need to understand all three strategies for the best chance of success.

1. *Licensing* is an arrangement whereby an inventor receives a royalty, which is a share of the revenue, in exchange for the use of the invention. Royalties can range from 1 to 15 percent. Typically, inventors need to have some sort of intellectual property rights (i.e., patent, trademark, or copyright) to get a licensing agreement; otherwise, they do not have exclusive rights to the idea. But a license-type agreement can be negotiated as a *development agreement*, whereby the inventor agrees to develop a product for a royalty, or as a *commission agreement*, whereby the inventor gets a commission on every item sold. Ideally, inventors can license their idea from a patent or initial product drawings, but more commonly they have to at least have a working model, and in many cases inventors have to fully develop and even sell their product prior to being able to get a licensing agreement.

2. *Turbo-outsourcing* refers to accelerating the invention process not just by outsourcing a phase of the business to another company and paying the company for the service, but rather outsourcing a phase of the business to a company that will invest and take ownership in the process. Turbo-outsourcing not only minimizes the cash outflow from the inventor but also provides the inventor with a dynamic partner who is spending its time and money to help accelerate the product into the market. In traditional outsource manufacturing arrangements, an inventor pays the manufacturer for each product and for all start-up manufacturing costs. In turbo-outsourcing agreements, the manufacturer pays for the start-up costs and production in return for any number of benefits, which could include a share of the business, an extra profit

per piece, a long-term guaranteed production contract, or exclusive access to certain markets.

3. *Starting your own business* could mean producing and marketing an idea in your own basement—or raising money and forming a billion-dollar company. Most product-related companies in this country start with individual inventors. Medtronics, Apple Computer, Microsoft, General Electric, and General Mills are just a few of the companies started by an inventor. This road may be difficult, and inventors might need to bring on experienced management help, but inventors do succeed all the time in very big ways. Starting your own company presents by far the biggest opportunity for creating high value for the inventor, but it is also the most difficult and expensive approach to introducing a new product.

KEY FACTORS IN DETERMINING YOUR STRATEGY: CHOOSE WHAT WORKS FOR YOU, YOUR PRODUCT, AND YOUR MARKET

Use the Introduction Strategy Scorecard in Figure 5.1 to determine a point score for each introduction approach. The minimum desired requirement indicates the level needed to succeed for each approach. For example, in the Margin row, you can see that high margins are needed for turbo-outsourcing, medium to high margins for licensing, and low to medium margins for a start-up company. If margins are high, all three approaches would score 1, as it is over the minimum for each. But if margins are low, then only starting your own company would receive a point. Score 1 point if your product strongly fits the preference or condition of that category and 0.5 points if your product fits the category, but not strongly. Things may not work out exactly as the scorecard suggests, but it is a good starting point. Explanations for each of the 10 key factors in the figure follow.

Comments about Key Factors

1. *How big is the vision?* Some products have large potential that can have long-lasting impact on a company's bottom line. The first Palm Pilot, which started the trend for personal digital assistants (PDAs), had a big vision. Other products might extend a product type to new market applications, offer additional uses, or improve a company's product line with a key new feature. Such products have an average vision. Products that better serve a significant existing market also fall into the

Figure 5.1 Introduction Strategy Scorecard

	Licensing		Turbo-Outsourcing		Starting Your Own Company	
Key Factor	Minimum Requirement	Score	Minimum Requirement	Score	Minimum Requirement	Score
How big is the vision?	Medium to large		Large		Small	
Fit for manufacturing	High		High		Small	
Product line importance	High		Average		N/A	
Margins	Average to high		High		Average to high	
Product life	Average +		Short +		Average +	
Skills and expertise	Low		High		High or add a partner	
Time available	Low		Medium		High	
Financial capabilities vs. intro costs	Low		Low/ medium		Depends on project	
Access to customers	Low		Medium		High	
Availability of distribution	Low		Medium		High	

average category. Finally, some products serve small or narrow markets, and while they can be profitable, their scope and sales potential is limited. A new style of saddle cushions for endurance horse racers or new field-repair bike racks for mountain-bike racers serve only limited markets and are examples of products with lower potential or vision. Turbo-outsourcing typically requires a big vision because the product has to produce profits for three companies; licensing can get by with average to high vision since companies will license products to protect their current market share or to be first in the market with a product for a new application. People starting their own business can do so with all types of products—from those with small sales potential to those having monumental vision, like the Apple Computer.

2. *Fit for manufacturing.* This refers to whether a licensee or turbo-outsource partner has the manufacturing equipment already in place to build the product. To be a good fit, the licensee or partner should have all the right manufacturing equipment in place.

Otherwise the start-up will be costly and take more time. Licensing agreements are typically struck because they offer product line and market share benefits to companies who will license products even if they have to add manufacturing capability or outsource production. Starting your own company, by definition, means acquiring a manufacturing facility, but you need to be sure that your product won't require a technology that is beyond your technical and financial capabilities.

3. *Importance to the product line.* This refers to whether a new product strengthens and increases sales for an entire product line. An improved cellular phone headset, for example, could help sales of a company's cell phone line. This is a major deciding factor in many licensing agreements. Companies look at a product's overall benefit to their other products rather than just the bottom line for the licensed product. This is especially true if a new product helps a company break into a new market application with its entire product line. Turbo-outsourcing deals are generally done because of the huge market potential, so the new item's importance to the company's overall product line is average. An inventor start-up company does not need to consider this factor because it doesn't have product line.

4. *Margins.* Margin is the revenue received by the manufacturer (also called *wholesale price*) when a company sells to distributors, retailers, or wholesalers after deducting the manufacturing cost and dividing by the manufacturer's revenue.

$$\frac{\text{Manufacturer's revenue} - \text{manufacturing cost}}{\text{Manufacturer's revenue}} = \text{margin}$$

For example, if a manufacturer sells a product to a distributor for \$160 and its manufacturing cost is \$90, then its margin is as follows:

$$\frac{\$160 - \$90}{\$160} = \frac{\$70}{\$160} = 43.75\% \text{ margin}$$

All companies need high margins. Licensing requires a minimum 50 percent margin. Otherwise the company won't have enough profits to pay you a royalty. Turbo-outsourcing requires even higher margins, perhaps 60 percent, as three companies will be participating in the profits, and without higher margins there won't be enough to go around. Inventors starting their own company should also strive for 50 percent margins. They can survive with 30 to 40 percent margins, but they won't make a lot of money.

Margins need to be even higher if companies sell direct to consumers or end users. Those companies will have high sales, marketing, and service support costs. You want a 75 percent margin for products sold direct, with a rock-bottom margin of 65 percent for both licensing and turbo-outsourcing. Margins can't be lower than 60 to 65 percent for inventors starting their own companies.

5. *Product life.* This refers to how long you can expect to sell a product profitably. Today, a long product life is five to seven years. You need a long product life for licensing, because licensing deals typically take a year to finalize, and it might take another year for the company to introduce the product. Turbo-outsourcing products can have shorter life spans, even one-time-event products, as they typically work with partners who have manufacturing and distribution capabilities in place. Inventors starting their own company often take a little longer to move on their idea, and a five- to seven-year product life is best.

6. *Skills and expertise to run a company.* Inventors with few skills usually opt for licensing or starting their own company (after bringing on an operations person to run things). Turbo-outsourcing requires a high level of skill in marketing, sales, and negotiation but not usually in manufacturing or company operations.

7. *Time to devote to the project.* Starting your own company requires the most time. Less time is required for turbo-outsourcing, but you still need a minimum of 20 hours per week. Licensing requires the least effort once you get a license, but you may need to do extensive product development before you are ready to license your idea.

8. *Financial capabilities versus introduction costs.* This refers to an inventor's ability to fund, possibly with help from investors, the start-up costs for his or her product. Licensing and turbo-outsourcing both rely on other companies' money. Starting your own business requires financial resources—yours and/or those of investors willing to help launch your product.

9. *Access to customers.* In some markets—for example, school fund-raising projects—there are many roadblocks preventing sales by new inventor companies, but often the biggest one is that inventors can't discover who the right contact is to approach for a sale. Even when inventors know who the contact is, they may still have trouble reaching that individual. Other markets, like industrial supply houses, are slow to take on products from inventors, especially inventors with just one product. Inventors

can overcome these restrictions by selecting market connections who will get them in the door to make a presentation. Inventors who lack market connections to get them in front of customers are better off licensing their product or turbo-outsourcing with an established distribution company. Other markets, such as scrapbook stores, bike shops, and baby product stores, are open to inventors and make it easy for inventors to launch their own product.

10. *Availability of distribution.* Distribution is always present, but the channel might resist an inventor's sales efforts. Distributors to trucking companies, for example, resist carrying products from new companies because they worry about getting service if an inventor company goes out of business. This is not a big consideration in licensing and turbo-sourcing, because you rely on an established marketing company. Inventors who start their own company do best when they sell to markets that are open to new products. Paint stores, for example, are open to new products, and the distributors that serve the stores will take on new vendors.

As you make the way down the list you'll find that most products have some characteristics that favor licensing, some that favor turbo-outsourcing, and some that favor starting your own company. Typically you will see that one route is more conducive to your product, and that is the route you should explore first. I've also found that this list helps you see where you might have problems with your introduction so that you can take corrective action. For instance, if you want to start your own company and the distribution channel is closed, you might want to get a partner who has access to that channel.

LICENSE TO A MARKET PLAYER: LOWER YOUR RISK AND COLLECT A ROYALTY

Licensing is the preferred option for many engineering inventors who have no desire to run their own company and for multiple-product inventors who enjoy the creative process but dread the details of running a company. Some inventors believe they can't create winning products while also trying to run a company. Those inventors have a strong point. Inventions succeed in part because they offer clever solutions to hard-to-solve problems. Inventions also need a first-class design, an easy-to-understand benefit, and a cost-effective manufacturing process. Creating a product with all of those features is a full-time job and requires much of an inventor's time. Inventors who come up with technical product ideas or who are capable of coming up with two or three clever solutions are probably better off licensing their ideas when they can. It is also a good option for people who have just one great idea but no inclination to run their own company or to try to set up a turbo-outsourcing arrangement.

Advantages

1. Lower financial risk for most inventions.
2. Least time commitment.
3. Good chance you will receive income if a deal is signed.
4. Assistance is readily available. Sales representatives in the industry might represent you for a commission. A license represents a one-time sale with a potentially large payoff. Prototype developers and industrial designers are often more willing to take a percentage on a license agreement in return for their work, as they are confident they will get at least some money back if you find a licensee.
5. Fewest hassles with items like product liability insurance, unemployment insurance, and other details of running a company.
6. You have a good chance of signing additional licensing agreements once you sign one and your product succeeds.

Disadvantages

1. Long time to market. Companies often take a year to decide on a license and another year to actually introduce the product.
2. No control. Once the company takes over the product you typically have no input or control.
3. Lowest opportunity for long-term profits. A licensed product might sell for three to five years and then your royalty stream ends. Turbo-outsourcing or starting your own company both have the potential to evolve into major companies.
4. Lost opportunities with auxiliary or next-generation products. Every new product creates additional opportunities that the licensee might capitalize on by introducing additional products. Companies frequently start with one or two products and then expand to 20 or more related products as new opportunities arise. Inventor run companies can add those products and grow in size, but inventors who license probably will not share in these additional product revenue streams.

Why Companies License Products

1. The product may help their entire product line. Companies would rather introduce their own products than license a product, because they don't have to pay royalties on products they themselves develop. Therefore companies need an incentive to license an idea, either because the product has large market potential or because it protects or expands the company's market position. My experience is that most inventions are licensed for the second reason. For example, a company that makes a scrubber (those sponges with soap in the handle) might consider a scrubber rack that sits on the sink and allows the soap to drop back into the handle. That product would enhance the company's position in the market by providing more to offer mass merchandisers, supermarkets, and kitchen stores. Since most retailers will carry only one or two scrubbers, having the scrubber rack means the company will have an easier time securing shelf space for both products.

2. They may wish to expand into new markets. For example, an auto tool manufacturer might do a lot of business with auto parts stores, but have very few sales to auto mechanics. Such a company would be open to licensing an innovative product that simplified strut replacements if it thought they would help penetrate the auto mechanic market.

When Licensing Is an Ideal Strategy

1. Product-related issues
   - Up-front costs of manufacturing are too high for the inventor's resources.
   - Product complements others on the market, making it attractive to potential licensors.
   - Product calls for extensive sales or technical support.
   - Product's benefits require an explanation, which means the product requires extensive promotion or high sales support.
2. Market-related issues
   - Distribution channels are difficult to penetrate.
   - Customers won't buy from small vendors. This situation is common for industrial products, because customers worry about being stuck with an "orphan" product that lacks technical support if the company goes out of business.

- Each sale is small and requires a large sales effort. For example, if you sell to mass merchandisers, each order is big. As for hardware stores, you might get a chain to carry the product in its catalog, but you still need to market your product to individual stores to get them to order from the catalog.

3. Inventor-related issues
   - Lack of time or inclination to run a company.
   - Lack of expertise to find partners or raise money to launch a company.

What to Expect in the Licensing Process

1. **Response is slow.** Companies are typically slow to license products unless you can find an in-company supporter. They tend to string out the process with endless analysis.
2. **Proof will fall to the inventor.** You may need to prove every important point to the company, including that the product can be completely developed and sold for a profitable price and that the market will accept the product.
3. **A competitive threat may be needed.** Inventors almost always have to initiate action with one company by threatening to approach other companies.

Biggest Obstacles

1. **Manufacturing overhead costs may price the product out of the market.** Companies take all of their manufacturing overhead costs, including rent, utility charges, quality costs, scrap, and other expenses and divide it among each item produced at the plant. Big companies often have manufacturing overhead costs that are 40 percent of their total costs, and those costs can ruin a product's price/value relationship.
2. **Product may not add enough to the company.** Licensing a product is lots of work for a company, and the product, or its benefit to their line, must provide at least a 10 percent increase to the licensee's operations for the deal to be worthwhile.
3. **You have no inside supporter.** Inventors need someone in the company to get behind the idea and push it forward. A license deal is unlikely to happen without a potential licensee employee pushing the product.

Keys to Success

1. **A product that fits the company's overall product strategy.** Companies rarely pursue a stand-alone product; the additional profits typically aren't high enough. As a percentage of sales, 10 to 15 percent is on the high end of profit for companies. Most companies have profit margins as a percentage of sales that are closer to the 5 to 7 percent range. That being the case, how can a company afford to pay the inventor a royalty of 2 to 10 percent of sales? The money just isn't there. To have a strong chance of being licensed, your product needs to strengthen the licensee's overall product line.

2. **A clear path to producing a final design at a profitable cost.** I've worked at several companies on the marketing side of new product development. Every idea I've ever seen, and there have been well over 100, has unexpected wrinkles during the production of a final prototype and then a production model. About half the ideas I've seen without a prototype end up having major problems either in cost or performance of the final product. As a result, companies won't license a product without a high degree of certainty about a product's final design.

3. **Clear evidence that end users desire the product.** Inventors have this fantasy that companies know exactly what they are doing and will recognize a great product immediately. I've evaluated more than 20 products as a director of marketing for various companies and only twice was I sure the idea would sell. Proving the product will sell is the inventor's job, and you may need a test-marketing program or focus group testing to show that the market is ready for the product. Another way to develop evidence is to offer testimonials from key buyers in the market.

4. **Convincing proof that a distribution channel will carry the product.** Companies understand distributors better than they understand consumers and can typically predict how distributors will respond to a product. But you still need to offer proof. The best way to do this is to have an advisor or a partner who is out of the distribution network.

5. **Having an inside cheerleader.** Regional managers and marketing personnel are the best insiders to push for your idea. They don't suffer from a not-invented-here mentality and will push for a product they believe the market needs. You can make these contacts prior to a presentation by meeting potential insiders at trade shows and association meetings. Your chances of licensing a product go up from 100 to 500 percent if you are active in the industry before you make any presentations.

CAPITALIZE ON TURBO-OUTSOURCING: KEEP CONTROL WHILE MINIMIZING RISK

Turbo-outsourcing takes advantage of company specialization, the need for manufacturers to generate production volume, and the need for marketers and distributors to have innovative products to sell. Both manufacturing and marketing partners will invest in the product provided the margins and sales potential are high enough. You don't need multi-million-dollar sales potential because size is relative and depends on the size of your partner companies. I've seen turbo-outsourcing by an inventor with just a $750,000 per year market outsource through a small manufacturer with $1 million in sales—the $750,000 new product sales potential almost doubled the company's sales volume. Other times, turbo-outsourcing may need potential sales of $5 million per year or more to interest a partner.

Inventor Hustle Wins

Candace Vanice was a lover of french fries who was concerned about their fat content. She thought, "What could possibly be better than fat-free fries?" Vanice believed she had a home run idea. She went to work in her own kitchen and developed a recipe for fat-free fries that tasted just as good as regular fries. Vanice was ready to go to market, but a few problems existed. Supermarkets are a very tough market for inventors. Food brokers that sell to supermarkets think that $250,000 is a small order. Getting approvals to sell a food product is very expensive. Underfinanced inventors almost never launch a supermarket food product.

Fortunately, Vanice didn't know about these obstacles. She assumed all she needed was a manufacturer who would manufacture the product and a food broker to sell it. Of course, the trick was to convince them to do it. She started by persuading her local supermarket to allow her to offer free samples of her homemade fries at the store. She asked people to fill out surveys to give her feedback about the fat-free fries. When Vanice had a boxful of raving reviews she was ready for the next step.

She approached food brokers first, showed them her great results, and encouraged them to take on her product. They were reluctant until Vanice slipped into a full turbo-outsourcing mode. She promised to provide Saturday supermarket sampling in target markets, to generate publicity through aggressive TV appearances, and to provide follow-up with the supermarket owners to ensure her product didn't sit on store shelves. Her next step was to get a food manufacturer to make and fund production. Vanice also needed a cut of the profits from the food manufacturer's share of sales. The food manufacturer wasn't willing to fund everything, but they did agree to move ahead when Vanice offered to pay for a necessary $7,000 slicer. This was a great deal *for everyone. The manufacturer was small and had built a plant it could grow into, but needed new products and sales volume to maximize use of its plant. The broker gained a unique product with consumer appeal, which helped it capture additional market share for all of its food products. And Vanice was getting a share of the profits from a product that is normally far too difficult and expensive for inventors to introduce.*

Advantages

1. *Control.* The inventor can contribute to the decisions that affect increasing sales, running promotions, and pricing the product.
2. *New opportunities.* The inventor is right in the throes of the market and able to identify new market opportunities and profit from them.
3. *Low financial risk.* Typically, the partner companies, which in the case of the fat-free fries were the food broker and the food manufacturer, put up most of the money.
4. *Faster route to the market.* The partner companies should have financial and market resources that allow a project to move forward quickly.
5. *Quick decisions from partners.* Turbo-outsourcing asks companies to do only what they know how to do, and typically asks partners to use only the resources they already have. Their risk in trying out a new idea is lower than for licensing, so their decision process is much simpler.

Disadvantages

1. *Pressure.* Partner companies are investing and they expect results. They are not tolerant of a two- or three-week delay for personal reasons. They not only expect inventors to carry out their plans, they expect those plans to be successful.
2. *Tricky to get your share.* The inventor needs to get a cut of the profits, which could come from the distributor's sales or from the manufacturer's revenue from the distributor or from some other source. Both partners want to see how things work out before finalizing an agreement, but by then the inventor could end up with a very small share. Inventors have to negotiate early and firmly and use memorandums of understanding (MOUs) (see Chapter 8, pages 153 to 158) to protect their position.

3. *Early pullback of partners.* The partners' low risk means they can easily pull out if sales aren't developing as fast as expected. Again, early negotiations can minimize this problem, but you will have trouble keeping partners committed to a deal they have lost interest in.

4. *Possibility of thin profits.* Three partners splitting the profits usually means a small share for everyone. Inventors' partners typically benefit, as turbo-outsourcing increases their sales volume substantially, but you might have trouble keeping partners involved if margins shrink.

Why Companies Agree to Turbo-Outsourcing

1. *Maximizes committed resources.* A company with an underutilized manufacturing plant has plenty of fixed expenses to pay even if it is not producing a product. Adding a new product to the factory can often be done with little additional cost and allows the company to pay its expenses even if the actual margins are low. The same goes for distribution or marketing companies. They have a number of fixed resources in place, and they have a lot to gain if they can add another product and generate more profits and revenue without increasing expenses. The inventor's job is to fill in the missing resources to get the ball rolling. In the case of the fat-free fries, Vanice bought a food slicer for the manufacturer, offered free in-store sampling, and ran a publicity campaign for the food broker.

2. *Significant market growth potential.* Companies want to receive an immediate 10 to 20 percent boost in revenue without a big investment, but they also want to see that the product could increase long-term sales by 20 to 30 percent (or more) per year. Companies are willing to invest after some initial success shows the market potential developing.

When Turbo-Outsourcing Is the Ideal Strategy

1. *When your product represents a sizable (20 to 25 percent and sometimes more) increase in a potential partner company's revenue stream.* You can find out a company's revenue stream by looking in the manufacturers' directory for the state in which the company resides or in a *Dun & Bradstreet Company Directory*, both of which are available at larger libraries. Estimate your product's sales by finding

the sales volume of products that try to meet the same need as yours. You can find out other products' sales volumes from association data or from annual reports and company press releases. You can also just ask a company salesperson, who will sometimes tell you. If your product doesn't represent high enough sales potential it won't produce enough impact to make it worthwhile for the partner companies.

2. *When target partner companies have most of the resources in place to do their share of the project.* Companies may invest some funds, but their decisions and support will be slower and shakier if their required investment increases.

3. *When your product is capable of hitting a home run for everyone involved.* It is innovative and its market potential is large.

4. *When the market demands big suppliers and big players.* Sizable companies provide enough support for the product.

5. *When you can find a significant role to play in the product introduction.* Companies will agree to pay you a share of the business as long as you add value, but they may start to resent your share of the profits if you don't play a key role.

What to Expect in the Turbo-Outsourcing Process

1. *You will need to prove the market wants the product.*

2. *You will face resistance to signing MOUs and other legal documents.* Companies often want to proceed with just a purchase order or purchase contract. You have to fight for a contract to protect your rights.

3. *You need to persevere to learn what resources partner companies lack.* Companies may say no to being a partner because they have to invest too much in resources. They may not want to tell you their real reasons for not moving ahead. You need good rapport and a friendly inside contact to uncover the reason for resistance so you can find a way around it.

4. *Companies may push you too fast.* If the deal looks good and your partner companies need the business, they might push you to move faster than you can reasonably move. You must firmly set timetables and schedules you can live with.

5. *You will have to play companies against each other.* Most partners want to be the last one to make a commitment and will try to wait until the other partner commits. You have to communicate your partners' need to each other to keep the deal going in a way that

makes sense to everyone. For example, it makes sense that your manufacturing partner won't invest $20,000 until the marketing partner signs on. Use this fact as leverage against the marketing partner to keep the deal moving ahead.

Biggest Obstacles

1. *Finding the right-size partners.* Your deal won't be attractive to a partner that is too big or too small. A project with a 20 to 25 percent impact on a company is just right. Less than that and the project is too small to create an impact for the partner company. More than 40 percent and the company probably can't perform its part of the project without adding significant resources.
2. *Too much investment.* You must have manufacturing partners that have the right equipment in place. That doesn't happen with every product, and without the right equipment in place a potential turbo-outsourcing partner will be reluctant to commit to moving ahead. One slow decision-making partner could derail the deal's momentum and kill the project.
3. *Not enough margin.* Some markets are tough and competitive, and your product might not have enough profit to share among three partners.
4. *Partner's confidence in the inventor.* The inventor plays a key role in the introduction plan with turbo-outsourcing, and companies are going to worry about whether you have the expertise, experiences, and management skills to fulfill your part. An inventor may need a part-time partner or an advisory panel to demonstrate that he or she has enough experience.

Keys to Success

1. *High impact.* You need the market to accept your product in a big hurry, which happens only if you have an important, unique benefit for end users so they will want to buy.
2. *Inventor as end user.* The better you know your product area, the better chance you have of gaining the confidence of your partners. Being an end user will help you deliver the right product the first time and keep your partners' confidence high.
3. *Ready customers.* A ready customer is one who will buy your product even if he or she already has something similar. Lawn-mowers will never have ready customers because people almost

always wait until their current lawnmower breaks down. Customers with passion see an idea as having an impact on their lives and will buy a product even if they already own a product for the same use.

4. *Great negotiating skills.* Friendly and fast negotiations will create market momentum. Your partners might drop the deal if they think negotiations will be long and painful. Be sure to get an attorney who believes the goal is to get a signed contract and who won't hold things up nitpicking and prolonging every negotiating point.

BUILD A COMPANY: MAXIMIZE YOUR PROFIT AND WEALTH POTENTIAL

Inventors, and not necessarily inventors with lots of money and/or skills, started many (if not most) of the product-oriented companies in America. In the past 10 years I've talked to hundreds of inventors who have started businesses, and many now have sales of $5 million or more. Many inventor groups push licensing as the preferred choice for inventors, but I don't agree. A license might produce income for you for three or four years. You can build a lifelong income with a company, producing one product after another, and you can produce a substantial business with plenty of value if you stay with the concept. Of course, starting a business is hard work and there are many obstacles, but I believe that most inventors achieve long-standing success by starting their own company. It is the only way for an inventor to keep complete control of his or her product and its future.

Advantages

1. *Best opportunity for creating real wealth for the inventor.* Some inventors go on to form million-dollar companies. Licensing and turbo-outsourcing produce short-term income but not necessarily lasting wealth.

2. *Complete control over your invention.* This includes subsequent product improvements, and future product development.

3. *Control over timing.* You can control how fast you want to introduce the product, expand in the marketplace, and add investors and sales outlets.

4. *Develop management experience.* Launching one successful company helps inventors launch additional companies in the future.

Disadvantages

1. *Highest risk.* An inventor's investment in money and time to launch the product is typically high. Starting your own company also has a lower chance of success than turbo-outsourcing, because turbo-outsourcing partners often have an already established market presence.
2. *Market resistance.* Retailers, distributors, and end users are often reluctant to deal with a one-line inventor company because they worry that it may not last long.
3. *Long time to significant profitability.* Inventors often need to start out slowly in the market because of limited financial resources or limited experience. They may require two years or more to start making money.
4. *Fund raising required.* Inventors starting their own company frequently spend 50 percent and more of their time raising money, a task not relished by many inventors.
5. *Enduring many tough times.* Rejection, lack of funds, product returns and other unexpected setbacks occur frequently for new companies. Inventors are sheltered from many of these problems in both licensing and turbo-outsourcing. But they face them all on their own when they start their own company.

Why Inventors Start Their Own Company

1. *They want to be entrepreneurs and own a company.* The desire to succeed is just as important as the inventor's financial or management capabilities. Many inventors with virtually no experience or financial resources do succeed when they have plenty of perseverance to overcome obstacles.
2. *They aren't able to get a license or turbo-outsourcing arrangement.* Failure to land another type of agreement does not mean a product can't make money. Your product might have a small market niche; other people might not see the product's market potential; the margins might be too small to share via licensing and turbo-outsourcing strategies. But these obstacles may be easily surmountable for an inventor-run company.

When Starting a Company Is an Ideal Strategy

1. *When the distribution channel is open to inventors.* Distribution is looking for products that target new trends or those that serve

small niche markets with well-defined needs. Distribution is more resistant to inventors when the market is large and has many suppliers.

2. *When the inventor has a ready-made client base.* Inventors are occasionally well connected to both their potential customers and the existing distribution network.

Bull's-Eye on the Target Market

Jason Lee and Patrick McConnell were thrill-seeking snowboarders who just didn't know what to do in the off-season. So they decided to create a MountainBoard, a snowboard-type device with all-terrain wheels and a suspension system for cruising down mountain trails in the summer. At first the inventors didn't have much funding, but they sold all the product they could afford to make, and after three successful years they hit $3 million in sales. The secret to their success—they knew exactly what wild-and-crazy 16- to 25-year-old males wanted, because they'd been dealing with them every winter while snowboarding. They also knew the specialty snowboard, surfboard, and skateboard shops where their target audience frequently stopped to check out new products. They succeeded because they were a part of their own market, and they knew exactly how to deal with both the distribution channel and their end users.

---

3. *When you have access to sufficient capital.* Inventors who can line up sufficient capital from friends and family for the initial stages of a business have the best chance of keeping a controlling interest in their company. Professional investors might insist on significant control of the company if you need their money before you can prove the product will sell.

4. *When the inventor can control the product development process.* The control might come from the inventor's own expertise or because the product is easy to produce. The inventor might also keep control because he or she has a partner who can do the development or because of an arrangement with a manufacturer who will pay for the product development.

What to Expect in Starting Your Own Company

1. *Market reception varies.* Your product and company will be readily accepted if you are entering a market that's new or open to inventors. Expect a chilly reception in a big market with many competitors.

2. *Market contacts are crucial.* You may need to spend the first three to six months of your introduction making industry contacts with sales and marketing people who can help you reach key buyers and distributors.

3. *Cash flow is negative for a long time.* The faster you sell your product the more operating cash you need. New products often take six months to turn cash paid for inventory into paid receivables. A fast-starting company that reaches $1 million in sales in the first year will need operating capital of $200,000 to $250,000.

4. *Customers will stop buying if they experience one or two problems.* New inventor companies can't afford mistakes with poor quality, missed deliveries, or wrong shipments. Distributors and retailers are skittish about unproven new companies, and they will drop you quickly after a few mistakes on your part—sometimes after only one mistake.

5. *Investors will require time.* Fund-raising itself takes time. In addition, you need to work hard to keep investors up-to-date about what's going on with your company. You will have to spend even more time with investors if you are not meeting their expectations.

6. *People will support you.* You will get plenty of help from investors and people in the industry if you involve them in your company early, before you really need them. People will help you in many ways if they have a stake in your company's success.

Biggest Obstacles

1. *Stringent requirements.* For consumer products you might need Underwriters Laboratory (UL) approval (required for electrical products' use in homes), product liability insurance, and possibly expensive electronic data equipment to deal with mass merchandisers. These requirements vary by product, and often the expense is considerable for new inventors.

2. *Manufacturing costs too high.* Inventors, because they can't afford high-volume production or the manufacturing tools that allow it might never be able to get their costs down to the point at which they can sell the product and still make money.

3. *Not enough market contacts.* Contacts open doors that give inventors a chance, and without them an inventor may never make a significant sale.

4. *Costs of producing a market-ready product.* Inventors 20 years ago might have gotten by with a product that looked like it was made

in a garage. But not any longer. People expect, and will only buy, professional-looking products. That look often requires special tooling and other costs that are beyond the reach of the inventor.

5. *Short-lived windows of opportunity.* Other people may see the same market opportunities as the original inventor. If inventors take too long to enter the market they may find competition that didn't initially exist, or the market may have just moved on to a different level, erasing the market window.

Keys to Success

1. *Market connections.* The best market connections are buyers for bigger retail chains or for businesses that will use your product (if you have an industrial product). Second best are marketing people for manufacturers that serve the market segment, preferably marketing people for companies serving your target customer and distribution channel. The third best are inventors who have successfully introduced a product and know lots of people in the market.

2. *Ideal distribution networks.* An ideal distribution network is one that is easy to access and that easily reaches your target customer. For example, pool supply stores are ideal distribution networks because pool owners visit them frequently and they are open to small inventor-started companies. Ideal products fit into a distribution channel that already exists for the target customer. Camera stores are not as strong a distribution network for inventors as pool stores because camera owners don't buy camera supplies very often, and when they do they purchase supplies at many different types of stores including drugstores, mass merchants, and even supermarkets.

3. *Significant benefits to end users.* The market searches for innovative products, but at the same time markets like to buy from established suppliers. The net result is that inventors need products with a minimum 30 to 40 percent improvement over competitive products. The ideal situation is when the benefits are in an area that is important to end users. A Java Jacket provides an extra layer of protection for a hot coffee cup—a meaningful benefit because the cup is no longer too hot to hold. A Tool Tree, which holds 15 long-handled garden tools, is nice, but keeping the garage neat is not as important to most people as being able to hold a hot cup of coffee comfortably.

4. *Manageable product development and manufacturing costs.* Unless inventors can do the prototype development themselves or partner with an engineer or prototype developer, high-technology or difficult-to-make products will be very expensive.

5. *Flexibility.* Many successful inventors end up adjusting their product to the market: They find a market they hadn't thought of before; end users suggest one more or one less feature; it dawns on them that a small change could cut manufacturing costs in half. Inventors who are willing to constantly listen, learn, and adapt have by far the best chance of success.

PART II

THE FAST TRACK: LICENSING YOUR IDEA

6

STEP 6A. PROVE THE CONCEPT: DEMONSTRATE WHY YOUR PRODUCT IS "HOT"

The licensee, whether it is a manufacturer, marketer, or product development company, takes on most of the risk when they are selling the new product. Companies are usually cautious in taking on a product until they feel comfortable that it will sell. This chapter covers how inventors can demonstrate, without spending a lot of time or money, that a product has a great chance of being a big winner in the market. Extensive proof may not always be needed. Sometimes inventors sell the idea from a prototype without any proof at all. The potential licensee just recognizes right away that the product is great and will sell. But since that doesn't happen in most cases, I've prepared an approach for the worst-case scenario: when the potential licensee has no idea whether the product will sell. If you believe your product's potential might be fairly obvious to potential licensees, you can use only the elements of the chapter you think are necessary to sell your product. The goal of this chapter is to help you prepare documentation to use in your licensee presentation that is explained in more detail in Chapter 10. This chapter covers the following concepts.

- Locate expert help: Communicate the product's potential by using industry helpers.
- Capture the market potential: Show you are on the leading edge.
- Prove market demand: Use tactics that produce provisional orders.

- Illustrate manufacturing costs: Produce significant profits on each order.
- Show a path to the future: Explain how your product is the first of many.

Help Is All Around

Tim Abbot's mother, diagnosed with cancer, had trouble watering her flower gardens. Abbot thought a perfect solution to this problem would be to have the common black plastic edging used around flower beds double as a sprinkling hose. All he needed to do was to place holes along the top edge, run water through the edging, and a perfect product would be born, as the edging would act as a hose.

Abbot, who had been an office equipment repairman for 20 years, decided to pursue his invention full-time. The only trouble was, Abbot had no experience in business and even less in injection-molded plastic parts. Abbott started first to gain the knowledge he needed. He visited the Indiana Small Business Development Center in South Bend more than 80 times to discuss his plans and to receive advice on how to proceed. He used the Collegiate Management Assistance program at the University of Notre Dame for market research. He received technical advice from Purdue University's technical assistance program. Early on, Abbot formed a partnership with a tool and die company, Journeyman Tool and Die, to develop prototypes and early production models. The two original partners took on three additional partners—a retired patent attorney and two marketing specialists—and together they founded and incorporated a plastics and packaging company to improve their odds of licensing the product.

What finally put the product over the top was a last-minute trip to QVC to convince the home shopping network to put the product on the air. The group was able to license the product after the QVC exposure, and the licensee was able to place the product in Home Depot and other major retailers. Abbot succeeded because many helpers not only offered him lots of support but also reduced his financial risk.

LOCATE EXPERT HELP: COMMUNICATE THE PRODUCT'S POTENTIAL BY USING INDUSTRY HELPERS

Why You Need Them

One of the major mistakes people make is not getting a manufacturer's representative, distributor salesperson, or a marketing person from the industry to help license the product in return for 10 to 20 percent of the royalty proceeds. In my opinion, the odds of finding a licensee at least doubles when your helper has a financial stake in the product's success. An industry professional's endorsement is a powerful sales point to most potential licensees. The industry person also provides additional benefits.

- *Contacts.* The industry professional will know people at target companies, key people in the industry who influence its direction, and potential customers who might give you a letter of endorsement, a letter of intent to buy, or even a provisional order stating that the company will buy the product if it is produced as specified. The best way to use an industry person on commission is to first have that individual line up support for the product and demonstrate that other people, particularly customers, like the product. Then have the person help you set up meetings with the companies you have targeted together.
- *Industry knowledge.* People in the industry know the jargon, know which products have done well or poorly, and know what direction the industry is taking. They also know what companies are trying to accomplish—so you can gear each presentation to exactly what the company wants to hear.
- *Daily interactions in the industry.* Timing is important in licensing, and it may turn out that the market is just not ready to license the product when you are. Timing, however, can change, and someone who works in the industry will recognize changes that may make a license agreement easier to sell, a change that the inventor could easily miss.
- *Easy to work with.* When entering into licensing talks, companies are often wary that negotiations with the inventor will be difficult. They fear inventors will bring in a hardball lawyer and/or negotiate to death every contract point. They fear this because it often happens, primarily because inventors aren't familiar with licensing negotiations and don't always know what is fair. Companies are generally more confident that negotiations will go smoothly if an industry person is helping the inventor.

How to Find a Professional to Help You

The best market connections are buyers for bigger retail chains or, in the case of industrial products, for businesses that will use your product. Second best are marketing people for manufacturers that serve the market segment, preferably marketing people for companies serving your target customer and distribution channel. You can also rely on salespeople or manufacturer's sales agents if they have been in the market for a long time. There are several ways to find an industry professional.

- *Develop personal contacts.* Most inventors tell me they don't know a market contact. But I've found contacts at church, Boy Scouts, the PTA, and youth baseball games. Just tell people that you are an inventor with a new product, describe the product briefly, and then ask if they know anyone involved in selling that type of product. You'll be amazed how often someone knows somebody who can help you. Your local inventors' club can also help you find some initial market contacts.

- *Talk to potential retail customers to learn the names of local sales representatives or distributor salespeople.* Call the people, ask them to lunch, and present your idea to see whether they like it and will represent the product to industry.

- *Visit trade shows.* Go to shows, talk to people in booths or at tables in the food area, and see if you can meet someone to help you. I know several inventors who made their key contact in a bar at a convention hotel after the show closed for the evening.

- *Request literature from trade magazines.* When the literature comes, there will often be a salesperson's name on the cover letter. Contact that person to see whether he or she likes your idea and would be willing to promote it.

CAPTURE THE MARKET POTENTIAL: SHOW YOU ARE ON THE LEADING EDGE

Companies can take two years or more from when they first start evaluating an idea to when they actually introduce it. Some of that time lost is due to a slow decision process, but most of the delay is simply because it takes time to complete engineering documentation for production and then set up a manufacturing line. Potential licensees have the same types of delays with their own products, and as a result companies are always looking for products related to new trends that will be selling strongly in three to five years. The ideal situation for a licensee is to have a product that can help sell an entire product line so you can cash in on the new trend. Your job is to convince a potential licenser that your product can do just that. In the case of Tim Abbot's garden hose, the sales point was that the increasing number of townhome developments would open up a market for small garden products. Abbot could pitch that his improved watering system was a perfect product to serve this market.

Follow these four steps to prove that your product meets the emerging market.

1. *Show an evolution of products.* All product categories evolve. They start with one-product-fits-all to increasingly specialized items. Specialization creates a variety of price points, an array of applications, and various modifications (or complete overhauls) to meet new market demands, different levels of technology, and degrees of visual appeal. You want to show that your invention is the next logical step of a product's evolution. In Abbot's case, he could show a steady stream of new products, from the old-fashioned circular and oscillating sprinklers to a host of new sprinklers over the past 10 years.

2. *Focus on a target market segment.* Gardeners with small display gardens in either townhomes or private residences were the target market. The focus was on flower gardens and the benefits to flower gardens. Potential licensees would be impressed with this growing segment because it's a market that provides high margins. Abbot could sell the story that the new sprinkler was more than a stand-alone product: It was a window into a desirable market segment.

3. *Capitalize on the technology trends.* The evolution of some products concentrates on technology developments. Today, DVDs and CDs are common, and you would have a hard time licensing a related product. But there was a time when DVDs and CDs were only being tested. At that time, it was probably two to three years before the products were ready for market, and that would have been the time to secure a licensing agreement.

4. *Show the development of new market categories.* Once again, companies have the most interest in emerging market categories that may be small today, but will have a major influence in several years. All companies want to be first in these categories, but you'll find that big companies' new product development generally lags behind that of smaller, more agile competitors. Inventors do well licensing products that accelerate licensees into new markets.

   New market categories can typically be identified by keeping close track of new product press releases in industry trade magazines or by attending trade shows. Virtually all companies announce new products with press releases in trade magazines. If you contact the companies for literature you'll find references to new developing markets. You can also attend industry trade shows and discover trends by asking people about the new products they have and why they are being introduced.

PROVE MARKET DEMAND: USE TACTICS
THAT PRODUCE PROVISIONAL ORDERS

The best proof that your product will sell is to have orders in hand. This is far better than the use of focus groups, market studies, or consumer questionnaires. Bringing in a big account is a good way to start licensing negotiations. Most of the time, inventors don't have orders in their back pocket, but that doesn't mean there aren't ways to generate them prior to production, the best being provisional orders, followed by letters of intent and support. If you aren't well connected in the industry you will probably need the help of someone who can get the process started.

Provisional or Conditional Orders

A company won't give you an order without seeing what the final product is actually like. But it might give you a *provisional order*, which is an order with conditions that protect the buyer. For instance, the order could include this statement

> Prior to order confirmation and shipment the following conditions must be met:
> - Actual production sample must be approved by [customer's name].
> - Pricing, including freight, must be verified and accepted by [customer's name].
> - Delivery dates and quantities shipped must be accepted and approved by [customer's name].
> - No order cancellation charges will apply if the above conditions are not met.

A provisional order is really just a strong letter of intent, as the potential customer is not offering a firm purchase order. It's a lot of work for a company to put one together, however, and potential licensees will be impressed if you have provisional orders before your licensing presentation. Companies are reluctant to offer a provisional order due to the paperwork of placing any order, but they will do it if first they like your idea and have a sincere interest in buying it, and if they realize the product won't be produced unless you sign a licensing contract. Companies will understand that a provisional order will help you land an agreement and, if they want the product, might be willing to give you one. Companies are doing the inventor a big favor by offering a provisional order, which is why it helps to be working with an industry contact who has an established relationship with potential buyers. You can increase your chances of landing a provisional order by promising programs and benefits to the prospect when your product is introduced. Additional strategies include offering to support a company's promotional campaign, whereby you might do seminars, presentations, or demos; promise to prepare a model to exhibit at trade shows and sales meetings; and agree to help the company prepare promotional literature or sales incentive programs when the product is released.

The Power of Letters

Although not as impressive as provisional orders, letters can nonetheless pack some punch.

Letters of Intent
Statements in a strong letter of intent include the following:

- The company has reviewed the product.
- The company, or the market, has a need for this product.
- The company intends to buy the product if it becomes available.
- The company estimates the yearly volume it intends to purchase.

Letter of Support
This is similar to a letter of intent, but it states that the company is willing to consider buying the product if it becomes available versus expressing an actual intent to buy.

Follow-Up Confirmation Letters from the Inventor
Companies are reluctant to offer provisional orders and letters of intent and support because they don't want to commit to buying a product that might not be available for two or three years. Another option you should always take is to send a follow-up letter after every conversation or appointment with a contact. Do this even if you talk to someone briefly at a trade show or association meeting. In the letter:

- Thank the person for talking to you about your idea.
- Thank the person for the support he or she showed you for your idea.
- Restate positive remarks the person made to you. For example, if the person tells you that "your touch-pad programming feature is better than the competition," reaffirm that statement in your letter. For example, "I was pleased that you were able to immediately notice the improvements I've made in the touch-pad controls."

- Mention that you will recontact the person once the product becomes available.

These letters show licensees you've been getting feedback on your idea and that there is support for your idea from people in the industry.

ILLUSTRATE MANUFACTURING COSTS: PRODUCE SIGNIFICANT PROFITS ON EACH ORDER

One of the biggest stumbling blocks to new product licenses is the perception that the manufacturing costs are too high relative to the product's perceived value: when the potential licensee believes that the costs will be too high, that your product will need a major engineering overhaul before it can be sold, and that a major engineering effort still might not lower costs. The result is that potential licensees will forgo an idea when manufacturing costs are uncertain—even if they like the product. Inventors can overcome this problem by having their product reviewed by an engineer for cost improvements, by preparing a detailed bill of materials with sourcing information, or by getting an actual quote from a contract manufacturer for both small and large volumes.

Engineer Review for Cost Reduction

Most inventor products start out with a rough model made in the garage or basement. Initially, inventors are mostly interested in building a model that works the way they'd like it to. But far too often, inventors never move beyond this stage and the product looks like it will cost too much. Have an engineer who works in applications development, research and development, or cost reduction review your idea to suggest changes to address this problem. If you can't find an engineer to help you, industrial designers can also perform this function.

You might have an engineering contact who can help you; otherwise, the best place to look for an engineer is at your local inventors' club (www.inventorsdigest.com and www.uiausa.com list both U.S. and Canadian clubs) or the Service Corps of Retired Executives (SCORE) at www.sba.gov/gopher/Local-Information/Service-Corps-of-Retired-Executives/. You can show that your product can be built cheaply even if your prototype has a more expensive design, but you'll have the best chance to license your idea if you build a prototype with the most cost-effective design. I believe strongly that you are always better off showing your product exactly in its final design.

Bill of Materials by Subassembly with Sourcing

You especially need to do this if the company you are talking to isn't familiar with certain parts in your product. A *bill of materials* (BOM) is a list of every part in the product; a *subassembly* is a major component; and a *source* is simply the manufacturer you might buy the product from. You can find examples of BOM and assemblies by looking at some of the installation manuals that come with products you buy. They typically have drawings of the product, broken out into components, and a parts list. All you need to do is add sourcing information. People from SCORE or the inventors' clubs can help you if you run into problems.

Your BOM provides material costs to your product. On top of materials costs you also have labor costs for assembly, packaging costs, and overhead costs. As a rule of thumb, aim for materials costs (less packaging) to be one-eighth of the final selling price to have an attractive manufacturing cost. For example, if you want your product to retail for $20.00, your material cost should be about $2.50. Earlier in the book I stated that a product should sell for four to five times its manufacturing costs, which in this case would mean the product should cost $4.00 to $5.00. The difference between material and total costs is overhead and labor expenses. Most products end up with overhead of anywhere from 20 to 50 percent of their total manufacturing costs. So keeping materials to one-eighth of the costs leaves room for packaging and overhead costs and for your royalty payments.

Quotes from Contract Manufacturers

Secure these cost quotes for both an initial volume and a larger volume that you might expect a licensee to sell the second year after the product is introduced. These quotes need to be about 25 percent of the final retail price since the manufacturer will include its overhead costs in its quote. Since you must hit a manufacturing cost of 25 percent of your suggested retail price, you may need to get quotes from several manufacturers. You can get by with a cost of 35 percent of the final retail price if the product is from a U.S. manufacturer but could be produced overseas.

If you need overseas sourcing, visit the following for sourcing agents that are experienced in working with inventors: www.hometwon.aol .com/egtgolbaltrading.com, www.acessasia.com., www.deltechusa.com, and www.opsaamerica.com. You can also check out these sites if you want to deal directly with the manufacturer: www.mfgquote.com, www.chinabiz .com, www.outsourceking.com, www.ec21.com, www.chinafacturing.com, and www.rockleighindustries.com.

SHOW A PATH TO THE FUTURE: EXPLAIN HOW YOUR PRODUCT IS THE FIRST OF MANY

There is an old adage in sales and marketing that it is easier to sell a million-dollar product than it is to sell one for $10,000. That's because the million-dollar product commands the attention of the chief executive—the key decision maker. The same situation exists in licensing. You want to paint the picture of your product opening big doors for the licensee, one that will produce steady growth for years. Without showing the potential for substantial growth, your product may get on the list of something a company would like to do, but more than likely will never get around to doing.

A key part of your licensee presentation should be the huge spin-off opportunities from your product. More important, you will generate a much more favorable initial response to your product if you create some key phrases about the benefits of your product that correspond to a company's overall strategic direction. For example, take the inventor of a pond filtration pump and filter for outdoor ponds. He or she might create some interest by explaining that "the filter-pump combination is 30 percent more effective than current products." He or she will create a lot more interest by stating: "This new pump will be the first equipment pond developers and homeowners will buy. It produces the first truly trouble-free pond. It will open the door to the entire pond equipment market." The second introduction will generate at least three times the interest of the benefit-oriented opening and is the only type of phrase that will catch the ear of a decision-making executive. Here are four approaches you can take to sell a big vision.

Additional Markets

Or as they are called in today's marketing vernacular, verticals. Verticals are different markets for the same product. For example, a few of the markets for cryogenic storage containers are: transplants; shipments of medical samples; animal fertility products; welding supplies and restaurant carbonation. Each of those markets is a vertical, or different market, for a cryogenic container.

It is important that you chose your message for your target customer. If you were selling to a metal container company, you could tell them that your new improved cryogenic product would give them a chance to penetrate the high-end, high-profit medical markets. But if you are selling to a supplier to the restaurant industry, you would want to say that your product will allow the licensee to dominate the market for better tasting juices.

Product Line Extensions

A potential licensee might have the best vise grip on the market, and it might be sold in every hardware store in the country, but that might be the only product it sells. The potential licensee would, of course, do better to sell a whole line of gripping products, including all types of pliers and plumbing wrenches; but a company with one good product often has difficulty expanding its product line against competitors. A breakthrough product, for instance superior adjustable gripping pliers, can break down the barriers a company faces and encourage retailers to buy more products from that company. In many cases, getting more types of products on store shelves is the only way that a company can grow. Possible selling phrases here are: "Here is a new product that will allow your company to double and even possibly triple the number of products it can sell to stores" or "The product can triple the number of stores that will carry your products."

Close Alignment with a Customer Group

Callaway Golf Company originally targeted older golfers with its graphite shaft that provided more club speed and therefore more distance. This was a great pitch to older golfers who couldn't swing as hard as they once did. Since that initial introduction, Callaway has kept its focus on older golfers by offering oversized clubs, dubbed "Big Bertha," and longer-flying golf balls to help them keep their scores down.

Companies want to be a preferred supplier to a target customer group, and licensees are always interested in a product that gives them an edge in a market because it allows them to introduce many more products to that same target group. Graphite clubs catapulted Callaway from a very small company to a major force in the golf market. The target phrase to use: "This product will place you squarely in the target customer's world and put you in a position to be the group's preferred supplier."

Dominating a Developing Market Trend

There might be 20 to 30 companies in an existing market. But typically only two or three companies offer products at the beginning of a new market trend. Three years after a new development, there could be 20 competitors in the market. That's true whether the trend is driven by consumer demands, new consumer tastes, application changes, or improved technology. The companies with the first products on the market typically dominate the market for several years because they learn faster than anyone else what the customers need and want.

This tactic can be an especially effective sales tool if you track historic trends in the industry: which companies introduced the first products, how many products now serve that market trend, and what market share those companies now hold in the market. Most of the time you will find the number of new products in the market grew rapidly and that the early companies still enjoy great success.

This strategy can work two ways for you. First, products meeting the needs of a new trend help some manufacturers gain market share even if the trend is well recognized in the market. Potential licensee targets are marketers or companies that have significant market share in the overall market category but aren't strong competitors in the emerging market. They need to play catch-up. The tactic can also work on a just-developing trend, where customers are making do with existing products. You may have to do some research to prove the trend is developing, perhaps interviewing key users to explain the story behind it, how the trend developed, and why it is likely to continue to grow. The target phrase here is, "This product will put you in an early leadership position in what looks to be a major new market."

7

STEP 7A. CHOOSE YOUR TARGETS: DETERMINE WHICH COMPANIES WILL BENEFIT THE MOST

Inventors frequently fail to choose the right target companies and deliver the right message because they are chasing the biggest companies in the market. The flaw in that approach is simple: Big companies with well-established market positions seldom license products. Their rationale is what is commonly dubbed "cannibalizing the product line." This refers to the fact that when a company introduces a new product, much of the product's sales come as a result of sales of existing products. For example, when a company introduces a new chain saw, typically 75 percent or more of its sales are at the expense of the company's previous chain saw. Many, many times, the sale of new product only marginally bests sales of the previous product. It is not profitable for a market leader to replace existing products with a product on whose sales it needs to pay a royalty. Companies that sign license agreements are typically smaller to midsize companies looking to break into a new market. They are anxious to expand sales into a new market and don't run the risk of cannibalizing their own product line, as they don't have a strong position in the market already. Licensing products depends on knowing how to find the right targets. I believe products are often licensed as result of a positive first impression. That impression depends just as much on having the right target as it does on having the right product. This chapter includes the following concepts:

- Decide on a positioning strategy: Choose a strategy based on potential licensees' goals.
- Look for companies with the right ingredients: Learn what characteristics make a company the right target.
- Pick your potential targets: Understand their business goals.
- Make your initial contacts: Confirm that a company is a good candidate.

Great Product Can't Connect

Todd Basche had a rambunctious young son who was always trying to leave his fenced-in backyard. Basche bought padlocks for the gates to keep his son safe, but he had trouble remembering the combinations. Each lock had a four-number combination, but with so many other passwords and pin numbers to remember, this became too confusing. Basche thought, "Why not use words instead of numbers? Words are much easier to remember."

Basche's first task was to figure out how to select letters for the tumblers to generate as many four- or five-letter words as possible from tumblers with only ten letters. Being from the computer industry, Basche was able to put together a software program to pick the right letters. He applied for a patent, did extensive market research, put together an investor presentation, and started hitting the licensing trail with the Wordlock™. For two years he talked to company after company that had anything to do with locks and security. No luck. This included companies producing padlocks, locking briefcases and suitcases, locks for lockers and safety deposit boxes, and all types of bike-locking devices. Then he read about an invention contest being conducted by Procter & Gamble and entered. Out of thousands of contestants Basche's product came in fifteenth. That was a strong finish, especially since the product wasn't a natural fit for a consumer-products company. One year later, Basche entered the Invention Quest contest conducted by Staples, which included more than 8,000 contestants. He was the winner of $25,000 and an exclusive licensing agreement to sell his product under the Staples brand.

Why didn't the Wordlock succeed before the contest? The product obviously has strong appeal. Basche believes that he didn't approach the right candidates and failed to get in front of the decision makers at the companies he did approach. Fortunately, persistence paid off and Basche received his license. However, he could have succeeded much sooner if had approached the right companies from the beginning.

DECIDE ON A POSITIONING STRATEGY: CHOOSE A STRATEGY BASED ON POTENTIAL LICENSEES' GOALS

You need to be careful in choosing companies to target. Potential licensees don't like to take products that have been "shopped around" to a lot of other companies, because they might assume something is wrong with the idea if no one has taken it before. A company doesn't really decide to buy a product on its own merits but instead buys a product to fit its larger strategy. Inventors have a better chance of choosing promising target companies if they understand how their product fits various goals that a potential licensee might have. Figure 7.1 shows various positioning strategies that will match the goals of potential licensees. The chart also shows which of those goals present the best licensing opportunities. Explanations of each positioning strategy follow.

Protecting a Market Position

Typically, companies are interested in four items to protect their market position.

1. *Keeping the lead product strong.* A lead product is the one that a company is most associated with. A lead product strategy is more prevalent in industrial companies than in consumer-product companies, but it can apply to both. An instrument company might have as its lead product nondestructive coating measurement systems for gold plating. A bike company might consider a high-end racing bike its lead product because that product determines the company's reputation. Companies do everything they can to protect their lead products. Unfortunately, large companies are resistant to new ideas on their lead products because they believe they know everything there is to know about them. Market followers are more open to ideas to keep their lead product strong because they know they don't have the engineering staff to keep up with larger companies.

2. *Product line breadth equal to or better than the competition.* When a company can supply all or most of a customer's needs in a certain area, the company is said to have a broad product line. Companies are receptive to products that can fill in their product line. But it calls for careful research by the inventor. You need to identify the major players in the market, what products they are missing, and how your product can fill in that gap. The best way to find companies with market gaps is by obtaining literature from

Figure 7.1   Positioning Strategies for Inventors

Positioning Strategy	Effectiveness, Market Leaders	Effectiveness, Market Followers
Protecting a market position		
1. Keeping a lead product strong	Low	High
2. Adding product line breadth	Medium	Medium
3. Products for new market trends	High	High
4. Products for new market application	High	High
Upgrading a market position		
1. Products with superior features	Medium	Medium
2. Competing with a sole supplier	High	Medium
3. Products with better promotional possibilities	Medium	Low
4. Products that can set a new market trend	Medium	Low
Expanding into new markets	High	High
Improving a company's value to the distribution	Medium	High

market participants, reading trade magazines, attending trade shows, and talking to salespeople in that market.

3. *Products that meet new market trends.* Companies will look at new ideas and new trends, especially if they don't have any of their own developing ideas in that market area. Companies with a major market share always want to participate in new markets to maintain or increase their overall share. Market followers are a tougher sell with products that meet new market trends because they probably don't have the marketing or sales power to set a new market trend.

4. *Products that meet new applications.* Again, companies who don't have products in the pipeline for that application might consider licensing one.

Upgrading a Market Position

Companies with major market positions are usually tough to license unless you have a very innovative product, because they worry that your product's sales will come at the expense of their existing products. Companies with minor market positions are always looking to upgrade their line, because they believe their new product sales will mostly come at the expense of companies with larger market shares. Companies with smaller positions will be receptive to licensing if you can offer any of the following four benefits.

1. *Products with superior features.* The odds of success increase dramatically if your product is innovative or does a much better job meeting the needs of the customer.

2. *Products that compete with a sole supplier.* All potential licensees want to take on a sole supplier. The market as a whole wants more than one supplier. A sole supplier has all the power in the market, typically charges high prices, and is frequently hard to deal with. Even if the sole supplier does a good job, the market always wants a second source. Companies will be willing to listen if your product doesn't infringe on the sole source's intellectual property protection. Market followers' number one goal is to be perceived as a market leader, and competing with a sole supplier may be a niche market that won't help the company's overall image.

3. *Products with better promotional opportunities.* A catchy name that you've trademarked, a better visual look, and/or a product that can be sold as a promotion all offer some benefit to a smaller company trying to upgrade its market positions.

4. *Products that can set a new market trend.* These are products like DVD players that totally change how everyone does something. These products change the market, and they can happen in almost any area. These products are not nearly as easy to license as you might think. Companies are risk-averse, and introducing an innovative product is dangerous in several ways: It will require a much larger than normal promotional budget; there is a good chance the product will have to be reworked several times to meet consumer needs; sales might take time to develop until the market accepts the new concept; and most important, the product just might not be accepted.

Expanding into New Markets

This feature applies primarily to product-oriented companies. As a rule, companies are either market- or product-oriented. A market-oriented company tries to provide more products and better service to a specific market. For example, a party supply company might want to provide every party trinket a party store might buy. A product-oriented company concentrates on its product or technology, which it wants to sell in as many different markets and for as many applications as possible. An inventor with a housewares plastic product might want to consider as a target plastic manufacturers that serve the hardware industry. Some of those companies might be looking for an innovative product so they can expand their product line into a totally new market.

Improving a Company's Value to the Distribution Channel

Every company wants to expand its distribution network or improve its value to the distribution channel. Sometimes, inventors have products that the distribution channel wants and no one carries. If you can meet that demand, companies will be interested in buying. For example, many companies distribute products through air-conditioning and heating contractors and distributors. Those companies receive questions from consumers about possible mildew in their duct systems and how they might eliminate it with their furnace settings. No one is offering those distributors products to meet that need. A company who takes on an inventor's product that solves this problem will be doing the distribution channel a service and the distribution channel will likely increase its orders of the company's other products.

LOOK FOR COMPANIES WITH THE RIGHT INGREDIENTS: LEARN WHAT CHARACTERISTICS MAKE A COMPANY THE RIGHT TARGET

The best chance of licensing an idea is to approach a company where your idea can make an impact, either from the product's sales or because of the spin-off effect on other products in its line. Margins produce the biggest resistance when licensing an idea. Companies who make 5 percent to 15 percent profits per sales dollar look at a 2 to 7 percent royalty as significant margin erosion, an erosion they will tolerate only if the product creates an impact. If it doesn't, the company won't think it's worth the time to deal with the inventor. Figure 7.2 lists key considerations for choosing a company. A detailed discussion of each item follows.

Figure 7.2   Key Considerations Choosing a Target Company

Consideration	Desired Properties
Company size	Your product could represent 20% to 50% impact on sales for target company
Ability to attract a key contact	Support of regional manager or marketing manager
Past licensing activity	Should have licensed products in the past
Marketing and R&D departments	Strong marketing and weak R&D departments
Product introduction cycle	No significant recent product introductions
Product line breadth	Significant holes in its product line
Market vs. product orientation	Market companies look for products to expand line Product companies look for products to expand markets

Company Size

You need to produce an impact for a company, or in the case of a large company, for a division or product line. The impact doesn't have to be from your product alone, but also from the secondary benefits of your product on other company products. Typically you need 20 to 30 percent or more impact in an established market, or you need to be able to help a company get at least a 10 to 20 percent market share in developing markets or applications. To have this impact you will typically have to license to smaller companies with room to grow their sales.

Ability to Attract a Key Contact

Most people in companies spend the bulk of their time getting problems off their desk and don't have time to worry about the business growing. Often, only the top executives spend time worrying about future growth, which is why you have to reach them to be effective. You will get that to executive review when you can persuade a regional sales manager or a marketing manager to push for your product success. The easiest way to meet a top sales or marketing person in a company is through your local salesperson. Start by getting the local salesperson's name from a customer or by requesting literature from the company. That literature will usually come with a cover letter from the local representative. Call the representative, invite him or her to lunch, and explain that you are an inventor with a new idea that may be perfect for the salesperson's company; ask for an opinion, and if the rep likes your idea, see if he or she will arrange a meeting for you with the regional manager or marketing manager.

What I like about regional managers is that they are aggressive: They have nothing to lose and everything to gain by supporting an idea. If the company decides to license the product, the regional manager is a big winner; if the company doesn't license it, he or she has created a favorable impression by showing initiative to help the company grow.

Past Licensing Activity

Some companies are not only willing to license ideas, they look for ideas all the time. Other companies simply aren't willing to license any ideas. You can typically find this out at trade shows just by asking reps whether any of the company's products have been acquired through licensing agreements.

Marketing and R&D Departments

Marketing departments are always looking for new products that sell and generally don't care where the product comes from. R&D departments have a vested interest in seeing that their own internally developed products are introduced. Licensing interest is easier to generate in companies where marketing departments have more influence than R&D departments. Usually, you can find out whether a company is marketing- or R&D-oriented by asking salespeople for input about the size of each department.

Product Line Breadth

Companies with holes in their product line will want to fill them. This is especially true if the company has tried to fill this gap before and failed. Holes in a product line can put a company at a significant disadvantage.

Market-versus-Product Orientation

Market-oriented companies want to expand their product line to their targeted market, whereas product- or technology-oriented companies want to expand into new markets. Market-oriented companies can be more difficult to sell to since they think they know what the market wants and probably have already made an effort to introduce those products. Product- or technology-oriented companies typically don't understand the markets very well, and they are interested in new uses for their product or technology.

PICK YOUR POTENTIAL TARGETS: UNDERSTAND THEIR BUSINESS GOALS

Pick Your Targets

- Start a list of candidates. Check out web sites of trade associations or trade magazines for directories of companies in the industry, or use a directory from an industry trade show. Look for the following lists:

  Companies that sell the same types of products as yours. For example, if your invention is an outdoor chair that adjusts to hills, find all the companies that make outdoor chairs.

  Companies that sell auxiliary products. For example, companies that sell other outdoor products, such as mosquito canopies, tarps, camp grills, tents, and hammocks would all be auxiliary companies (for outdoor chairs) that might be looking to expand their product line.

  Companies that make products out of the same material as yours. If the outdoor chair has an aluminum frame with telescoping legs and a fabric seat, look for companies that make aluminum frames. The best choice would be backpack companies or those that make products for the camping industry. A second choice would be companies that make lightweight aluminum frames for any market. The best source for that data is the *Thomas Registry of American Manufacturers,* which you can find in large libraries or at www.thomasregister.com.

- Estimate your product's sales potential. You don't have to be accurate in your estimates—just use ballpark figures. A range of $2 to $5 million is fine. Find products that you think have comparable popularity in similar markets and research their total sales. You can often get sales data on other products by visiting the company's web site or through a trade association market study.

- Start looking for a good fit in terms of size. Look for companies with sales 3 to 10 times greater than your product's potential. A good web site to start with is www.trainingdialog.com. This is the site for Thompson Dialog and is by far the best site I've found for generating company information quickly and easily. The site is a little difficult to use at first, but once you have the routine down you can retrieve full company information in one to two minutes. Another useful site is www.business.com, which offers all types of business searches, including product category searches and financial and product line information about numerous companies. Other business information sites are www.hoover.com, www.bemis.com, and dir.yahoo.com/Business_and_Economy/Directory/Company.

- Research companies to find those that are active in your marketing and have licensed ideas in the past. You may be able to find information on the company's web site or by talking to company salespeople or customer service reps. Talk to your industry contacts to get help deciding which companies might be best. Also be open to your contact's suggestions of companies that are not on the list.

Understand Your Target Companies' Business Goals

Your last step is to learn the business goals or strategies for your final list of candidates. You will have to rely on web sites, annual reports if available, trade magazines, and industry contacts to understand exactly what goals or strategies companies have. I believe that inventors should attend trade shows because there you will get a chance to talk to many people and learn about companies in the industry. Inventors will have trouble getting a real feel for the industry just from reading web sites and trade magazines. Also, inventors can obtain lots of assistance from an industry person who helps license the product on a commission basis. Industry people will probably know some of this information themselves, or they will have contacts who can fill them in.

Once you understand companies' goals, you will want to compare their goals to your positioning strategy that you worked on earlier in the chapter. You should find 5 to 10 companies with goals that fit your positioning strategy. Those companies will comprise your initial market targets to contact for future sales.

MAKE YOUR INITIAL CONTACTS: CONFIRM THAT A COMPANY IS A GOOD CANDIDATE

I've found that you can easily make contact with at least a company salesperson to confirm that a company is a good licensing prospect and possibly find a person who will help you navigate the initial introduction steps at the company.

Before you make any contact you should work out a phone strategy that explains why you are contacting this particular company. Structure the call more as market research call than as a sales call. Inventors need to act professionally if they expect to be taken seriously. Your statement should follow a sequence similar to these eight steps.

1. Greeting. "Hi, I'm [your name]. I'm developing a product for the [market's or application's name]. Can I ask you a couple of questions? *Comment:* Don't say you're an inventor looking to license an idea—that comment will immediately turn off many businesspeople.

2. "Let me explain something about my background first." *Comment:* Tell the person why you are interested or involved in the industry and why you should be able to develop a product that will sell. You might be in sales or marketing, or you might be an industrial or an end user of industry products. Try to paint as positive picture as possible about your background.

3. "I believe there has been a need in the industry for a product that will [whatever your product idea will do]. Do you also see a need for this type of product?" *Comment:* You should verify that the person sees the same need you do; otherwise, he or she won't end up being very helpful. The person might also explain why he or she thinks the industry does *not* need the product you've identified, which would be useful market research information.

4. "I believe the most important feature of this product needs to be [state here what you believe to be your product's major benefit]. Do you see other benefits as being equally or more important for this type of product?" *Comment:* Again, you are collecting information. Asking for and respecting the contact's input will encourage the contact to either support you or point you in another, better direction.

5. "Once the product has been through its market-testing phase, I'm considering finding a distributor. I believe your company would be ideal as a distribution outlet because the product provides [list here the positioning strategy you've developed for your product].

Do you think your company would be willing to market this type of product?"

Comment: Licensing a product after complete market testing is the best-case scenario from the company's point of view. If a company isn't interested in taking on a product at this stage, it won't be interested in taking it on earlier in the development cycle. You may not be able to take the product this far, but at least you know the company is a licensing candidate if its representative says yes to this question.

6. "Has your company ever sold another company's product or licensed a product before?"

   Comment: Just more market intelligence to help you select the best company as a licensing target. If the company isn't interested in distributing another company's product, ask the salesperson if other companies in the industry distribute or license products for small companies or inventors.

7. "Can I call you and ask questions as I proceed on the project?"

   Comment: Half the time people will say yes, and then they can be ongoing contacts for you.

8. "Is there anyone else at your company I should contact?"

   Comment: Get as many names as possible for future follow-up. You can then call them and mention that your initial contact suggested that you call.

Following this procedure should help you land at least two to three companies as potential licensees. With luck, you can get a company in the target market itself, plus two or three companies who sell auxiliary products, and possibly one or two that use a similar manufacturing process.

8

STEP 8A. PRESERVE YOUR CAPITAL: USE LOW-COST TACTICS FOR LANDING A LICENSE

At first glance licensing seems like a cost-effective way to promote your idea, but I've found that inventors can easily spend $20,000 or more before finding a licensee. Inventors need to preserve their cash, since there certainly is risk to licensing—you may not succeed, and even if you do your product may not sell well. I believe inventors are better off sharing the risks and costs, as well as the royalties, whenever possible with an engineer, industrial designer, and/or industry professional, because taking on investing helpers keeps inventors' costs low as well as giving them the best chance of success. No one can be certain that an idea will sell. Inventors are wise to conserve their capital so they can try again if their first product fails. Sharing the royalties on the first product cuts into an inventor's share, but I've found that inventors who succeed once can more easily succeed a second and third time. Inventors are better off doing whatever it takes to get their first product on the market. Once inventors have an initial product success they will have more access to the market and need less help, or possibly no help. They will then be able to own 100 percent of their inventions. This chapter covers these concepts:

- Avoid a sales test: Don't incur costs you can't recoup.
- Enlist helpers: Use their investment of time and money to cut your outlays.

- Create options to lower costs: Let potential licensees pay for desired testing.
- Sign memorandums of understanding (MOUs): Offer an incentive to potential licensees.

A Steady Stream of Success

Fred Fink was an auto mechanic who was frustrated that vehicle "hood shocks," which hold open a car's engine hood during repairs, often have damaged pneumatic seals, thus forcing mechanics to employ makeshift solutions such as sticking a steel bar between the hood and car body to keep the hood open. At some point, Fink decided to invent a simple clamp with an adjustable screw that attaches to the hood shock and holds it in place. Fink was sure the product was right for the market and was encouraged because there weren't any competitive products on the market. He didn't have to search very hard for a licensee for his product: Automotive tool manufacturer Lisle Corporation of Clarinda, Iowa, has been licensing auto products for years. In fact, 25 to 30 percent of the company's 300 or so products are licensed from inventors.

Lisle uses its screening criteria when considering licensing agreements.

- *How difficult is it to solve the problem?*
- *How good are the competing products on the market?*
- *Will the product operate reliably for consumers?*
- *Does the potential sales volume justify the costs of tooling?*
- *Can the product be made and sold at a profitable price?*

To Lisle, the first three criteria are the most important. The company is more likely to license a product when the product's design solves a problem, especially when the problem is difficult to solve. If a problem is easy to solve, there are probably dozens of ways to solve it, and a product's patents won't offer much of an advantage when competitors start to offer alternative products.

AVOID A SALES TEST: DON'T INCUR COSTS YOU CAN'T RECOUP

Inventors looking to license their product typically don't have the time, inclination, or money to conduct an extensive sales test. Potential licensees *do* want a test since it removes all doubt that the product will sell. Unfortunately, companies sometimes use the request for a sales test as a way to brush off the inventor. The trick here is not to avoid a sales test, as most companies will do one before investing too much money in an idea, but to get the potential licensee to pay for and hopefully conduct the test. To pass on the testing costs to the licensee, you need a product that can attract lots of attention in the market, and you need a prototype to demonstrate clearly that your product works reliably and fits the market's needs.

Grabbing Consumers' Attention

Consumers are simply inundated with too many products. If you deliver an attention-getting product, a company might be willing to pay for a low-cost market test. Here I list six ways you can develop this attention. Use as many attention-getting devices as possible. Your position will be even stronger if you also possess provisional orders or letters of intent as discussed in Chapter 6 (pages 128 to 130). Be sure to use the trademark symbol behind any slogans and names you use, and place the copyright line (your name and the year printed) at the bottom of each page. For example Copyright, Don Debelak, 2004. Try not to give a 100 percent verbal presentation. Instead, pass out some materials to clarify that your names and slogans have copyrights or trademarks that belong to you.

1. *Solve a difficult problem.* Identifying a problem is the first step; coming up with a clever solution is the second. A *clever* solution is a giant leap ahead of just a solution. One reason I've harped on the need to get some engineering or industrial design help is that those people are trained to take a solution you've developed and upgrading it into a clever, or more clever, solution. Another term you'll hear in licensing talks is an "elegant solution," which is another way of saying the inventor came up with an easy-to-make, simple-to-operate product for a complex task.

2. *Thoroughly meet a need that has never been met before.* Lasik eye surgery is big business because it corrects vision. Contact lenses and glasses are just a Band-Aid solution compared to Lasik surgery. It doesn't have to be a complex solution like a computer mouse, either. Students carried schoolbooks in their arms or in a briefcase 30 years ago. When backpacks were introduced, people recognized immediately that they were a better solution.

3. *Develop a product that makes tasks much easier.* Food processors provided a big jump in performance, as did weed whackers and MP3 players. One of the simplest inventions, the Phillips screw and screwdriver, was monumental success for its inventor Henry Phillips, who licensed his idea to many companies simply because it was easier to use on the production line.

4. *Choose a name with pizzazz.* Names grab attention when they are unexpected like the Weed Weasel, Post-it notes and Zip drives. Names also work when they identify the product's purpose, making it tough for competitors to introduce their products. For example UV-ID, which could be trademarked with a distinctive design obviously refers to identifying marks on property that can only be seen under a UV light. AB Rocker and Adjust-A-Bed by Select Comfort are other examples of names that explain the product's function and leave competition behind.

5. *Consider an unusual product look.* This always generates a second look from consumers. The Palm Pilot and Apple's iPod caught people's attention because the products were small. Sony's Walkman took the market by storm because the headphones were radically different. Mountain bikes, the Mini Cooper, and bread-making machines all had a different look. When introduced, the iMac computer generated tremendous buzz because of its different colors.

6. *Invent something bold, different, dangerous, and fun.* Snowboards, in-line skates, windsurfing boards, and skateboards all proved that big changes in equipment are much easier to sell than small changes.

A Great Prototype

Having a "looks like, works like" prototype is another key to either avoiding a sales test or getting a potential licensee to pay for it. If you can't afford the prototype, you may be able to get a potential licensee to fund the prototype if you can convince the company that your product has merit. The secret to stimulating interest is to have elements in your product idea that will attract consumers' attention, to have people involved in your project who are respected in the market, and to have some proof your product will sell.

ENLIST HELPERS: USE THEIR INVESTMENT OF TIME AND MONEY TO CUT YOUR OUTLAYS

I like to start my invention seminars with the statement that even the Lone Ranger had Tonto. I do that because at least half of the inventors I talk to want to operate like the Lone Ranger, doing everything on their own without any help or support. They are often possessive of their idea as it is and don't want to change anything about it. Inventors seem particularly prone to doing everything on their own when they are trying to license an idea. Being a Lone Ranger has many drawbacks. Here are the primary ones:

- Inventors fail to get the input they need to adjust their product so it is right for the market.
- Their ideas don't have the implied endorsement of industry professionals.
- Inventors don't have the moral support of partners when things don't go well.
- They miss out on solutions that engineering or industrial design helpers can provide.
- Inventors pass up the opportunity to have investing partners with either time or money to ease the financial risk.

I've discussed these points in various places earlier in the book. The last point, getting investments from helpers, is just as important in seeking a licensee as it is in starting your own company, even though the costs are much less. The reasons are twofold: (1) Licensing often ends up costing far more than inventors expect, and they eventually need financial help, and (2) you can increase the amount of effort and support helpers offer you by letting them become investors. One thing I encourage inventors to do is to attend meetings of local entrepreneur clubs, enroll in new entrepreneur classes at local universities, and go to venture fairs where new businesses are looking for money. At shows inventors learn about the entrepreneur process. But more important, they can observe firsthand just how many people have the entrepreneurial spirit. Many people, especially in sales and marketing, search for opportunities to be involved in market areas they know something about and in which their experience can play a major role in success. I believe many inventors look at asking for money from helpers backwards. They think helpers might give advice but that they don't want to invest or take a risk. Yes, helpers are willing to give advice, but they are also looking for a chance to hit it big and cash in on a new product or venture. Most industry helpers want to have a piece of an idea they believe will succeed. Inventors asking for an investment are not asking for help, they are *offering an opportunity.* When helpers invest, they become a much stronger part of your team and are willing to work much harder on getting your idea sold.

I believe bringing industry helpers on board as investors is particularly important in licensing; even though inventors may not need their money, they do need plenty of industry connections to make it through the licensing process—connections to get in the door and connections to keep pushing your idea for three to six months while a company makes a decision. Your helper's connections might also motivate companies to pay for additional prototypes, market testing, and any other expenses involved in the potential licensee's decision process. Don't be afraid to ask for investments when you talk to industry people in your initial market research. People want to invest and be a part of a winning idea, and their involvement will dramatically increase your chance of success.

Not Quite—But Close

Stanley Hochfield, a golfer from Long Island, commonly ventured outside on windy, rainy days. Sometimes umbrellas held up to the wind, but when they didn't, they would blow inside out, especially on the golf course. Hochfield decided to create a sturdier umbrella, the GustBuster. Hochfield didn't want to proceed on his own, so he formed a three-way partnership with an acquaintance and a patent lawyer to develop the idea for licensing. Although he didn't have the money or inclination to start his own company, he did let golf pros at a Long Island tournament use the GustBuster at a golf tournament. As a result, the umbrella received some favorable publicity.

Steve Asman, who didn't yet have a company, was an entrepreneur searching for an idea. He approached Hochfield about the possibility of licensing the product. Asman immediately realized that Hochfield's design, though clever, wasn't sturdy or durable enough for the market. Asman worried that new design would be too expensive or would not work. Hochfield wasn't able to take the design to the next level himself, so they struck a deal. Asman would investigate redesigning the product to withstand harsh winds if Hochfield would agree not to present the idea to anyone else until Asman had solved his design questions and established the manufacturing costs of the product. Asman redesigned and delivered a winning product, and the license agreement went through. He wouldn't have been willing to commit to a license or to pay for the redesign without a short-term exclusive option to check out the product.

CREATE OPTIONS TO LOWER COSTS: LET POTENTIAL LICENSEES PAY FOR DESIRED TESTING

Since you are unlikely to sign a license agreement on the first visit, your goal should be to stimulate enough interest in the potential licensee to agree to generate some form of action on both sides. In some cases, the potential licensee may want to evaluate the product for three to six months. If so, you should offer an option, or exclusive rights, to the product for a period of time in return for a fixed sum of money. You need to offer the option because the potential licensee won't want to devote efforts to the evaluation if you are trying to sell the idea to someone else at the same time.

Other times, a company might have interest in an inventor's idea but has too many doubts or questions to move forward with either a licensing program or an option. In such a case, you need to discover what the company's doubts are and try to develop a joint program to resolve them, hopefully with the company picking up the tab. Inventors can gauge whether potential licensees are truly interested in their product or just putting off a decision by asking for a memorandum of understanding (discussed in the last section of the chapter) to detail what the inventor and licensee will do during this evaluation period.

Options

An option offers a company a period of time in which the inventor will not present his or her idea to anyone else. Often, a company will offer some compensation in return for an option. Options can be granted for anywhere from $500 to hundreds of thousands of dollars. You can base the actual amount of money you request on the size of the company you are talking to. As a starting point, ask for a minimum of $10,000 from companies with sales of more than $20 million, $5,000 for companies with sales of $2 million to $20 million, and $2,500 from companies with sales of less than $2 million. This earnest money shows that the prospect is serious about pursuing your idea, which is only fair if the company wants you to hold off presenting the idea to other people. The actual amount of the payment is not as important as the fact that the potential licensee has paid something, which is the start of a licensing negotiation.

Options can be effected by means of a purchase order or a memorandum of understanding, or you can write your own agreement. I prefer a purchase order from the customer with an attached statement of mutual confidentiality (see Appendix E) if you don't have a patent. On the purchase order, simply have the customer sign a commitment: "(1) Three-month exclusive evaluation agreement for [product name] from _____ [effective date] to _____ [ending date]." Then list the price agreed to. Below the item purchased, state that "Terms of attached Statement of Mutual Confidentiality apply."

SIGN MEMORANDUMS OF UNDERSTANDING (MOUs): OFFER AN INCENTIVE TO POTENTIAL LICENSEES

If inventors are not able to secure an option, they may be able to agree to conduct joint testing or evaluation. Here are some of the actions you or the potential licensee may want to take:

- Conduct an engineering review to potentially lower manufacturing costs.
- Hire an industrial engineer for an aesthetic redesign.
- Produce a "looks like, acts like" prototype.
- Produce a small production run with temporary tooling for a market test.
- Change some of the product features and produce a new prototype.
- Attend a trade show for market research.
- Run a market-testing program.
- Redesign packaging, rename the product, and run market testing.

Inventors need to encourage potential licensees to disclose what more they would like to see before making a decision. Licensees might say that they don't think the idea will fit into their plans or that they just need to think things over (which is often a brush-off), but sometimes they will state their concerns. Comments like, "I'm not sure we can produce the product and sell it at $17.95," and "The product just doesn't seem to be unique when compared to product X" are openings for you to suggest a follow-up plan of action. For initial resistance to the manufacturing cost, you could suggest an engineering study that would include cost methods and sourcing to hit the target price. For resistance to product features, you could suggest a market test or focus group study. If the company agrees that it might be worthwhile to investigate further, then you can propose a memorandum of understanding that will offer the company a three- to four-month exclusive option (i.e., during which time you won't show the product to anyone else) while you and the potential licensee carry out further product evaluation.

Memorandums of Understanding (MOU)

The first step in the licensing process of an invention process is the most difficult. After a company agrees to consider becoming a licensee and to invest in the invention, the second step seems much easier. The second investment from an individual is much easier to obtain than the first; the second agreement with a potential licensee is much easier to negotiate than the first. Therefore, the goal is to make the first agreement as simple as possible to sign.

Basically a memorandum of understanding is a simple document stating that the two parties are going to work together to investigate an idea with the intent of negotiating a licensing agreement. The memorandum of understanding must contain a confidentiality clause or attached agreement to protect the inventor's idea(s), and offer a degree of exclusiveness to the potential licensee (i.e., you won't approach other companies for a period of time) and a degree of exclusiveness to you (i.e., the company won't negotiate with another inventor to license a similar idea). The MOU gives an overview of how the parties will proceed, with the intended result being a license agreement.

MOU Format

This format will help you understand the elements that should be included in an MOU so you can discuss it with potential licensees. Contact an attorney for a final version before submitting it to the licensee.

1. *Title.* Start with a title and description:

> Memorandum of Understanding
>
> Investigation of the Market Potential of Quick Window Shield Painting Accessory

2. *The date and parties involved.* For example:

> This Memorandum of Understanding (MOU) is made this 25th day of February, 2005 (Effective Date), between (1) inventor's name and city of residence and (2) name and location of potential licensee.

3. *Background*

    a. Inventor background: State your name, your background as it relates to the invention, and a brief description of the invention.

> John Backstrom has been a professional painter for 22 years. One recurring problem he has faced is the need for a helper when spray-painting a house. The helper is needed to hold a shield over windows to protect them from the spray of the paint gun. Paying a helper cuts into the painter's profits. Backstrom has created the Quick Window Shield to allow painters to pop a shield over the window in less than 10 seconds to eliminate the need for a helper.

    b. Potential licensee name: A brief description of the company, its market, and the fact it has expressed interest in the invention.

    c. Purpose of MOU: List the specific actions you and the potential licensee are taking and what you are trying to accomplish.

The purpose of this agreement is to construct a "looks like, acts like" prototype and perform functional tests to ensure that the product provides an easy-to-use solution that doesn't require a painter's helper while spray-painting a house.

4. *Understanding and agreements.* This is the key point of an MOU—defining what both sides are promising in your attempt to complete the negotiations. The sections that follow are typical of an agreement, but you will need to adjust them to fit your exact needs.

   a. Overview: State what you hope to accomplish if the activities during the MOU period produce the results both parties are hoping for.

   The parties are entering into this agreement to better understand the market potential of the Quick Window Shield. Provided both parties are satisfied with the performance of the new prototype, they will consider either further evaluation or proceed to an agreement relating to the production and marketing of the Quick Window Shield.

   b. Responsibilities: This section lists what each party will do during the MOU period.

   Inventor
   • Coordinate with licensees assigned engineer and model shop to produce the new prototype.
   • Set up tests with five professional painters to evaluate the Quick Window Shield.

   Licensee
   • Provide engineering and model shop support for producing a new prototype.
   • Provide funding required to produce the prototype.
   • Produce five models for testing upon prototype approval.

   c. Exclusivity: The inventor typically has to give some exclusivity in return for a MOU agreement.

   Inventor agrees not to present the Quick Window Shield to any other companies with the intent of negotiating a licensing or other agreement regarding the manufacturing and sales of the Quick Window Shield. Licensee agrees not to enter into discussions regarding manufacture and sale of any products similar to the Quick Window Shield.

5. *Confidentiality.* A key part of a MOU agreement includes a confidentiality agreement. As a rule a statement of confidentiality is attached to the agreement. You can find statements of mutual confidentiality on several web sites, including www.findlegalforms.com, www.legaldepot.com, and www.mynondisclosure.com. There is also a statement of mutual confidentiality in Appendix E of this book. Again, consult your attorney before submitting a final document.

> Both parties agree to abide by the Statement of Mutual Confidentiality as stated in Appendix A of this agreement.

6. *Term.* You want to state how long the agreement will last. This is important, because you have an exclusive agreement as part of the MOU. A reasonable amount of time is three to six months. If the term is much longer than that, you can't present your idea to other companies who may be good candidates.

> This agreement shall be for six months from the Effective Date first stated above.

7. *No assignment.* This is just a housekeeping item stating that the agreement can't be assigned to another party.

> This MOU and any rights created by it cannot be assigned by either party.

8. *Termination.* You want to be able to end the agreement if the other party is not performing its responsibilities as agreed to. You might want to include a schedule of key steps that both parties agree to take during the term of the MOU, either in the Responsibilities section or as an attachment, that allow you to terminate the agreement if the other party is not performing. Your other recourse is to keep the time of the agreement as short as possible but long enough to hopefully get to a license agreement.

> The MOU can be terminated by either party if the other party is not performing to the terms and responsibilities of this agreement by written notice to the defaulting party. Prior to termination, the party terminating must provide a letter of concern to the other party and the other party has 15 days to remedy the complaint of nonperformance. The

obligations of confidentiality set forth in this agreement shall survive termination of this agreement.

9. *Governing law.* You will need to list the state whose laws will apply to the agreement. Typically, you will have to concede that applicable law will be in the potential licensee's state.

10. *Signatures.* Include signatures and date for both parties—the inventor and the potential licensing company or individual.

9

STEP 9A. DEVELOP A LICENSING PLAN: FIND THE QUICKEST WAY TO MARKET

Licensing plans serve three purposes. First, they help inventors raise the money they might need to license their product; second, they show potential helpers the inventors' competence, proving the inventors have done their homework and prepared themselves for a licensing campaign.

Licensing plans serve a third purpose that I believe is crucial. They stop inventors from rushing into the market before they are ready and turning off key contacts because of it. Inventors are anxious to sell their ideas, but the unfortunate fact is that they will have an extremely difficult time generating enthusiasm in a key contact after that person has said no. You can't afford to ruin your best contacts and then later return with a more careful plan. You have to be right the first time. This chapter helps you to accomplish that.

- Propose a target introduction timetable: Encourage a quick deal.
- Prepare the licensing plan: Include the key elements for success.

One After Another

Mary Ellroy has a string of new product successes in the toy industry, including the following board games: Giant Intergalactic Electronic Game Book, Conversation Pieces, Great States, and the Magic Rainbow Sprinkler.

Ellroy's strategy for licensing a product follows a formula favored by many inventors.

First, she stays not only within an industry but also within a segment of an industry. Almost all of Ellroy's products are targeted to be sold at specialty toy stores such as FAO Schwarz or Zany Brainy. Concentrating on a specific market allows Ellroy to understand exactly what the market wants and deliver a product that will be easy to license.

Second, she researches her industry through trade shows, trade magazines, and by studying other product introductions. An inventor rarely knows enough about an industry, and constant research is the only way to keep current.

Third, she keeps up routine contacts with major suppliers to the market segment—in Ellroy's case, the toy companies that sell to educational and specialty toy stores. Staying in one market, and not the biggest market segment, allows Ellroy to know each company, what products they like, and which products they are likely to license.

Fourth, she ensures the product is right with extensive testing. Ellroy is a member of an inventors' club and uses members as a sounding board for what is good or bad about an idea, soliciting suggestions on how to improve her product. She also tests her products with potential end users long before she approaches a company about licensing an idea. She strives to get a wide variety of input so every base is covered.

Finally, she presents a final product. Ellroy strives to create a show model that is almost identical to what she believes will finally be sold. She has thought through instructions, game pieces, and packaging before presenting the product.

One other reason Ellroy has enjoyed much success is that she targeted the specialty toy store market when it was emerging and searching for products. Her initial success allowed her to keep on introducing products as the market increased in size. Was Ellroy hurting herself by going after a small market segment versus the Wall-Marts of the world? I don't think so. If any of her products were to really catch on, her licensee would be able to easily move the product into a bigger distribution network. Ellroy had an easier time selling her products to smaller market channels. First you need to get the product out into the market, and if it is accepted, bigger sales will follow.

PROPOSE A TARGET INTRODUCTION TIMETABLE: ENCOURAGE A QUICK DEAL

Potential licensees are no different than most people; they delay making decisions, and sometimes they delay making a decision so long they miss their window of opportunity. To avoid this, I believe you need to incorporate a timetable into your licensing plan, and certainly into your licensing presentation, to try to speed the deal along. Fortunately for inventors, virtually all industries have major events at which most major product introductions occur. For example, the toy industry has a major toy fair in New York every February where companies launch many new toys. Always work out an introduction timetable backward, starting with the end event. For example, if you're targeting the February 2007 New York Toy Fair, work backward to determine when a license needs to be signed to get the product introduced at that event. (See Figure 9.1 for a sample timetable.)

Trade shows are not always the defining moment; sometimes it is the buying season. Fall clothes are sold in March or April, spring gardening items hit hardware stores in October, and many mass merchandisers choose their summer merchandise in December of the previous year. Knowing when the product has to be available helps the inventor in two ways: first, it encourages the potential licensee to sign a deal; second, it gives the inventor the leverage to say, "To hit the fall 2006 season, I need the product licensed by February of 2005. If you are going to have a long delay in your decision I'll need to consider approaching another company or I'll miss out on the entire 2006 season." This statement doesn't sound like excessive pressure because the licensee understands your position exactly: A month's delay can cause the product to miss a whole year's worth of sales.

Figure 9.1 Key Targets Introduction Timetable

Product Description: A new line of silicon carbide flexible bakeware for general merchandise stores.	
Target Introduction Date: Chicago Housewares Show at McCormick Place, February 2007.	
Key Target Dates	
Production released	October 2006
Tooling ordered	May 2006
Preproduction units for 2007 Chicago Housewares Show for market research	December 2005
Market tests complete	November 2005
Prototype units for consumer market research	September 2005
License agreement signed	May 2005

You can usually find the key introduction dates for your business from industry helpers or by reading the trade magazines and association news. There will typically be lots of advertising for new products near the key market target dates.

There are a few important points to remember when developing your timetable. First, you will need the help of someone in the industry to figure out what type of a schedule looks reasonable. All industries have different time schedules, and different types of production require different tooling and production start-up times.

Second, you don't want the schedule too detailed, since a detailed schedule has points a potential licensee can dispute. A brief schedule like the one shown in Figure 9.1 makes the point without leaving much room for the licensee to challenge any of your points. Third, you are merely trying to agree on a final date by which your potential licensee will sign on. If the company feels the right date is September 2005, that should be fine; you are simply trying to establish a deadline for striking a deal.

PREPARE THE LICENSING PLAN: INCLUDE THE KEY ELEMENTS FOR SUCCESS

The licensing plan format might appear intimidating at first, but it is really not difficult. It can range in size from 10 to 40 double-spaced pages, or from 2,500 to 7,500 words. The key points of a licensing plan are:

- Product description
- Rationale behind product's development
- Features that make the product exceptional
- Inventor's background
- Product manufacturing cost versus retail price
- Market size
- Existing products
- Market drivers
- Proof the product can sell
- Potential target companies (delete this section if you are showing the plan to a potential licensee)
- Positioning strategy
- Ideal target customers
- Where the product stands today
- Development required
- Strategy for meeting key contacts (delete this section when showing the plan to a key contact or a potential licensee)

- Option-oriented strategies
- Introduction timetable
- Licensing costs estimate
- Funding request/offer
- Continuing assistance from inventor

The Product

You need to sell your product from the start of the plan. In this section you should have a picture of the product accompanied by some advertising copy that explains your main benefits and offers testimonial(s) from one or two people who either used and liked your invention or who believe it addresses a problem. For example, a testimonial for a product that prevents piecrust edges from burning might state: "I had the perfect Thanksgiving dinner for 18, but the whole effect was ruined by the burnt crusts on the pumpkin pie."

A favorable impression is important from the first moment a reader picks up your licensing plan. You must make every word count. Don't merely say you have an innovative new hammer. That is far too bland. Instead, immediately state the product's benefit. "The Power Hammer drives nails with 80 to 100 percent more power, even when the hammer is not centered on the nail." I've written and observed people reading all types of plans, and you'd be surprised at the number who stop reading after the first or second paragraph.

Rationale behind Product's Development

This section is focused on two points: the need for the product and your innovative, clever solution. I've found it is effective to state that you identified the problem or market need at a specific time. Describe that moment, what you were doing, and how the problem dawned on you. Then state that you explored four or five design options before coming up with your innovative solution.

For example, the rationale for the Quick Window Shield product discussed in Chapter 8 might read:

> I first realized the market need for the Quick Window Shield when I had to spray-paint a house before the weather turned cold. My assistant didn't show up that day, so I tried to do the whole job myself. I ended up spraying paint on the windows and spent two days cleaning it off. I started to think about the $120 to $150 I paid a helper for each job and thought, "Why not eliminate the helper?"

I tried three different solutions to the problem, but they were too cumbersome or took too long to implement. Then I received help from a mechanical engineer and together we came up with our current configuration, which uses low-cost air-actuated springs to set up the shield in less than 15 seconds. After two iterations of cost cutting, we finally developed a cost-effective solution without any loss in performance.

This section should clearly make the point that you don't just have an idea, you have a specific, well-designed solution that has gone through some testing and has successfully evolved.

Why the Product Stands Out

A product can stand out in a variety of ways, but the important ones you must mention are *performance* and *appearance*. When discussing performance, list a couple of significant, powerful benefits. You can list more in an ending paragraph, but not with your main one or two benefits. I've found that the innovative product must stand on one or two features. Having 10 small features is not equivalent to one major feature. If your product features are smaller, you have to reconfigure your invention to include at least one major feature.

For example, one inventor created the GeoMask, a dispenser that quickly applies masking tape to woodwork in a room, ensures the masking tape is tight, and doesn't let any paint leak through to the woodwork. Those benefits need to be changed to read: "Mask a room in under 5 minutes with 95 percent better protection."

The second important item you must mention is appearance. You need to add a distinctive feature to a product so that people recognize it as being different than the competition. Even just a distinctive mark that doesn't add any functionality to the product will do. A distinctive X shape, a different color scheme, or a memorable mark all give identity and long-lasting branding. I've found that products, no matter how well they seem to perform, have trouble succeeding without a distinctive appearance that people can remember.

Inventor's Background

Explain your background as it relates to the successful design of your product. You'll have better success if you are an end user or somehow affiliated with an aspect of marketing or selling current products—something that shows you have an inside perspective of the market's need. List your background if it is impressive, and list your advisors or partners and their experience if you don't have a strong background.

Product Manufacturing Cost versus Retail Price

To have a chance to make money, your manufacturing cost needs to be 20 to 25 percent of the product's retail price. This section should work backward, listing what you think should be the suggested retail price, with some justification, and then the manufacturing costs. The best way to propose a suggested retail price is to show pricing for products that are similar in complexity and manufacturing difficulty to yours. You can also demonstrate a suggested retail price from some market or focus group studies.

Your manufacturing costs should be quoted by a contract manufacturer or based on an engineer's evaluation. This section should show effort on your part and not a wild guess. This will be an extremely important consideration to most professional contacts since there is not much point in devoting time and effort to a product that can't be sold for a profit.

Market Size

List the larger market first and then the more specific market you are targeting. For example, if you have a device that holds papers with data that are being fed into a computer, your larger market is office supply retailers of all types. The more specific target market might be office supply catalogs. You can list market size in many ways depending on the data available to you.

- Use total actual market sales for your type of product and by each distribution channel. This would apply to a product like the Geo-Mask with an established product category: The total market would be mask application devices, and the distribution channels would be paint stores, hardware stores, home improvement catalogs, and mass merchandisers.
- Use total number of possible end users and the number of targeted end users. For example, the relevant numbers for the Quick Window Shield would be the number of painting contractors and the number of contractors that do spray painting.
- Use similar products' sales volume. The Quick Window Shield inventor might list the sales of spray-paint systems to professional contractors.

Existing Products

List the major sellers of similar products in your target market and the products' market share; if you can't get that information, offer your best estimate of their market share, placing the market leader first. Market share data is sometimes available from trade associations or in trade publications. Distributor salespeople and management will frequently be able to tell you the top three or four products in any category, though they probably won't be able to offer a market share percentage. Manufacturers' sales agents also can typically name the top three or four products in a market.

Once you have a list, state each product's deficiencies that your product overcomes. For example, the deficiencies of products in competition with the Quick Window Shield might include these:

- Requires a helper all day
- Takes more than five minutes to set up per window
- Three times the cost of the Quick Window Shield
- Not adjustable, handles only a small range of window sizes
- Doesn't adjust well to older types of window molding

Market Drivers

Inventors have the best chance of licensing a product when there are strong reasons to believe that the market will continue to grow rapidly. For example, the market driver for a folding stowaway keyboard used with personal digital assistants (PDAs) like the BlackBerry or Palm Pilot is that the use of PDAs is expected to grow 100 to 200 percent per year. Such powerful growth will drive the need for that product. Examples of market drivers for other products are:

- There are increasing numbers of affluent parents—market driver for an upscale baby bike seat.
- Rising gas and oil costs will increase demand for fuel-efficient cars—market driver for a plug-in battery recharger for hybrid car accessories.
- Increasingly, cell phones are becoming the family's only phone—market driver for an ultrasmall, use anywhere cell phone recharging system.
- Women are performing an increasing number of home improvement projects—market driver for a line of screwdrivers that require less torque to turn.

- Popularity of fondue parties is changing dining out in restaurants to eating at home more often—market driver for a four-compartment electric wok for stir-fry dinner parties.
- The percentage of golfers walking rather than riding is increasing 5 percent per year—market driver for a self-propelled feature that can be added to a golf pull cart.
- The number of people who create scrapbooks as a hobby is increasing 30 to 50 percent per year—market driver for a paper cutter that precisely produces a user's custom-designed border frame.

Proof That the Product Can Sell

Chapter 6 covered the topic of creating evidence that your product will sell, which may include actually selling the product, having provisional orders or contracts, showing industry endorsements and support, and having focus group results that demonstrate the product's acceptance by the market. This is one of the most important parts of the plan if you are trying to obtain financing or acquire industry helpers. (See Chapter 6, pages 125 to 126.)

Potential Target Companies

You need to show that there are a number of potential licensees in the market and that you have plenty of companies to approach if your original target companies won't license your idea. But don't list hundreds of companies—that merely shows that you have not carefully screened companies by some criteria to determine which ones are good prospects. I recommend a list of 20 to 25 companies, and list them by category, with five to seven companies to a category. (Review Chapter 7, pages 140 to 143.) Four categories you should list are:

1. Target companies with similar products and weak market positions
2. Target companies with different products serving the same market
3. Target companies with the right manufacturing capability
4. Distributors or marketers without manufacturing capability

Positioning Strategy

How is your product positioned to be a long-term growth tool for the potential licensee? That strategy is the real key behind your product's success as a licensing candidate. List any market projections that relate to your product in this section, especially if you are talking about positioning the product as an entry into a new market. (See Chapter 7, pages 137 to 138.)

Ideal Target Customers

This should be a list of four to five companies you have selected as your best opportunities for licensing. These companies are the ones you have selected from the preceding list of "Potential Target Companies." (Also see Chapter 7, pages 143 to 146.) List the following information for each target:

- Company name
- Company size
- Other products sold into the market
- Key contacts
- Other products licensed
- Why you chose the company as a target

Where the Product Stands Today

Report what you have done to date. Include in this section:

- Patent/trademark status
- Development status
- Sales to date, if any
- Market research
- Manufacturing status
- Cost evaluation
- Packaging status

Development Required

List here whether the product needs further prototypes, regulatory approvals, engineering design, or preproduction samples for more market tests. Since you are using the licensing plan to help raise funding, you need to justify why you need additional money—for example, to build three preproduction units. Inventors have to be careful about this. They of course want to raise the money they need, but they don't want to make it appear that very little of the development work has been completed. Try to list no more than three activities here or you may scare people away, thinking that your product isn't developed enough to be a wise investment. If you have more than three development needs, you are typically better off raising money for two and then doing another licensing plan to raise additional money. Some of the items to consider listing in this section are:

- Patent and trademark costs
- Additional product design
- Cost of engineering
- Industrial design
- Manufacturing costs
- Engineering drawings
- Packaging design
- Regulatory approval testing
- Durability testing
- Units required for market tests

Strategy for Meeting Key Contacts

Key contacts, from both the industry and target companies, can make the difference between success and failure. This section needs to include both the contacts you have made and the ones you plan on meeting. Inventors tend to dismiss this section, as they want to do most things on their own, but investors will consider having strategic contacts as a key item in your licensing strategy. (See Chapter 3, pages 55 to 60.) Include in this section:

- Attendance at trade shows
- Membership in a professional association
- Contacts met through potential customers and distributors
- People you already know who have a wide range of contacts

Option-Oriented Strategies

Chapter 8 covered option-oriented strategies with which to approach manufacturers. This section is important to both industry helpers and your potential investors. It shows that you have an idea of what you might need to do to get a license, and it shows you'll be flexible in pursuing a licensing agreement. You don't need to follow all these strategies, but you'll have several backup strategies ready in case you don't get an immediate license. (See Chapter 8, pages 152 to 154.)

Introduction Timetable

This part of the plan is as much for you to follow as it is to show to potential industry helpers and investors. It should lay out every step you need to complete from this point on, including the action start and finish dates. If you have experience, you won't need to make your points too detailed—for example, your section might look like this:

Action Item	Start Date	Completion Date
Complete packaging design	May 2005	July 2005

If you are inexperienced, you probably should show a more detailed timetable. For the preceding same example, it might look like this:

Action Item	Start Date	Completion Date
Complete packaging design	May 2005	July 2005
Choose packaging vendor	May 2005	May 15, 2005
Review initial concepts	May 30, 2005	June 10, 2005
Review concepts with contacts	June 10, 2005	June 25, 2005
Choose final concept	June 25, 2005	July 15, 2005
Complete packaging	July 1, 2005	July 30, 2005

Some of the areas that could be listed in a complete timetable include:

- Patent and trademark issues
- Product development, including prototypes and engineering design
- Packaging
- Trade show attendance
- Association contacts
- Meetings with key contacts
- Market tests
- Efforts to prove the product will sell
- Preparing a licensing presentation
- Determining two initial licensing targets
- Initial licensing presentations

Licensing Cost Estimates

If you need more money, don't show only the money you need, show the total amount that will be spent, including funds that you will be investing. If you need $18,000 and are investing $8,000 of your own money, make that clear. I also believe you should list the amount of time you will spend on the project as an in-kind investment (which means you are working for free, or providing a service without charge). You will also need to include costs for travel and trade show attendance if it is in the plan. As an example, the costs for a licensing plan that takes six month to complete might look like the one that follows. These costs are somewhat high for most inventors, but I have found that an investment of about $30,000 or so is not uncommon for products that eventually become licensed. If your investment is less, you can scale back the numbers to reflect your actual investment.

Expense Item	Cost in Dollars
30 hours per week managing the project	in-kind investment
Packaging	$ 5,000
Changes in prototypes	3,000
Trademark registration	650
Patent fees	2,500
Trade show attendance	2,500
Licensing presentation	2,000
Travel to secure support of key contacts	1,000
Travel to potential licensees	2,000
Procure four models for testing	4,000
Test market	in-kind investment
Total	$22,650

Funding Request/Offer

If you need money, you need three sections: the money you are looking for now, the total investment required, and what you are offering in exchange for an investment. For example, the funding section might look like this for our $18,000 investment.

Investment required for this phase of licensing	$18,000
Money from inventor	4,000
Money from family friends	2,000

Money from industry helpers	2,000
Money being sought from new investors	10,000

Investments to date

Patents	3,400
Prototypes and other product development	5,000
Market tests	1,000
Initial packaging	400
Attendance at three trade shows	1,800
Manufacturing cost estimates	2,000
Total	$13,600

Investment sources to date

Inventor	3,600
Family/friends	6,000
Industry helpers	4,000

Incentive offer

In return for a $10,000 investment the investor will receive 15 percent ownership in the product plus royalty proceeds.

Continuing Assistance Available from the Inventor

This could include your ongoing help in product design, product engineering, start-up help at the factory, seminars or clinics you could offer to target customers, sales assistance, marketing plans, or market research. This topic was also covered in Chapter 8 (see pages 153 to 154). It is not really necessary for the plan, but I think it is helpful to show that you are prepared to do whatever it takes to secure a license, which means offering your investors and industry helpers an excellent chance to have a return on the investment. Your willingness to do whatever it takes shows the flexibility and persistence required from successful inventors.

10

STEP 10A. SELL YOUR CONCEPT: CREATE THE HIGHEST VALUE FOR YOUR PRODUCT

You have the background data you need to strike a license agreement, you have low-cost strategies to propose, and you have a plan to pursue. The next step is to get out and sell your product to a licensee. One aspect that works both for and against an inventor is the need to present the item to only one (or just a few) companies at a time, to avoid the appearance of "shopping around." Inventors have to be careful to present to only a few companies at a time while at the same time pitching exclusivity as leverage to keep the product moving. Success, however, depends on the licensing presentation and your sales efforts.

Selling a license is quite a bit different than most other sales efforts. People generally buy products for their own needs. For example, if you need a new car, you look around at the cars available, find two or three that appear good to you, and then go to a dealer to find out more details. In these cases, the buyer has done research, knows something about the product, and has the mind-set to buy. For a licensing presentation, companies might see you because they are looking for new products, but they might look at 20 new products, including their own, before choosing two to three to introduce. Therefore they are probably meeting with you with little expectation that the invention will work out. They may have ideas of products they would like to introduce, which may or may not fit with your product. Consequently, most companies are not coming to your meeting ready to buy. One way to compensate for this inventor disadvantage is to have an industry person and a company supporter, such as a regional manager, helping to promote your idea. This support raises a company's expectation for your presentation, encouraging its representatives to believe your product is a winner. It also helps you target your presentation to the potential licensee's goals. Support helps, but there is still a tremendous burden on the inventor to have a great presentation with punch and flair to win the potential licensee over to the inventor's side. You can't just be another salesperson: You must be a showman/woman. This chapter explains the following concepts.

- Create the dynamic opening: Convert prospects from the start.
- Generate a can't-miss licensing presentation: Appeal to licensees' goals.
- Initiate the licensing negotiations: Convince the prospect it's win-win.
- Finalize the licensing deal: Negotiate the key points in your favor

Facts Sell the Product

Cassie Quinn was a mother with a problem. She always had trouble finding what she wanted in her baby's diaper bag. Frustrated, she did what so many mothers have done before: She created her own diaper bag. She constructed a bag that held seven small drawers and six large see-through pockets. The drawers were held in place by a zippered flap. The inside of the bag had two large compartments to hold diapers and other large articles. At first Quinn had only a handmade model, but she eventually produced a sale-quality bag after several focus group sessions with other mothers.

　　Quinn didn't have the time or energy to market the product herself and wanted to license the idea. She didn't know how to go about finding a licensee, so she formed a partnership with her father-in-law, Steve Danzig, who had a new-products marketing company. He prepared a detailed report and licensing presentation that consisted of seven items.

1. *A market analysis, including trends, growth, and recent products*
2. *Shelf space allocated to diaper bags at major retailers, including:*
   - *Discount mass merchandisers like Target*
   - *Midrange retailers such as JC Penney and Sears*
   - *Drugstore chains like Walgreen's*
   - *Juvenile product specialty stores such as Babyland*
3. *Competitive analysis, including the number of brands and market leaders*
4. *Total sales dollars of the market category*

5. *Analysis of the market leader's position, how it came about, and how the company maintained its market share*
6. *Explanation of how Quinn's product was positioned in the market in relation to the competition*
7. *Results of focus group sessions with parents and grandparents of young children*

Danzig went to the Juvenile Products Shows in Dallas, Texas, and met several manufacturers that he had targeted as potential licensees. He was able to make presentations to several companies, including Kalencom Corporation, which ended up licensing the idea.

CREATE THE DYNAMIC OPENING: CONVERT PROSPECTS FROM THE START

Inventors do best when they start their presentation with a tremendous opening. This part of the presentation is all showmanship, and the better your show the better your chance of landing a license. Inventors need to get a big "wow" response in the first moments. This could well be the most important part of your visit to your prospect. I know inventors who have taken as long as an hour to set up a presentation before people walked in the door to ensure they'd be blown away by the inventor's product. There are several ways to add drama and action to your opening, including demonstrations, product comparisons, and videos—of either your product's strong benefits or the problem it addresses.

Demonstrations

I saw an inventor who had an improved drain and filter product for large tanks. For his demonstration, he set up two big tubs, one containing the current market leader's drain and the other with his product. Nearby he had four 5-gallon buckets full of sludge and water. He started his demonstration by pouring a bucket of sludge into each tub; his product drained in half the time of the market leader's. One person in the audience questioned whether the inventor may have used a bucketful of denser sludge in the competitor's drain. The inventor invited that person to choose which of the last two buckets should go through each drain: The results were the same, and the inventor clearly had the audience's attention.

Showing pictures is not nearly as effective as a display, so plan a demonstration whenever possible. If your product is big or complex, consider making a small demonstration model that will show how it works.

You can often get help with demonstration ideas from a local inventors' club if you can't come up with one on your own. Check out www.uiausa .com or www.inventorsdigest.com for listings of inventors' clubs in the United States and Canada.

Video Presentations

Not every product is conducive to a demonstration, and then you might need a video to highlight how your product will work. The video should be about five minutes and sell the product benefits by showing end users happily using the product. If possible, have the end users explain how the product benefits them. Try to put something funny in your video, as that puts prospects in a better mood to accept your product. Games work well if you can video people playing and having fun. A video of the product in use accompanied by music is much better than a show-and-tell video that simply states "here is my product and here is how it works." For example, if you have a video of a baby holder that sits in a shopping cart, don't *explain* how it works. Instead, *show* the baby in the shopping cart grabbing things and trying to eat the holder while the carefree mother tosses items over the baby and into the cart. Use the product in a real situation. You may need two hours of tape to get five minutes of great video, but that is what will sell your idea.

You can also put product comparisons on video, showing one person using your product and another using the top competitor's product so people can see for themselves which is better. Again, a lot of talking during the video slows everything down, so resist the temptation. You'll have plenty of time later to explain your idea. For now, concentrate on showing your product in real-world situations. I discussed earlier the inventor who had a holder for the Scrubber Rack, which holds a combination scrubber-soap-dispenser product so it doesn't leak soap all over the kitchen sink area. He had 20 pictures of different sinks, all with a scrubber and no rack, and one of a scrubber *in* his Scrubber Rack. Without the rack, everything was a big mess. That's what you want to show people.

GENERATE A CAN'T-MISS LICENSING PRESENTATION: APPEAL TO LICENSEES' GOALS

The licensing presentation should last only 20 minutes. In fact, inventors should be able to give their presentation in 15 minutes or less, not including questions. Present the facts your contacts at the potential licensee will need to convince management to sign a licensing agreement.

But before you start the official presentation, you need to confirm the company's goals, which is best done verbally. Start out with a statement similar to this one: "As you can see [after your whizbang opening], I have a product I'm excited about. I've decided not to shop my idea around to other companies because I think that you are the best match for my product. Your goals are similar to mine. Correct me if I'm wrong, but your market goal appears to be . . . [simply state what you believe are the goals of the potential licensee in terms of the target market]. You strive to provide daredevil toys to 16- to 25-year-old males" or "You provide great kitchen convenience tools to the working housewife" or "You target parents who look for educational toys that are also fun." Stop then and ask if your contacts view their company's goals similarly. They should say yes, as you have done your research to determine those goals. But if not, ask for their view of the company's goal, and then incorporate what they have said into your presentation.

Licensing Presentation Format

Offer your information in a PowerPoint or slide presentation, limiting the text. You can add more information verbally to enhance your presentation. Here's an outline for a typical presentation. Figure 10.1 follows up with a sample presentation for a Baby Walker Bumper Pad.

1. Provide a short overview.
   a. Product description
   b. Target market
   c. Market size
   d. Yearly profit and sales potential
2. State why you developed the product, which should be a personal story similar to the one you shared in your licensing plan.
3. Verify that the market sees the same need you do by showing the results of questionnaires, focus groups, or actual sales results.
4. State your design objectives—what your product is designed to do. Have at least three or four objectives and always include the objectives of creating a product that is easy to manufacturer and reliable for the consumer.
5. Demonstrate and show the product, not so much for the "wow" factor, but more for how it will work and function.
6. List the major selling features of the product.
7. Show a projected retail price and manufacturing cost. Include data on how you calculated these costs, such as a focus group study, a competitive product analysis (i.e., comparable retail

Figure 10.1 Licensing Presentation: Baby Walker Bumper Pad

Here is a sample presentation outline for a pad that attaches to the bottom of a baby walker to protect furniture from being scratched and damaged. A baby walker is a product that children who cannot yet walk sit in to propel themselves around the house.

1. Short overview
   a. Product description: The Baby Walker Bumper Pad protects furniture from being damaged by a baby walker.
   b. Target market: The 20 million parents per year who have children between the ages of 6 and 12 months.
   c. Market size: The industry sells 4 million baby walkers per year.
   d. Suggested retail price: $14.95. Wholesale: $7.50.
   e. Yearly sales potential: Based on sales amounting to 10 percent of the baby walkers, sales potential is $3 million per year.
2. Why?
   a. Three children
   b. Three months each in a baby walker
   c. More than $1,500 worth of damage in one house
   d. Many of my friends reporting the same problem
3. Market research
   a. Patent search results
      (1) Two previous patents
      (2) One- to three-inch foam blocks rather than a whole pad
      (3) No Velcro attachment
   b. Trade magazine and trade show search results
      (1) No similar products despite a 12-month search.
      (2) No similar products at last year's Juvenile Products Trade Show.
   c. Industry research
      (1) Four baby products' retail store owners
      (2) Two manufacturers' sales representatives
      (3) Sell to 20 to 25 percent of the people purchasing baby walkers
   d. End-user research
      (1) Three focus groups

(Continued)

Figure 10.1 *Continued*

---

     (2) 20 parents

     (3) 14 of 20 participants willing to buy

4. Design objectives

  a. Meet new industry trends

     (1) Nonflammable polypropylene padding

     (2) Thinner Velcro straps

     (3) Wear-resistant cotton/polyester blends

  b. Flexible system to fit all types of walkers

  c. Size and color scheme for hooks or shelves

  d. Bright, bold packaging to attract attention

  e. To meet safety standards

  f. Simple manufacturing process with no difficult-to-manufacture features

  g. Significant utility patent protection

     (1) Fastening from both Velcro and other three means

     (2) Unique folded ridge on the top of the pad to provide a snug fit on the bumper

  h. Patent status: currently pending

5. Key points (demonstrate)

  a. Ease of installation

  b. Upper ridge on pad to keep product in place

  c. Rugged protection

6. Major features

  a. Velcro straps

  b. Holds in place despite abuse

  c. Dirt-resistant fabric

  d. Soft, high-impact-resistant foam

  e. Looks great in a low-cost package.

7. Projected retail price and manufacturing cost

  a. Suggested retail price: $14.95

     (1) Focus group of 15 consumers

     (2) Six other products

     (3) Rank products by value

  b. Manufacturing cost: $2.75 (based on three quotes)

(Continued)

Figure 10.1   *Continued*

---

8. Introduction timetable
   a. To introduce at October 2006 Juvenile Products Manufacturers Association Show
   b. Production to start July 2006
   c. License by December 2005
9. Additional help provided by inventor
   a. Arranging a pilot production run
   b. Initiating agreements with distributors or manufacturers' sales agents
   c. Arranging for final industrial design and engineering documentation

---

prices and costs), bill of materials estimates, estimated production times as determined by a manufacturing engineers, and so forth.
8. Present your introduction timetable. Use the key elements of the timetable from Chapter 9 to show a date by which your product must be licensed in order to hit your target introduction date.
9. State additional help you can offer if the company is interested in your product.

To wrap up this part of the presentation, tell the audience you've put together some thoughts on ways the candidate company and you could further develop the product but that first you'd like to answer any questions they might have.

INITIATE THE LICENSING NEGOTIATIONS: CONVINCE THE PROSPECT IT'S WIN-WIN

I've previously discussed the need to have a more open approach to licensing in order to achieve your objectives. That gives you more opportunities to sign a deal, and it also helps the potential licensee see that you are trying to find a true win-win scenario where everyone profits and that you will do whatever it takes to get the project rolling. You need to be aggressive at the end of the licensing presentation and promise to take on many tasks. I recommend this approach because it indicates that you won't wait forever for a commitment and because it gives the company options to overcome whatever obstacles may block its acceptance of a licensing agreement (e.g., no market connections or lack of engineers available to finalize documentation).

End your presentation with a statement similar to this one, and then you'll be ready to move on to discuss options.

> I firmly believe that your company is the best choice for my product. You have a strong market position, an established reputation as a market leader, and the financial resources to effectively promote the [product name]. I also believe the [product name] offers your company an innovative solution to an industry problem that will help your sales penetration and company image. I'm prepared to work with your company in any number of ways to get the product introduced. Let me show you some of the options we could consider together.

You should have put together at least a starting point for your options in Chapter 8 (see pages 152 to 154), but feel free to add to the list for your presentation.

- Oversee the final product design through your partnership with an industrial design firm. Cost: $15,000 (be sure to list the correct costs for your product).
- Do additional market research with key companies or executives. Cost: $5,000.
- Conduct an additional market test in a specified market or store. Cost: $20,000.
- License the product outright for an up-front fee and an ongoing royalty percentage.
- Sign an exclusive product distribution agreement that can be supplied through a contract manufacturer.
- Sign a nonexclusive distribution agreement.
- Locate a contract manufacture that will make the product for the licensee.
- Supply a private-label product (one with the manufacturer's name on it) for the manufacturer's exclusive distribution with an option to license at a later date.

The options can be broken down into two categories:

1. *The inventor finishes product development.* The inventor's goal is to get the potential licensee to pay the cost of development in return for the first rights to buy the product or the right of first refusal. First rights on an agreement means the company will have the first chance to buy your idea once development is complete. If it doesn't execute that option you will have the right to offer the product to someone else. Your agreement here may include licensing terms

such as *up-front fees, royalty rates,* and *minimum royalty.* For example, a purchase order or contract might read, "ABC Company shall have the first rights, for a period of 60 days after the completion of this step [list the actual step], to license the invention or new product at a 6 percent royalty rate, with a $20,000 up-front payment and a minimum royalty of $25,000 per year."

A right of first refusal generally means that before you sign a contract with another company you have to give the first company the right to match the second company's contract terms. A right of first refusal is somewhat difficult to negotiate because it doesn't specify any terms that both sides agree to. Consult an attorney before finalizing either a first-rights or a right-of-first-refusal agreement.

This approach helps both the inventor and the company. The inventor receives funding for the final, sometimes expensive, stages of product development. Without this help the inventor may never get his or her product to a stage at which it can be licensed. The company also benefits by getting a look at what might be a promising product for a $1,000 to $20,000 investment. That same look might cost the company up to $100,000—and maybe much more—if it tried to start a similar project on its own. The advantage of this type of proposal is that it gives a potential licensee a low-cost intermediate option to better determine whether a product has strong market potential.

2. *The inventor produces the product and the company distributes it.* This type of proposal is not the same as turbo-outsourcing because the intent here is still to license the idea after the product becomes established in at least part of the market. You may be able to set up an agreement like this with a buyout clause allowing the company to buy out the product in one or two years for a fixed amount of money plus a royalty rate. You should be able to get a contract manufacturer to produce the product if you have signed an agreement with the potential licensee.

If there are high up-front expenses to get a contract manufacturer to produce the product, you may need to ask the potential licensee to pay that money. You can offset that investment by offering to accept a low margin (e.g., 10 percent on sales) or by selling the licensee 25 to 50 percent ownership in your company in return for funding.

Low-margin agreements state that you will mark up the contract manufacturer's price by only 10 percent (or another agreed-upon percentage) to the potential licensee in return for the investment required by the contract manufacturer.

Another choice to fund the contract manufacturer's cost is to request an up-front fee for an exclusive distribution agreement for a set period of time, typically one to three years. This strategy works if the contract manufacturer's start-up costs are modest— less than $25,000.

FINALIZE THE LICENSING DEAL: NEGOTIATE THE KEY POINTS IN YOUR FAVOR

I don't like to offer too many details about negotiating a licensing agreement because you should get a lawyer to assist you. But inventors need some knowledge about the contract so they can intelligently discuss terms. In most agreements, the *licensee* is the company paying the royalty and the *licensor* is the inventor or company to whom the idea belongs and to whom the royalty is paid. The basic elements usually contained in a license are as follows:

- The nature of the license: exclusive or nonexclusive
- A definition of exactly what is being licensed
- Geographic or market limitations
- Future inventions
- Terms and termination of the agreement
- Right to audit
- Royalty rate, payment terms, and any up-front royalty payments
- Patent expenses
- Infringement by others
- Rights to sublicense
- Patent assignment

Nature of the License

You might license a product to just one company, which is an exclusive license, or you might license a product to several manufacturers, which is a nonexclusive license. An example of a nonexclusive license is VHS videotape technology, which was licensed to dozens of companies. New processes, such as a better way to strengthen plastic molds, might also have a nonexclusive license.

One important point is that you can't grant someone exclusive rights unless you have a patent, trademark, or copyright, which are intellectual property rights as defined by U.S. law. If you don't have property rights, your agreement could have another name such as a "marketing and manufacturing agreement." In an agreement like this you could be disclosing your product technology and trade secrets in return for a payment based on sales volume. Your agreement could also specify that you will grant exclusive intellectual property rights if a patent is issued.

Definition of the Product or Technology Being Licensed

The definition is typically listed in the paragraph in which you grant a license to the licensee. This is a crucial paragraph. You want the license to be for the product and its subsequent variations, modifications, and derivatives. That gives you a continuous royalty stream as the product continues to evolve, even if the advancements are designed by your licensee. The licensee will try to limit licensing to just the specific product under consideration, which will limit how long you will receive royalties.

Geographic or Market Limitations

The license might be restricted to a specific geographic area, such as the United States, or it might be restricted to a market, such as sporting goods. For example, if your product combines two different fabrics into a unique feel or look, you might license it to a sporting goods company that could use it to insulate undergarments, and you might license it to a clothing manufacturer for the unique look it gives children's blouses and dresses.

Future Inventions

The licensee might ask for rights to or the right of first refusal on your future inventions. Typically, you can have this clause removed. It restricts the inventor, and the company is not offering anything in return. If you are forced to keep the clause, accept only a right of first refusal and allow the company only 30 to 60 days in which to evaluate the idea before releasing it back to you so that you may pursue other licensing options.

Terms and Terminations

The licensee usually tries to negotiate a set period or to time the license agreement to the life of the patent or patent improvements. You, as the licensor, want to benefit from a royalty as long as the licensee sells the product. After all, the market success a company gains from selling your product will help it sell the product long after the license expires. This goes back to *product definition*, discussed earlier. You want the royalty to cover subsequent variations, derivations, and modifications.

As a licensor, you should have the right to terminate the agreement for nonperformance. Usually this is tied to a minimum royalty payment per year. For example, the contract might state that the licensor has the right to terminate the agreement if the royalty payments are less than $50,000. The manufacturer has to pay you a minimum royalty, even if sales are low, or risk having the agreement terminated. An inventor might agree to a 90- or 120-day advance termination notice to give the manufacture an opportunity to liquidate its inventory before the license expires.

You should also have a clause in the contract stating that either party can terminate the agreement if the other party violates its terms and conditions.

Right to Audit

Include a clause that gives you the right to audit the books of the licensee to ensure that you are receiving your rightful share of the royalty payments.

Royalty Payments

The three considerations in this section are (1) up-front royalty payments, which may or may not be an advance against future sales, (2) the royalty percentage based on net sales, and (3) a minimum royalty over the life of the contract.

License agreements are fully negotiable, and there are no hard-and-fast rules that apply. Royalties can run from less than 1 percent to 15 percent or more, and up front fees can vary from $5,000 to millions of dollars. I recommend using the following general guidelines as starting points for negotiating royalty rates.

- A product that has a 50 percent manufacturing margin (manufacturer's selling price minus manufacturing costs divided by manufacturer's selling price equals 50 percent) should have a 5 to 6 percent royalty. The royalty rate should go up one to two points for every 10 percent increase in margin. For example a 60 percent margin product should have a royalty rate of from 6 to 7 percent.
- The up-front fee should be equal to a minimum of 50 to 75 percent of the expected yearly royalty payment. Try to negotiate an up-front fee that is not a royalty advance but a separate payment—however, expect resistance since companies will want any payment to be a royalty advance.
- Another negotiating point is a total minimum royalty or some other provision to prevent the company from keeping your idea for 12 to 24 months without selling any product. That could cost you the market opportunity. Try to get a minimum of half your expected yearly royalty, and ask for a minimum payment every six months until the product is introduced.

Patent Expenses

License agreements occasionally ask the licensor to pay for patent expenses. Be wary of this clause. If you have to pay for patents, make sure it is *only* for U.S. patents. Foreign patents can easily cost more than $100,000, and those expenses might be more than you can recover in royalties. Ask the licensee to pay for foreign patents.

Infringement by Others

This clause specifies who is responsible for taking action against a person or company infringing on the patent(s). You don't want to be responsible, because patent lawsuits can be very expensive—easily more than $100,000. Your licensee also doesn't want to be responsible. I recommend that such a clause *not* be included. If it is, the clause should say only that both parties would mutually agree to a course of action at the time the infringement is discovered.

Right to Sublicense

In many cases the licensor will want to sublicense the product or idea to other manufacturers or companies. Fifty-fifty is a typical split in a sublicense agreement. Often the clause grants the licensee the ability to sublicense at its discretion. This can be a good or bad situation for the inventor. If the licensee sublicenses the idea overseas or to new markets, the inventor ends up with income he or she never expected; but if the company sublicenses the product to another company in the same industry, you could end up with only half the royalty rate you expected.

A sublicense clause should state that the licensee cannot sublicense a product without the inventor's permission. The agreement should also state that the licensor cannot unreasonably withhold permission.

Patent Assignment

You don't need to assign a patent in order for a company to license the product from you. I don't recommend that you ever assign the patent rights except to your own company. Your ability to retrieve your patent rights, once assigned, is severely limited. You would have to negotiate a release from the patent assignment agreement, which the assignee company would be reluctant to do.

PART III

THE FAST TRACK:
TURBO-OUTSOURCING

11

STEP 6B. PROVE THE CONCEPT: ESTABLISH THAT THE PRODUCT WILL MAKE MONEY

To demonstrate that their product is a winner in a turbo-outsourcing deal, inventors must establish three important elements. First, they need to show that the deal will provide meaningful benefits for all parties. Second, inventors need to convince companies that they will make money even when the profits are split three ways. Third, to negotiate an advantageous deal, inventors need to convince the partners that they offer a crucial benefit to the project.

Proving your concept is crucial when you attempt to turbo-outsource, because companies considering both turbo-outsourcing and licensing agreements evaluate each potential deal against their other opportunities. Their analysis asks the question, "What else could we do if we don't sign this deal?" Companies are unlikely to move ahead with a complicated turbo-outsource deal if they have a product of their own with potential. Inventors need to prove convincingly high sales and marketing potential for their product to overcome potential partners' desire to proceed with their own products.

Inventors are also faced with the burden of proving that they bring real value to the deal. This burden exists only in turbo-outsourcing, so inventors need to be careful when they choose this option. At first glance, the need to demonstrate their value seems counterintuitive. Most inventors would love to have a full turbo-outsourcing deal, with a distribution partner doing all the selling and a manufacturing partner doing all the production. After all, turbo-outsourcing sounds like an inventor's dream: You just sit back and collect your share of the profits. That might work for a while, but with time the partners start to wonder whether the inventor is earning his or her share. For turbo-outsourcing to work the inventor has to be providing true value over the life of the agreement. Turbo-outsourced partners aren't just buying the product—in a sense they are buying the inventor. In some cases the inventor will add value as the project's design engineer, handling product improvements, modifications, and quality issues. At other times, the inventor's value comes from being connected to customers in a meaningful way that both partners value. If you can't sell both your own value and your product's potential points, you either won't get a deal or you won't get a substantial percentage of the profits. The chapter covers the following concepts.

- Find your space: Show why you are a crucial ingredient to a product's success.
- Generate buzz: Showcase the market's potential.
- Establish who gets what share: Choose a strategy that benefits the inventor.
- Evaluate manufacturing cost versus perceived value: Determine whether there is enough profit for three partners.
- Follow up with buyers: Discover support levels required to make sales.

Creating Value to Strike a Deal

Gary Kellmann, in his early twenties, was trying to figure out a great present for his girlfriend when he noticed that her hair-care products were scattered throughout her room. He built a holder for her accessories, which consisted of two rings with a clasp that opens and closes the rings. One ring was large, for large hair accessories, and one was small, for smaller accessories. The small ring hung down from the top of the large ring, creating a pleasing visual effect of a small ring within a large ring. His girlfriend and her friends loved the idea, so Kellmann decided to take the product to market under the name Hair Holder Holder.

Kellmann didn't have any money, so he decided to try to license the idea. He walked up and down the aisles of drugstores and discount stores to find out who was selling to his target market. He found several potential licensees that seemed promising. While Kellmann wasn't able to line up a license with any of those prospects, he did find a marketing company, which was already successfully selling to drugstores, willing to sell his product. Unfortunately, they didn't manufacture products.

Kellmann didn't give up. He found a contract manufacturer willing and able to make the product. The contract manufacturer wasn't willing to pick up all the start-up and operating costs, but the marketer and manufacturer were able to work out financing between them and a deal was struck. Kellmann receives a 7 percent royalty from the marketer and in return handles the design and manufacturing process. Although Kellmann didn't have any money invested, he had responsibilities that kept him in control of the product and its improvements, and he received an excellent return. All in all, he found that it was an ideal situation.

FIND YOUR SPACE: SHOW WHY YOU ARE A CRUCIAL INGREDIENT TO A PRODUCT'S SUCCESS

In turbo-outsourcing your partners are taking on much more risk than you are and they are probably willing to offer 25 to 33 percent of the profits to you. You have to justify this payoff by adding long-term value to the venture over and above just having a great product. You can offer value through engineering expertise, market expertise, or by being well connected to the end-user community.

Engineering Expertise

Inventors know their product better than anyone else, and companies often need engineering expertise because of cutbacks in their own engineering and R&D departments. Inventors are big contributors to a project if they can do engineering documentation, quality control, and product modifications and design next-generation products. If you can't do the work yourself, you might be able to find an engineer to work with you for a share of your cut of the profits or who will work on a part-time basis for fixed hourly rate.

Market Expertise

This expertise has to be able to produce sales. There are several types of expertise you can put to work for you. One obvious one is being a specialist in one of the market channels. For example, you might know how to get your product on TV networks like QVC, the Home Shopping Network, or ShopNBC. Your distribution partner may have connections in the retail market, but you perhaps you could handle TV sales. Market expertise may also come from an inventor's close relationship with one or two major retailers. If you can place the product into even one chain and build a solid sales base, you add value to the project. An inventor with across-the-board sales expertise can offer to work for a sales commission that would be paid on top of his or her share of the profits.

Involvement in End-Users' Community

I believe this is the easiest way to add value because companies, though always worried about engineering and sales to the distribution channel, are rarely heavily involved in the customers' world. Being involved means knowing key end users, participating in associations, working with universities, offering seminars, and working cooperatively with end users to meet their goals. For example, Spinergy manufactures the Rev-X, a premium bike wheel. These are the ways its founder, Martin Connolly, goes into the customers' world.

- Knows all the bike racing teams and arranges for them to obtain free sets of Rev-X wheels
- Actively courts bike shop personnel and arranges for them to get products at big discounts
- Sponsors lunchtime bicycling seminars at big companies like Hewlett-Packard and Boeing to promote bike riding
- Contacts TV shows that appeal to young viewers to get product placement for the Rev-X wheels
- Forms alliances with other companies to promote and stage bike racing events

Inventors want potential partners to see that they are connected to the market. Judging contests, volunteering to be on planning committees for events and doing promotion for the industry are all ways that you become part of the market. That connection creates strong values for turbo-outsource partners because, while companies would love to be connected, most are not. You might have to pursue connections for six months to a year to become truly a part of the customers' world, but you will be looked on as a valuable resource once you acquire the credentials.

GENERATE BUZZ: SHOWCASE THE MARKET'S POTENTIAL

A product's sales potential for turbo-outsourcing agreements is similar to that of licensing. (See Chapter 7, pages 143 to 144.) The product's sales should show potential, but companies also consider the benefits of being involved in a new market: The new product can create sales for other products in their line, and they'll have opportunities to land new accounts. Generally, though, you need to generate some real buzz to sell a product. In Kellmann's case, the buzz was the excitement of potential users. Focus group studies received rave reviews from potential buyers because there was nothing else like his Hair Holder Holder on the market, and it was a product target customers really wanted. Key points you can use to show buzz to potential partners are strong end-user support; leading-edge innovation; secrecy, suspense, and intrigue and a stunning visual look.

Strong End-User Support

People are for the most part very blasé about most products. They don't really get excited about many items offered. As a result, when you strike a chord (e.g., builders creating plastic "wood" for decks), people jump on the bandwagon and the products sell. CDs, DVDs, mountain bikes, SUVs, and bread makers are all examples of products that caught the consumer's eye. Even if the market is relatively small (e.g., paper coffee cup sleeve, glow-in-the dark bubbles), all companies are strongly interested in products people want, both because they will produce sales volume and because in-demand products typically have higher margins.

Leading-Edge Innovation

You create the most buzz when you have an idea that meets a need that consumers think is important. Personal digital assistants (PDAs) and video cell phones are examples of products that created buzz. Buzz can come from small inventor companies, too. The Stowaway Keyboard for PDAs came from an inventor, as did Clean Shower, the Super Soaker, and the board game Trivial Pursuit.

Secrecy, Suspense, and Intrigue

The Segway Human Transporter from Dean Kamen had a big prelaunch publicity program. The concept was named Ginger, with no real clues about what the product was or how it would work. Tekno Bubbles succeeded in part because the product was such a big surprise to people. The Stowaway Keyboard also succeeded in part because people wondered just how the product could be folded up to fit into a shirt pocket. You create buzz by having a product that does something amazing, that isn't obvious until shown. People love to hide a Stowaway Keyboard in a pocket and say, "Oh, let me pull out my keyboard."

You also create intrigue by promising something that people want without telling them what it is. Intrigue can even be done with promotion, as in: "Let me give you a blind taste test. I'll give you $100 if you don't choose our new product." Recently, when introducing a new type of filter, I told a customer that if he would agree to side-by-side tests (his current product versus my new product), I'd explain afterward how we produced the 50 percent longer life he was sure to see.

Stunning Visual Effect

If three competitive products are lined up, people will choose first the brand they have always bought; if they've never bought that type of product, they will often buy the product that looks best—either aesthetically or in terms of appearing to provide the most effective solution. For example, consumers with no product knowledge will buy a juicer (a device that turns vegetables into juice) that offers the biggest cutter or shredder, because that product looks like it will do the best job. The Mouse Driver, a computer mouse that looks like the head of a golf driver, became a strong hit with golfers because of its unusual, visually compelling look.

ESTABLISH WHO GETS WHAT SHARE: CHOOSE A STRATEGY THAT BENEFITS THE INVENTOR

How Deals Can Be Structured

There are five ways to share the benefits in turbo-outsourcing. Sharing profits, sharing revenue, buying and selling, commission from the manufacturer, and commission from the marketer.

1. *Sharing profits.* You want to avoid a deal that's based on sharing profits, because you can't control the expenses of the marketer or the manufacturer. You could be selling the product well only to learn that the other partners had unusually high expenses. You can't control those expenses, nor can you effectively police deals based on profits.

2. *Sharing revenue.* Each party gets a designated share of the money received from either the distribution network or the end user. For example, out of $100, the marketing partner might get $30, the inventor $8, and the manufacturer $62. This type of agreement is

much better for inventors, as they don't have to worry about the expenses of either partner. This is the second best choice for an inventor.

3. *Buying and selling.* The manufacturer sells to the inventor at a set price, and then the inventor sells the product to the marketing partner. This arrangement guarantees inventors their profit and keeps them in control of the product. This type of agreement may let the inventor sell to certain markets on his or her own. This is the best type of agreement for an inventor and can be fairly simple to negotiate because it consists of two separate two party agreements.

4. *Receiving a commission from the manufacturer for all products sold.* This arrangement is simple to negotiate. It could just be a contract between the marketing partner and the manufacturer and the distribution partner, with a separate sales agreement between the inventor and the manufacturer. This arrangement has the drawback that the inventor can easily lose all control of the product.

5. *Receiving a commission from the marketing partner.* This type of deal is unusual, but can happen if the inventor can sell to several markets that the marketing partner doesn't sell to. The inventor can also lose control of his or her product with this type of arrangement if the inventor is just a sales representative. The worst-case scenario is when the marketer severs the relationship with you and keeps on selling the product. To prevent this from happening, first sign a memorandum of understanding (MOU) (see Chapter 8 pages 154 to 158), which is a document that establishes your ownership of the product. Second, have a formal sales commission agreement stating that, if for any reason the commission agreement is canceled, a new agreement will be mutually agreed upon to compensate you for the use of your product idea.

Percent of Profit for Each Partner

The Inventor

Inventors should strive for a deal whereby they either buy and sell the product or share in the revenue. Both of these agreements give each party a percentage share of the revenue, the only difference being that inventors keep more control when they buy and sell their product. Before you talk to potential partners, estimate what percentage of the revenue each partner should receive. Figure 11.1 is a starting point for what the inventor's share should be in a turbo-outsource deal based on the project's margin.

Figure 11.1   Inventor's Take from Turbo-Outsourcing

Percent profit and inventor percentage are as a percent of sales				
Margin*	Marketing Penalty†	Real Margin	Percent Profit‡	Inventor Percentage
70%	10%	63%	15%–20%	7%–10%
60%	10%	54%	10%–13%	5%–7%
50%	10%	45%	7%–10%	3%–5%
40%	10%	36%	3%–5%	1%–3%

* *Margin* is the relationship between the selling price and the cost of manufacturing, as discussed in Chapter 5 (pages 102 to 103).
† The *marketing penalty* reflects that a turbo-outsource pays two levels of cost: (1) the traditional distributor discount and (2) the percentage that the marketing partner takes (in effect, paying more for distribution than a non-turbo-outsourced project).
‡ The *percent profit* is based on my observations and on some of the profit percentages reported in the *Almanac of Business and Financial Ratios* (Prentice Hall), which is available in larger libraries.

The inventor's percentage may seem high, but the marketing partner and manufacturing partners both make some extra profit, which is explained in the next two sections. An important point to note in Figure 11.1 is that inventors receive significant profits only if they have high margins.

The Marketing Partner

Marketing and sales costs typically run 10 to 25 percent of sales. Marketing partners, who actually bring in the sales dollars, are going to want to show at least 10 percent profit as a percentage of sales over what they expect their sales costs to be. If marketing and sales costs are 20 percent on their current product line, they will want to receive 30 percent of the revenue to cover their marketing costs and profits. You will have trouble negotiating a better deal than this with a marketing partner, primarily because companies aren't going to be willing to commit their resources without at least a 10 percent profit on their sales dollars. The 10 percent requirement of marketers also produces the most common deviation from a standard turbo-outsourcing deal—the inventor handles sales and marketing.

The Manufacturer

Manufacturers are the key to any deal because they are the ones that have to accept what is left over from the marketing partner, and they are ones that put up most of the money. The manufacturer could also receive the biggest return, depending on the manufacturing overhead involved in the project and the very beneficial impact of overhead absorption.

Figure 11.2 shows where the retail sales dollars go in a turbo-outsourcing agreement (explanation of manufacturing overhead to follow shortly). There are two key points to observe in Figure 11.2. One, that turbo-outsourcing has better revenue sharing when the distribution process has as few layers as possible. A distribution layer is a part of the channel that receives a discount or commission or takes a markup. An example of a four-layer distribution channel is one that sells through manufacturers' representatives who receive a 10 percent commission to distributors who receive a 35 percent markup who sell to retailers who take a

Figure 11.2   Revenue Flow for Turbo-Outsourcing

Direct sales: Marketing partner sells directly to the end user.
Direct to retailers: Marketing partner sells to retailers that sell to end users.
Through distributors: Marketing partner sells to distributors who sell to retailers who sell to end users.

All numbers reflect the share of a $100 sale to the end user based on a 60% margin.

	Direct Sales ($)	*Direct to Retailers ($)*	*Through Distribution*
Paid by end user	$100	$100	$100
Retailer discount	N/A	50	40
Distributor discount	N/A	N/A	15
Marketing partner*	50	20	18
Inventor share	7	6	5
Manufacturer share	43	24	22
Total	$100	$100	$100

* Note the marketing partner's sales and marketing costs are much higher with direct sales.

100 percent markup. The direct-sales scenario, whereby marketers sell directly to end users—thus bypassing distribution layers—produces much better revenue than does the marketing partner who sells to a distributor who then sells to a retailer. The second key point is that the manufacturer's share is listed last. That is the reality of turbo-outsourcing. Manufacturers have a number that they either need to accept or turn down. Their acceptance of that number is key in signing the deal.

Before you try to sign a deal with partners, you need to create a chart similar to the one in Figure 11.2 that will show partners what share of the revenue they can expect to receive. You might not be 100 percent accurate with your percentages, but they do give you a starting point in revenue-sharing discussions.

Overhead absorption offers a manufacturer the opportunity to not only make up for what looks like a gloomy profit picture but to actually make more money than everyone else. *Overhead* refers to all fixed costs of a manufacturing facility, including rent, quality control, product engineering, purchasing, management, utility fees, and other administrative fees (personnel, insurance, etc.). *Overhead absorption* means that manufacturers absorb, or pay for, their overhead by including an overhead charge on every product sold. Overhead frequently can be 50 percent or more of a product's cost. A product's cost for a plastic part costing $2 would have three cost components:

Materials	$0.75
Labor	$0.25
Overhead	$1.00

In this example each product sold will absorb $1.00 in overhead. A company determines its overhead cost component at the beginning of a year by allocating the overhead based on the products it will sell for the year. In this example, say that all the company's products have the same price structure, that the company has overhead costs of $1 million, and that the company sells 1 million products: It would then allocate $1 of overhead per product.

Now what happens if you offer a manufacturer another 500,000 units with the same $2 manufacturing cost, and the manufacturer nets a 10 percent ($0.20) profit per piece. At first glance, the deal doesn't seem attractive. However, what is the actual impact of that extra $1 per unit of overhead absorption? The company's production now produces a total of $1.5 million in overhead absorption. But the overhead is still $1 million, so that extra $500,000 is profit for the company. In other words, a 10 percent profit on a million units produced $100,000, but the *extra overhead absorption* on the additional units produces $500,000 in profit, a very good margin.

Manufacturers will be interested in your product when their overhead costs are 30 to 50 percent of their total product costs because of the tremendous power of excess overhead absorption.

EVALUATE MANUFACTURING COST VERSUS PERCEIVED VALUE: DETERMINE WHETHER THERE IS ENOUGH PROFIT FOR THREE PARTNERS

Chapter 6 (pages 130 to 131) offered a detailed explanation of how to calculate manufacturing costs and how to compare those costs to your product's perceived value. You need to take the same steps with turbo-outsourcing. As shown in Figure 11.1, you have a much bigger burden in outsourcing, because you need the margins to be a minimum of 50 percent—and 60 percent for the deals to really make sense. The burden on inventors, then, is to show that their product can have a high margin because end users value its benefits.

I generally prefer value-based pricing, which establishes pricing based on what customers will pay. In the case of turbo-outsourcing, however, I believe you also need to show that your manufacturing costs can provide a 60 percent margin given the product price. You need to first establish what that price needs to be, and then obtain supporting evidence that the product can be sold at that price. These three steps should help.

1. Estimate your manufacturing costs. Follow the same steps as outlined in Chapter 1 (pages 26 to 28).

2. Determine the price you need for a 60 percent margin. The formula to find the margin is:

$$\frac{\text{manufacturing price}}{1 - \text{desired margin}} = \frac{\text{manufacturing price}}{1 - 0.6} = \frac{\text{manufacturing price}}{0.4}$$

3. Do market research with end users, focus groups, and/or questionnaires (see Chapter 1, pages 17 to 23). Find potential buyers willing to offer provisional orders or letters of intent (see Chapter 6, pages 128 to 130) when your price is set at a 60 percent margin. You need to tell both end users and distribution channel buyers in the research what the price will be. For example, show end users four or five competitive products along with yours, listing the prices for each product, and ask them which one they would buy. Hopefully, they will prefer your product with the 60 percent margin price. You also need to ask for provisional orders and letters of intent from the distribution channel using the 60 percent margin price. If 60 percent won't work, try the same testing

procedures, with both end users and distributors, at the 50 percent margin price.

Ideally, you will be able to show that both end users and the distribution channel consider the product a good value at the 60 percent margin price. If not, you can get by with a 50 percent margin. Any less than that and you will need to strike a modified turbo-outsourcing deal where you either take on the marketing responsibilities or provide more of the manufacturing up-front costs and simply hire a contract manufacturer.

FOLLOW UP WITH BUYERS: DISCOVER SUPPORT LEVELS REQUIRED TO MAKE SALES

The costs of marketing partners are high. Their insistence on a 10 percent profit on each sales dollar can kill the chances of a great product that may hit only a 40 to 45 percent margin. Inventors do have other options—using a manufacturer's representative sales group, selling through a distributor, having an exclusive relationship with a retailer, hiring an industry sales rep for your firm, or selling the product yourself—all of which cost less and will allow you to introduce lower-margin products. But all these options run the risk of not providing the technical, sales, or distributor support your product needs. Manufacturer's reps, for instance, may be able to call on buyers, but they won't be able to provide technical support, advertising, or extensive trade show attendance. If your margin is lower than 50 percent, consider the product's technical support requirements, the need for a dealer network, the amount of promotion your product requires, and how open the distribution network would be to considering a lower-cost option for your product. If your analysis shows your margin is less than 50 percent, but you need a big marketing partner, you will need to reconsider the options of licensing or starting your own company.

Here are the four factors you need to consider:

1. *Technical support.* Products that require lots of customization for the customer, that interface with many other products, or that require an 800 number and a web site all beg for a bigger marketing partner. The issue isn't that only a big company can provide these services so much as it is that customers typically won't buy a complex product from a small company with uncertain support, because it is harder for them to determine whether their commitment of money and other resources will be worthwhile. In some cases, providing all these services costs more than most inventors or small distributors can support.

2. *Dealer networks.* Dealers, such as Don's Appliances, are authorized sellers of products from certain manufacturers and are used when technical support is an issue and when products need to be demonstrated. Snowblowers, lawn mowers, and sewing machines are all sold through dealers. Dealer networks provide many of the services that a small company can't support. Their drawback is that they call for heavy sales support. Company representatives need to call on dealers frequently, provide training, and deal with problems. You might need 20 to 30 salespeople to cover the United States. That costs lots of money.

3. *Heavy promotion.* With turbo-outsourcing you are asking the manufacturer to make a big investment hoping for an immediate return. As a result, turbo-outsourcing agreements don't do well for products with a slow buildup in sales, because the manufacturing partner will be unhappy. If the investment is high the manufacturer probably won't invest unless you can show that you have a marketing plan in place to produce those quick sales. Unless you can quickly land a big customer with a lower-cost marketing option, you probably need a big marketing partner to generate the quick launch a manufacturer might require to make a big investment.

4. *Open distribution channel.* I've discussed this issue in Chapter 2 (pages 34 to 37). Again, if the investment required of the manufacturer is significant, the only incentive is a quick start in sales. You will need a big marketing partner if a small new company will have trouble penetrating the distribution channel.

12

STEP 7B. CHOOSE YOUR PARTNERS: FIND DISTRIBUTION AND MANUFACTURING PARTNERS TO ACCELERATE SALES

Turbo-outsourcing has the potential to launch a product in the market in a big way and establish a significant market share. I've been in marketing 25 years and I've learned that companies have a difficult time altering their market share. If a company comes on the market with 3 to 4 percent share, the market will probably perceive it forever as a minor player. To dominate a market, your best bet is to dominate the market from the start, a goal that can be achieved with major marketing and manufacturing partners. In regard to licensing, I encouraged you to look for midsize companies that were more likely to sign an agreement. When it comes to turbo-outsourcing, you want to go for the biggest possible marketing and manufacturing partner. But you also have to be careful to match partners of similar size: A strong marketing partner won't live up to its potential if the manufacturer can't make enough products, and a strong manufacturing partner won't be satisfied if the marketing partner can't produce the sales required to justify its investment of time and money. Most of all, though, you need partners that are trying to aggressively grow their sales and who will look at your product as a vehicle to do that. This chapter discusses how to accomplish these goals.

- Locate the right marketing arm: Sign sales power to drive the deal.

- Locate the right manufacturing company: Discover manufacturers looking for products.
- Sign preliminary agreements: Keep control of your product.
- Obtain commitments for performance: Insist on a major effort from partners.

Big-Time Partner Secures Market

When Nathaniel Weiss was in his twenties he enjoyed writing songs for his guitar. As he talked to and observed others doing the same, he noticed how they would have to stop and write down what they had just played, and Weiss thought this back-and-forth process took away from the spontaneity of the creative process. He thought the best solution would be to allow a writer to play the guitar while the music wrote itself on the computer. Fortunately for Weiss, he had the computer skills needed to create the G-Vox, a hardware/software package to do just that. A guitar player could play his or her song, and the program would not only save the notes but also display them on the monitor as they were being played.

Weiss created the software himself and knew several companies that could make the hardware if he could only find a company to launch the product. Weiss required significant sales volume to justify the costs of both preparing the hardware for production and offering adequate technical service. Since the product involved guitar players, Weiss decided Fender Guitar was the ideal marketing partner. It had a strong market reputation, and Weiss's product offered a benefit to the company: a unique concept in a competitive market, one that had great value to songwriting guitar players. Fender was a tough sell for Weiss, but he eventually landed the company as a partner and launched the product at guitar stores across the country.

Weiss didn't stop there. He thought that school musicians represented an even bigger market than guitar players for his product. He expanded his product so that it could pick up the notes for all types of band and orchestra instruments, and he added software that created the sounds of other instruments. These pickup features allowed students see the notes they were playing and compare them to what they were suppose to be playing. The feature that created the sounds of other instruments allowed students to, in effect, play along with the band at home. Once again, the market required extensive sales and technical support, and Weiss went looking for the right marketing partner. This time he chose McGraw-Hill, a leading publisher with a strong presence in the school market. McGraw-Hill saw the product as a unique way to expand its product offerings and differentiate its product line. It was a perfect match, and Weiss's company, G-Vox Interactive Music, quickly hit $5 million in sales.

LOCATE THE RIGHT MARKETING ARM: SIGN SALES POWER TO DRIVE THE DEAL

Inventors will typically not be able to entice a manufacturer to commit to an investment until they can explain how they plan on marketing the product. While a large marketing partner provides the best incentive for manufacturers, it is not the only option, and it may not be the best option if the product's margins are below 50 percent. When deciding on a marketing strategy, inventors need to first evaluate which partner option offers the best combination of costs and volume and then decide which companies within that option would make strong partners.

Choosing the Right Partner

Inventors can begin their analysis with the lowest-price option, which is the inventor selling his or her own product, and work their way up the scale to the option of selecting a company that has a large sales and marketing organization.

Inventor Handling Sales and Marketing

This is an appealing scenario for inventors, since with this option they should be able to receive 15 to 20 percent of the revenue. It also allows the inventor to introduce lower-margin products with only the manufacturer as a partner. This strategy is most effective in small markets with smaller manufacturing partners. A big manufacturer will want to have the maximum sales that it believes will come from having a bigger partner. Another drawback is that you will pay for sales trips, trade show attendance, brochures, and other marketing expenses associated with a new-product launch. Depending on your arrangement with the manufacturer, you may need operating cash to cover the gap between the time you need to pay the manufacturer and the time you will be paid by customers. To transfer those costs to the manufacturer, you can offer to sell on commission, but then you might get a lower share of the revenue or have less control of the product. This option works best under the following conditions:

- You have one or two big customers as supporters.
- You have market experience in sales and marketing.
- The manufacturer's start-up costs are modest.
- The market is open to small companies.
- You have the financial power to fund both the marketing costs related to the introduction and ongoing operations.
- The product has low technical and sales support requirements.

Hiring a Commissioned Salesperson with Industry Connections

An experienced marketer or sales manager working for a big company or distributor may be willing to come on board as commissioned sales representative if your product has enough potential. Adding a sales professional will encourage your manufacturer to invest and help you crack distribution channels that might resist inventors. This is an excellent option for inventors without extensive sales experience. This option works best under these conditions:

- The number of key customers is small and an industry salesperson will know most of the key contacts.
- The product's potential is $2 million or more, so the salesperson will accept a 5 to 7 percent commission. If the sales potential is lower than $2 million, the salesperson will want a higher commission rate than the inventor can afford.
- The manufacturer's costs are modest, though they can be larger than for the inventor selling on his or her own.
- The product has low technical and sales support requirements.
- You have the financial capability, or can raise money from investors, to fund introduction costs and operating cash.

Signing an Exclusive Agreement with a Nationwide Retailer or Dealer Network

In the dental market, Patterson Dental Supply is the largest nationwide dental products dealer, with market share of more than 30 percent. Patterson Dental might be interested in a two-way exclusive agreement whereby you will sell only to Patterson and the company won't buy any competitive products. Patterson might be interested in this type of agreement if dentists want your product. You can strike the same type of arrangement with a national retailer like RadioShack (which has a similar deal with Sprint cellular phones), Toys "R" Us, Spencer Gifts, or REI (outdoor equipment). This arrangement has advantages for the inventor, since the exclusive dealer or retailer might help pay for introduction costs. The dealer or retailer might also help fund manufacturing or pay the inventor a certain amount for exclusive rights. You probably will get funding only a small percentage of the time if the dealer or retailer is taking your standard product, but you should always press for some sort of payment if the dealer or retailer requests package or product modifications. A variation of this option is to provide a private-label product to the dealer, retailer, or distributor. This option works best when the following conditions apply:

- Your product has strong intellectual property protection.
- There is a dealer or retailer in the market large enough to support your sales objectives.

- The product has strong end-user appeal.
- Your product has technical and/or sales support requirements.
- Manufacturing start-up costs are no more than 10 percent of the annual projected sales volume.

Striking an Exclusive Deal with a Manufacturer's Agent Sales Group

Some manufacturer's agent groups sell countrywide when sales are primarily to large retailers such as Home Depot or Staples. The representative groups call on major retailers and buying groups and typically have strong contacts with those chains, but they generally don't have the personnel to call on smaller stores. The agent groups typically can't offer technical or sales support and won't fund introduction costs. Typically these groups require 10 to 15 percent commission. This option works well when these conditions apply:

- There is a concentration of buying by major retailers and dealers.
- Nationwide manufacturer's agents exists for your product category.
- The product has few technical or sales support issues.
- You don't require financial support from your marketing partner.
- Consumers may choose your product, but it doesn't lend itself to loyal end-user support.

Signing an Exclusive Agreement with an Industrial Distribution Partner

This option works like an exclusive retailer or dealer agreement for consumer products, except that you're offering a distributor an exclusive agreement for an industrial market. Distributor networks are a common method of selling products to companies in industrial markets. For example, distributor Graingers and Fastenall supplies industrial fasteners and other standard production parts to industrial customers across the country. Nationwide industrial distributors are a good choice when they are available. This options works best under the following conditions:

- There is a distributor in the market large enough to support your sales objectives.
- The product has strong appeal to industrial users.
- There are few technical and sales support requirements.
- Manufacturing start-up costs are no more than 10 percent of the annual projected sales volume.

Signing an Agreement with a Full Marketing Partner

You can also sign a contract (remember Nathaniel Weiss from earlier in the chapter?) with a marketing partner that has a complete marketing staff and sales staff. This option typically requires at least a 60 percent margin, as the marketing partner may require 25 to 30 percent of the revenue. This option offers plenty of technical and customer support and marketing muscle and typically will produce the highest sales volume. These partners may be a little slower pulling together their marketing materials, but generally they offer strong promotional programs. Manufacturing partners prefer this option as long as they aren't squeezed too tight on margins. This marketing option works well under these conditions:

- The product has significant sales potential.
- The distribution channels have many participants and market share depends on a large sales force.
- A large investment is required to launch the product.
- The product needs technical and sales support.
- The product gives a unique advantage to the market leader's product line.

Selecting the Right Company

Two of the most important advantages that turbo-outsourcing has over licensing are lower risk and quicker deals. The lower risks allow deals to move forward with much less analysis. The right turbo-outsource partner needs to be a company interested in moving quickly in the market and one for which your product represents a chance for an increase in sales of 20 to 50 percent. You can find candidates in your chosen markets for turbo-outsourcing using the same tactics covered in Chapter 7 (pages 143 to 145).

One similarity between turbo-outsourcing and licensing is that companies do not like having the deal shopped around. This is especially true of marketing companies, so you need to choose your target carefully. The ideal situation is the knowledge (from your industry contacts) that a company is anxious to move forward and is looking for new ideas. Other ways to find a marketing partner are to look for companies that have had recent management changes; those pursuing a private-label strategy; or those with a competitor that has recently introduced a major new product. Once you have identified your targets, call them to verify that they are true candidates. Set up an interview format similar to the one in Chapter 7 (pages 145 to 146) to double-check that your targets will be interested in being a turbo-outsourced partner.

Recent Management Changes

New sales managers, marketing managers, and top management, especially from outside the company, look for ways to make a quick impact. Plus, salespeople are anxious to find a way to impress their new boss. That opens the door for the inventor. Your turbo-outsourced project might be just the thing the company, the new boss, or the salespeople are looking for to create a positive impression. You can find companies with management changes in trade magazines. Look for sections titled "People on the Move" (or something similar) that list job changes, promotions, and other personnel changes.

A Private-Label Strategy

Some companies sell a variety of products under their own name that are actually private-label products, meaning simply that they purchase a product from a supplier and sell it as their own brand. Private labeling, from the marketers standpoint, is a form of outsourcing. The company may not be a partner and may not have made an investment, but it has probably made a firm purchase agreement. More important from the inventor's point of view, the company has already made the decision that it can profit by taking another company's product into its line even if the profits per sale are lower. You don't need to convince these companies that turbo-outsourcing makes sense—they already know that. You need only convince them that *your* product is a good fit for their product line.

Major Product Introduction by a Competitor

Marketers and salespeople believe market momentum is crucial to a company's success. When market swings a marketer's way, sales boom for all products. Companies often lose momentum when a competitor introduces a new product, and that makes them anxious to respond in the marketplace. When you go to industry trade shows you'll be able to learn about new products being introduced. You will also be able to identify companies that are competing against the company with the new product. Visit the booths of those companies and you'll find people who are anxious to talk about a new product that could help them rebuild their market momentum.

LOCATE THE RIGHT MANUFACTURING COMPANY: DISCOVER MANUFACTURERS LOOKING FOR PRODUCTS

Manufacturers are easier to deal with than marketers. First, they aren't nearly as worried about whether you are shopping your product to other manufacturers. Shopping a product to a variety of manufacturers doesn't create the same "no interest in the product" stigma that it does with marketing companies. Manufacturers expect their customers to search for competitive bids. Second, the manufacturers' decision matrix is simpler than that of marketing companies. Manufacturers have to decide only whether they can make the product with a minor investment and whether they trust the marketing partner to sell the product effectively.

Overhead absorption is a two-way sword for manufacturers. Excess production creates extra-big profits; however, profits can plummet into big losses when production falls. Manufacturers who are short of production are looking for any way possible to fill their capacity. To find a manufacturer, you need to find a company with the right production equipment, an underused plant with enough capacity to meet your projected sales volume, the financial resources to invest in any equipment needed, and the cash to handle its increased operating needs.

Right Production Equipment

Chapter 2 (pages 38 to 39) explained how to find out what type of equipment is needed to produce your product and what types of manufacturers have that equipment. I've found the best way to locate manufacturers looking for business is to contact the salespeople who sell the production equipment to those manufacturers. For example, if you need a plastic injection-molded part, talk to the manufacturer of plastic-injection-molding equipment. You can find the suppliers of equipment in trade magazines or at trade association web sites. Contact the company and request literature, which will come with a letter and a sales contact's name. Call the sales contact and ask if he or she knows of any manufacturers that might be looking for production volume and might be willing to help finance up-front tooling costs.

If you can't locate the right manufacturers through salespeople at production equipment manufacturers, another source is www .jobshoptechnology.com, the web site for *Job Shop* (another term for contract manufacturer) *Technology* magazine. *Job Shop Technology* also has frequent regional shows where manufacturers with excess capacity set up exhibits to troll for new products. Also check out the web sites of associations pertinent to your industry or manufacturing technique. They frequently have listings of manufacturers and their production capabilities.

Foreign manufacturers also might be willing to partner. Some helpful sites are www.mfgquote.com, www.chinzbiz/com, www.outsourceking .com, and www.ec21.com. Product sourcing agents are companies that will locate a manufacturer for you. Web sites to check are www.groupchina .com, www.prosavvy.com, www.gbvtrader.com, www.asiansourcenow .com, www.product-sourcing-com, and www.buy-thai.com.

Underused Plant

Manufacturers using 80 percent or more of their plant don't benefit nearly as much from extra overhead absorption as a plant that is at less than 60 percent capacity. It is not immediately obvious whether a company has underused capacity, and manufacturers normally don't give out that information. The salesperson for a production equipment supplier might be able to tell you. Otherwise, follow these three steps to find out.

1. Locate companies whose sales volume is 100 to 400 percent of your expected sales. Follow the same steps outlined in Chapter 7 (pages 143 to 144).

2. Request a quote and delivery time from the company for what you expect will be 50, 100, and 200 percent of one year's sales. To show you are in earnest, let the manufacturers know about your potential marketing partner without giving out the company's name. Offer information about what industry the marketing partner is in and its annual sales volume. Follow the procedures in Chapter 7 (pages 143 to 144) to estimate your expected sales level. Quotes will come back with start-up costs, which tells you whether a company has the right production equipment.

    Delivery times are the best predictor of plant use. Suppliers with plants that are near capacity will have longer delivery times, and their quotes might reflect even longer lead times for larger quantities, indicating they may need to bring in more equipment. Companies that are underused will have shorter delivery times.

3. Ask the manufacturer whether it will be willing to amortize the up-front production costs into the product cost. Companies with unused capacity and financial resources will do this. These companies are your best targets for a turbo-outsourcing agreement.

Financial Resources

Once you have received your initial quotes from manufacturers, ask them for a financial statement for your accountant to review. This is a common request for manufacturers; after all, no one wants to give a production order to a company that is about to go broke. Have an accountant or SCORE representative review the document and offer an opinion on the company's financial health.

You can also check web sites that have information about companies' financial status. Sites to check include www.business.com, which is a good start for all types of business searches, www.hoover.com, www.bemis.com, and dir.yahoo.com/Business_and_Economy/Directory/Company.

SIGN PRELIMINARY AGREEMENTS: KEEP CONTROL OF YOUR PRODUCT

Profits need to split three ways in turbo-outsourcing, and everyone wants as big a piece of the pie as possible. In addition, your partners will want to exert control over the project to protect their investments. Chapter 10 (pages 196 to 198) covered the type of percentages you can expect. In a typical deal, the marketing partner will net 30 percent of revenue, the inventor 10 percent, and the manufacturer 60 percent. The secret for the inventor to maintain control and share a healthy percentage of the profits is (1) to sign a preliminary agreement without giving away the other partners' names, and (2) to have the parties agree to a business arrangement that benefits the inventor.

Chapter 8 (pages 154 to 158) discussed using a memorandum of understanding (MOU) and a mutual statement of confidentiality and nonuse (see Appendix C for samples) during licensing negotiations. You should request the same agreements before starting negotiations with a potential turbo-outsource partner. Your first goal is to generate interest among potential partners, as discussed in Chapter 13 (pages 218 to 219). Once they are interested, mention that you are also talking with a possible manufacturer (when talking to the marketing partner) or marketing partner (when talking to the manufacturer). Don't proceed any further without a memorandum of understanding (see Figure 12.1) and a mutual statement of confidentiality.

OBTAIN COMMITMENTS FOR PERFORMANCE: INSIST ON A MAJOR EFFORT FROM PARTNERS

Inventors aren't helped by agreements that don't create action. Inventors have a tough time initiating action once agreements are signed, so you should propose a timetable similar to the one in Figure 12.2 and get the partners' agreement to it before signing any final contracts. Timetables are an effective tool for generating action on the part of all parties. Without a timetable you risk having one gung-ho partner moving forward in a hurry while the other partner moves slowly. That difference in implementation timing and strategy will cause immediate problems for you.

Figure 12.1 Sample Memorandum of Understanding

**Potential Market Potential for Quick Window Shield™
Painting Accessory**

This Memorandum of Understanding (MOU) is made this 25th day of February, 2005 ("Effective Date"), between the product entrepreneur John Backstrom, of 11468 San Quinta Blvd., Corrales, NM 22456 (**PE**), and JBL Paint Products, an Ohio Corporation with its principal address at 3425 Stinson Blvd., Cleveland, OH 34567 (**JBL**).

1. *Background.*
   A. *PE background:* **PE** has been a professional painter for 22 years. One recurring problem he has faced is the need for a helper when spray-painting a house. The helper is needed to hold a shield over windows to protect it from the spray of the paint gun. The helper cost cuts into the painter's profits. **PE** has created the Quick Window Shield™ to allow painters to pop a shield over the window in less than 10 seconds to eliminate the need for a helper. **PE** has created product prototypes and a final production design, which has been tested for market acceptance, ease of use, and product durability.
   B. *JBL background:* **JBL** is marketing over 10 paint-related products that are sold to home improvement chains, hardware stores, and paint stores throughout North America.
   C. *Purpose of MOU:* **PE** and **JBL** are investigating the possibility of **JBL** marketing **PE**'s product line. This MOU is for **PE** and **JBL** to share confidential information in order for **JBL** and **PE** to negotiate a contract agreement in which **PE** will furnish a finished product in a mutually agreed upon package to **JBL**, through another agreement with a manufacturing company, for **JBL**'s distribution in North America.
2. *Understanding and agreements.*
   A. *Overview:* The parties are entering into this MOU to facilitate the negotiations for a final marketing and distribution contract for the Quick Window Shield™ between the two parties.
   B. *Responsibilities:* Both parties agree to negotiate in good faith with the intent of finalizing an agreement within six (6) months.
   C. *Exclusivity:* During this six (6)-month term **PE** agrees not to present the Quick Window Shield™ to any other companies with the intent of negotiating a marketing-related agreement

(Continued)

Figure 12.1 *Continued*

regarding the manufacturing and sales of the Quick Window Shield in North America. During this six (6)-month term **JBL** agrees not to enter into discussions regarding manufacturing and sales of any other products similar to the Quick Window Shield™.

3. *Restrictions.* **JBL** further agrees not to enter into a separate agreement with any other parties revealed to it by **PE** as a result of this MOU regarding products similar to the Quick Window Shield™. This restriction shall survive this MOU and any resulting agreement for a period of twelve (12) months after the termination of this MOU or any resulting agreement.

4. *Confidentiality.* Both parties agrees to abide by the Statement of Mutual Confidentiality as attached as Appendix A of this agreement.

5. *Term.* This agreement shall be for a period of six (6) months from the Effective Date stated above. Restrictions listed in paragraph 5 of this MOU shall survive for three (3) years after termination of this MOU or as agreed to in any resulting agreement.

6. *No assignment.* This MOU and any rights created by it cannot be assigned by either party without the other party's prior written approval.

7. *Termination.* The MOU can be terminated by either party if the other party is not performing to the terms and responsibilities of this MOU by written notice to the defaulting party. Prior to termination, the party terminating must provide a letter of concern to the other party, and the other party has 15 days to remedy the complaint of nonperformance. The obligations of confidentiality set forth in this MOU shall survive termination of this MOU.

8. *Governing law.* This agreement is governed by the laws of Ohio.

IN WITNESS THEREOF, the parties hereto have caused this MOU to be executed as of the Effective Date set forth above.

For Product Entrepreneur

Dated: _____   _____
                                  John Backstrom

For JBL Painting

Dated: _____   _____
                                  Bill Smith, Vice President, Marketing

Figure 12.2   Performance Commitment

For the Broach Quick Jig, a new product for machining companies that improves productivity 20% when machining with broaches.

Date	Activity	Responsibility	Progress
May 04	Create concept	Inventor's name	Complete
May/June 04	Initial market feedback	Inventor's name	Complete
August 04	Production plans	Manufacturing partner	½ complete
August 04	Market introduction plans	Marketing partner	½ complete
June 04	Initial product specifications	Inventor and marketing	Complete
June/July 04	Engineering feasibility analysis	Manufacturing partner	Complete
July 04	Initial costing analysis	Marketing partner	Complete
July/Aug 04	Market research at 60% margin price point	Marketing partner	Complete
Sept/Oct 04	Preliminary commitment from marketer	Marketing partner	In process
Oct/Nov 04	Commitment from manufacturer or manufacturing plan in place	Manufacturing partner	In process
Dec 30 04	Complete prototypes for beta testing	Manufacturing partner	To be done
Jan/Mar 05	Beta testing, product modifications as needed	Manufacturing partner	To be done
April 05	Final decision to proceed, agreements signed	Marketing and manufacturing partners	To be done
May/June 05	Execute introduction	Marketing and manufacturing partners	To be done

13

STEP 8B. PRESERVE YOUR CAPITAL: ENCOURAGE THE MANUFACTURER TO PICK UP THE UP-FRONT COSTS

Inventors typically don't have the capital or access to capital to fund a major introduction—and often don't have the money to finance preproduction models for market testing. Successful manufacturers, however, have access to capital and have in-house model or prototype shops and engineering staff to make prototypes and preproduction models. Since marketing partners won't sign on until they can at least see a "looks like, acts like" prototype—and preferably preproduction units—inventors often need to forge an early alliance with a manufacturer to finish product development. The alliance can be structured in many ways: the manufacturer contributing in-kind resources of personnel and equipment, a cost-sharing agreement, or the manufacturer picking all of the costs. This early alliance provides some limitations to the inventor, as he or she will lose negotiating leverage, but in many cases it is the only way for underfinanced inventors to obtain the prototypes and preproduction models they need.

While prototype and preproduction costs are often high, they are typically much lower than start-up manufacturing costs, including tooling, fixtures, setting a production line, and providing engineering and quality control support. These costs are high even for a small start-up, but they can run in the hundreds of thousands of dollars for a major product launch. Inventors typically need manufacturers to fund these costs, as inventors just don't have the opportunity to earn enough money to pay for them in a turbo-outsource deal. This chapter explains how to work with manufacturers for funding.

- Sell the manufacturer on the benefits: Obtain help during development.
- Use the marketing partner's success: Motivate the manufacturer to fund start-up costs.
- Create easy entry points for manufacturers: Lower the risk for joining the team.
- Negotiation principles for smooth relationships: Prevent problems with the right type of agreement.

Manufacturer Help Seals Success

Devee Govrik wanted to be a product entrepreneur. She was searching for an idea when she opened her kitchen junk drawer and took a good look. Govrik's drawer was like most people's—a big mess. Inspiration struck and Govrik created the Junk Drawer Organizer®, which was a plastic tray with different-size compartments for scissors, tape, batteries, flashlights, and about a dozen other items people typically toss into their junk drawer. She made a model out of cardboard, and her friends and family thought she had a great idea. Govrik also thought the product could be produced with a one-piece plastic injection mold that would hold costs down.

Govrik didn't have enough money to make a model or the money to purchase the molds she needed. She decided her only hope was to find a manufacturer that could help her. Armed with her model and lots of enthusiasm, she started making the rounds of various manufacturers. She finally found one with an underused plant who thought maybe the product had potential. The company was willing to put together a better prototype and fund 500 flyers for Govrik to mail out. Govrik mailed her flyers, but orders didn't come in, so she started calling the potential customers. She paid particular attention to Lechters, a chain of kitchen-related stores based on the East Coast. When Lechters expressed interest in seeing a sample, the manufacturer made several preproduction models, and when the first orders came the manufacturer owner paid for half the cost of the tooling, provided all of the operating cash and packaging costs, and agreed to split the profits with Govrik once he had recovered his investment. Govrik had one big account to sell her product. After a short period of exclusivity ended, Govrik was able to sell the product to other retailers, including mass merchandisers Kmart, Wal-Mart, and Target.

SELL THE MANUFACTURER ON THE BENEFITS: OBTAIN HELP DURING DEVELOPMENT

Models, prototypes, temporary tooling, and preproduction models can all be expensive for inventors if they are self-financing the project. Prototypes require lots of small changes and time-consuming finishing work. When you pay those costs yourself, you may be paying anywhere from $50 to $125 per hour for model builders and engineering time. That can add up to a lot of money, even if you can raise the funds.

The situation is much different for manufacturers. They need to be prepared to make and introduce new products on a regular basis, and they often have a model or prototype shop. They probably have model builders on staff, prototype production equipment in place, and access to most of the materials they need to make a prototype. The manufacturer has the cost of its prototype shop and its personnel included in its overhead, and it incurs much lower *incremental costs* (costs over and above a manufacturer's normal expenses) to make prototypes than does an inventor. Inventors should obtain a manufacturer's help if possible: Find a manufacturer with all the right equipment in place; demonstrate strong intellectual property protection; show the right industry support; pique the manufacturer's interest to gain an appointment, and finally, make a presentation that illustrates the benefits of being a future partner.

Right Manufacturing Equipment

If a manufacturer has the right equipment and personnel in place, it will use them to help you if you can convince the company your idea has potential. Why? Because the manufacturer doesn't really have to invest more money in those things. The manufacturer, after all, has already paid for the equipment and is already paying for its employees. However, inventors will be hard-pressed to convince a manufacturer to invest money in a project if it doesn't have the right manufacturing equipment. Chapter 12 (pages 208 to 211) explained how to find potential manufacturing partners. You can use the same procedure now to find potential partners that might help finance the prototype development process.

Strong Intellectual Property Protection

Most inventors put tremendous emphasis on patents when it comes to intellectual property protection, and certainly you will have a better chance of getting help from manufacturers with a patent in hand or pending. But when it comes to sales potential, you will find manufacturers and marketers are much more interested in trademarks, because they can produce a significantly higher sales volume. Devee Govrik, in the inventor story earlier in the chapter, didn't have a patent, but her trademarked name, Junk Drawer Organizer, was a powerful market asset.

Strong Market Potential

Market potential is tough to show when you don't have a prototype from which you can gain real market input. But you should be able to show that a large number of people are potential purchasers of your product. Govrik's Junk Drawer Organizer, for example, is a product that can be purchased by virtually anyone in America.

Right Industry Support

Manufacturers are cautious about proceeding with a new product, as they have probably had numerous failures in the past. They will be skeptical, and probably won't do anything, unless you have an industry supporter, preferably a sales or marketing manager—but at a minimum you need a salesperson, product manager, or retail store owner or manager as your industry helper.

Pique the Manufacturer's Interest

Inventors without a prototype have a tough time creating interest because most people in the industry won't think you have a product yet. The inventor's challenge without a prototype is to figure out a way to create enough interest that manufacturers will schedule a formal meeting where you can present your concept.

You'll get your best results if you approach your initial contacts in person, either by arranging a meeting with a salesperson, talking to someone at a trade show, or discussing the concept with a contact at an association meeting. In some cases you may need to talk to a company rep on the phone, but try to offer only limited information and then press for a 15-minute meeting to share your presentation materials. (See Chapter 12, pages 208 to 211, for details on locating potential manufacturing partners.)

One way to pique interest is by having a great name for your product. If that's not the case, you need to develop strong opening comments. You have only two or three sentences to make an impression with the manufacturer, so you need to prepare you comments carefully. The first sentence should explain *why* you understand your product: "I am a mother with three children." "I'm a farmer and I've been operating a tractor for 15 years." "I've spent 10 years in a plant that anodizes metal parts." "I've been in the tree-trimming business first as a helper and for the past seven years as the owner of my own company."

Next you need to add intrigue to your product. You can do this by translating your benefit into a statement that emphasizes you've discovered something unique: "I believe I've stumbled upon a novelty product that every college student will want." "I believe I've discovered a manufacturing design that will cut the parts on a weed trimmer in half." "I've found a new style of joint that allows even a novice to build a perfect outdoor deck."

The people you talk to will pump you for information, but you need to resist and ask for just 15 minutes to present your concept. Finalize your conversation by stating something to the effect that "I have something I'd like to discuss that would let your company evaluate this concept for little or no investment. I need only 15 minutes to discuss the situation." When asked later what you meant by little or no investment, explain that you have carefully targeted the manufacturer because it can be involved in the project using the equipment and staff it already has in place.

Presentation Illustrating the Benefits of Partnership

Once you get in the door you need to make a short presentation that should cover these points:

- Who you are and why you were able to come up with the idea
- Who your industry helpers have been
- Your patent and trademark status
- What your benefit is and why it's so powerful
- The market potential: the number of people who could use the product
- Your turbo-outsource strategy and how you will sign a marketing partner
- That you need help building a "looks like, works like" prototype
- That the manufacturer will have the first opportunity to produce the product by assisting with the prototypes and preproduction models

You can structure the points in your presentation just like you would in a licensing presentation. Refer to Chapter 10, pages 177 to 180, for an explanation of each presentation point.

USE THE MARKETING PARTNER'S SALES SUCCESS: MOTIVATE THE MANUFACTURER TO FUND START-UP COSTS

Once you have worked with the manufacturer to create prototypes and preproduction models, your next step is to locate and approach potential marketing partners (Chapter 12, pages 204 to 208). Once you have a marketing partner interested, you need to again approach the manufacturer to request that it pay for all of the start-up manufacturing costs. This could be a much more difficult step than convincing the manufacturer to pick up prototype costs since the manufacturer might have been able to produce your prototypes with just a small amount of incremental costs. That won't be the case with start-up funding for production. The manufacturer will need to bring in inventory, come up with sufficient operating cash, set up some type of a production center, and possibly buy equipment. These needs could add up to a large investment. When asking for this investment you need to be in negotiations with a potential marketing partner; be able to highlight sales successes of that partner; have firm evidence of market size; demonstrate that the product has a good chance of sales success; and present projected sales numbers.

Negotiations with a Marketing Partner

Both partners in turbo-outsourcing deals typically want to be the last one to sign the deal so they are comfortable that the deal is as good as possible for them. The manufacturer won't be willing to put up substantial money unless it has confidence in the marketing partner. While you don't want to give away the marketing partner's name until a memorandum of understanding (see Chapter 12, pages 211 to 213) is signed, you should reveal the name of the marketing partner (or potential partners) once the manufacturer agrees to sign a MOU. Otherwise, the manufacturer won't have confidence in you. The marketing partner need only be interested in further discussions; you don't need a firm marketing agreement in hand. But the marketing partner must be willing to continue negotiations and join in talks with the manufacturing partner.

Highlight Sales Success of Marketing Partner

While you don't want to reveal the marketing partner's name to the manufacturer without an MOU, you *do* want to describe that partner with comments such as, "The partner I'm talking to has a top-three market share position in most of its lines, and it has its products in approximately

60 percent of the market's key stores." Make similar comments if your marketing arrangements are based on hiring commissioned sales reps, if you have an exclusive agreement with a distributor or retailer, or if you are using a manufacturer's sales agent group. Here are sample comments highlighting success:

- "The sales representative I'm working with was the top salesperson for the second-biggest company in the industry."
- "I potentially have an exclusive sales agreement with one of the top-three retail chains in the industry."
- "I'm negotiating with an agent group that has nationwide coverage, employs more than 20 sales reps, and handles five of the industry's top 20 products."

Firm Evidence of Market Size

The manufacturer is going to be investing money and therefore needs to compare that investment with the market size. You may be able to pull together information from trade show data or from association reports. If not, you should rely on information from the marketing partner. The marketing partner will probably assist you if you explain that you are working with a manufacturer to help fund inventory and start-up production costs, and before making a significant investment the manufacturer wants to have an estimate of the total market size.

You should also include here an analysis of the competitive products, their annual sales volume, and why your product is better (see Chapter 2, pages 44 to 46). Though the marketing partner is the key to the manufacturer agreeing to move forward, don't make the mistake of thinking you can just tell the manufacturer the marketing partner thinks you have a good idea. Take the time to sell the manufacturer about the market potential of your idea.

Demonstrate That Sales Have a Good Chance of Success

Turbo-outsourcing sales projects differ from licensing in that they must produce immediate sales. Companies get involved in turbo-outsourcing for an immediate increase. Your manufacturing partner's decision makers aren't going to be interested in developing a market for three to five years out. They want sales right now. Your goal is to show that sales will be strong right from the start. You need more than just a perfunctory sales test—you need to show you have some immediate substantial customers.

By this time in the negotiations you should have signed MOU and mutual statement of confidentiality and nonuse agreements with both marketing and manufacturing partners. This is the time to rely on your industry helpers and your marketing partner to make the case for when and where the product will be introduced, which customers to target in the first six months (customers the marketing partner is confident will buy), and what the sales plan is to land other customers. Your marketing partner will help you if you explain that the manufacturing partner needs reassurance that there are enough immediate customers to justify its investment. The marketing partner or some of your industry helpers should have strong contacts in any company projected to be an immediate customer.

Present Projected Sales Numbers

The manufacturer needs these numbers, projected out three years, in order to justify whatever investment it needs to make. These numbers must, at a minimum, be endorsed by the marketing partner and industry helpers. You are better off if the partner or helper prepares the numbers. You might want to solidify the numbers by listing potential buyers. If you do include a list, make sure that the total sales to the potential customers is three to five times the projected sales numbers. Some of the customers you expect to buy won't, and other companies will buy less than expected.

CREATE EASY ENTRY POINTS FOR MANUFACTURERS: LOWER THE RISK FOR JOINING THE TEAM

The manufacturer has three major risks when undertaking the project: (1) the tooling and manufacturing equipment investment, which it may or may not have to make, (2) inventory costs of starting the project, and (3) operating costs over inventory purchases. These are not the manufacturer's only costs, it also has management time, plant layouts, and engineering time, but those are not major risks. In some projects the tooling and plant investment might be low, but there will always be significant inventory and operating capital costs. Lowering the risk might not be necessary if the market potential of the product is significant and if the manufacturer has confidence in the marketing arm to sell products. However, if the manufacturer worries that the risk is too high, you may need to suggest options that lower that risk.

In reality, inventory is an operating cost, but for turbo-outsourcing deals I think it pays to keep it separate when discussing risk. Inventory costs are real costs you can't escape. Other operating costs, such as funding accounts receivables until the manufacturer is paid, are costs incurred primarily if the product is successful. The manufacturer won't mind covering costs if the product is selling. Five tactics you can use to cut the manufacturer's risk are to receive some up-front money from the marketing partner; commit to an accelerated investment payback; produce just enough units to generate firm contracts; start with a limited product line and run a larger market test from temporary tooling and limited inventory. You don't need signed final agreements with these options except for introducing a limited product line. But you should still have agreement between the parties that they will move forward to sign an agreement if the results of these options, which are types of sales tests, are positive.

1. *Receive some up-front money from the marketing partner.* The manufacturer will be the most cautious if it is the only party that will lose money should the product fail. Getting some money from the marketer, and the inventor, too, will reassure the manufacturer that everyone is committed to the project. The inventor and marketing partner don't have to contribute extensively to the project, but enough to assure the manufacturer that they don't want the project to go under.

2. *Commit to an accelerated investment payback.* In turbo-outsourcing, the manufacturer invariably makes the biggest investment. One way to ease the burden on the manufacturer is to agree to a schedule to repay that investment. This could be accomplished by the inventor and marketing partner agreeing to accept less revenue, perhaps 10 or 20 percent less for 6 to 18 months to help the manufacturer recoup part of its investment. You probably don't want to allow the manufacturer to recoup *all* of its investment—after all, it will still own the tools and the operating cash when the deal is finished—but you can allow it to recoup investments that it won't be able to use again.

3. *Produce just enough units to generate firm contracts.* Distributors, retailers, and end users will rarely issue firm orders or contracts based on anything but a preproduction unit. The manufacturer can probably produce 5 to 10 units for a minimum cost that will allow the marketing partner or inventor to get orders. The buyer will have to wait to get shipment with this strategy, but such a delay is not uncommon today because of the overseas outsourcing used by many marketers. Under this option, the manufacturer will go ahead with its investment and production once the marketing partner has produced significant orders.

4. *Start with a limited product line.* Buyers might not respond to a preproduction model, but may prefer to wait until you are really in

production. If that's the case, and the product line has several variations (e.g., sizes, colors, different versions), you can show the whole product line, but state that only part of the line is immediately available, with the rest becoming available in six months.

5. *Run a larger market test from temporary tooling and limited inventory.* Temporary tooling often amounts to only 10 to 20 percent of the cost of permanent tooling. Manufacturers that are nervous about how much they will invest, still might be willing to run a test market program in one or two cities, producing the product with temporary tooling. Marketers will also prefer this option if the product calls for a promotional program that they have to fund. They will want to be sure the marketing program works before launching a national campaign.

NEGOTIATION PRINCIPLES FOR SMOOTH RELATIONSHIPS: PREVENT PROBLEMS WITH THE RIGHT TYPE OF AGREEMENT

Chapter 15 covers the details of negotiating a contract. This section deals with the preliminary conversations between partners before they have committed to the project. Both partners in this process will want to understand an overview of the type of agreement you envision. You need to be able to explain the key points of the agreement in a short form that encourages your partners to continue. This issue looms increasingly larger as the size of the investment grows. The key issues you need to be able to discuss preliminarily are partnership terms; commitment on everyone's part; term of the contract; and derivative products. Try to avoid an in-depth discussion of contract terms at this time. Simply state that you are flexible and open to any conditions that are important to the manufacturer. You will want to have a lawyer with business contract experience help you when you are ready to actually negotiate.

Partnership Terms

The term *partnership* is really a misnomer, because what you really want is a two- or three-way agreement. *Associates* is probably a better term, but that doesn't imply much commitment, so I have always preferred the term *partners.* Inventors don't want an actual partnership agreement because they have only one of three votes and because a profit stream is much less predictable than a percent-of-revenue stream.

A three-way contract simply spells out each party's responsibilities, how each party will benefit, and how the parties will interact. These contracts are much simpler to negotiate than partnership agreements because all parties keep their autonomy. The deal may also have two separate agreements, one between the inventor and the marketer, another between the inventor and the manufacturer.

Commitment on Everyone's Part

This item is a big sticking point. Each party wants to know that all partners have the same level of commitment to making the project work. You can't really resolve this up front. The best way to handle comments regarding commitment is to say that this is an issue that concerns all partners. You can also emphasize the product's potential and say that the specific commitment levels will be negotiated in the final contract.

Term of the Contract

Partners are pulled in two directions: They want a shorter-term contract so they can escape if things aren't working out, but they also want a longer-term contract to ensure that they can profit from their involvement. This issue will not be a big one if the investment is low, but it could escalate if the investment is large. Manufacturers want at least enough time to recoup their investment. Expect a request for at least a two-year and possibly a three-year term, with options to extend the contract after that.

Derivative Products

A derivative product is a follow-on product that could be a variation of the product; a complementary product, which is one that works in some way to enhance the original product; or a new product uncovered by introducing the original product. For example, your product might be a new style of pneumatic tool holster that attaches to a construction belt. It allows a construction worker to carry an air-operated wrench. A follow-on product would be a separate holster for power screwdrivers or nail drivers. A complementary product would be a set of suspenders that help hold up the extra weight of carrying a pneumatic tool. An additional product responding to a newly discovered need might be a retractable air-hose line that also attaches to a work belt.

Marketing partners want to ignore derivative products. If a new product comes up, they want to introduce it themselves. Manufacturers want to have the option of making the derivative product if it fits their manufacturing ability. Both manufacturers and marketers will probably be happy leaving the inventor out of any derivative products. The inventor, however, wants derivative products to be included in the agreement, as it allows him or her to continue to have an outlet for new products. Present your derivative-products clause to the team in the mutual statement of confidentiality and nonuse agreement. That will allow you to share in the revenue of any new products the team introduces.

14

STEP 9B. DEVELOP A MARKETING PLAN: CREATE THE BACKUP FOR A SUCCESSFUL DEAL

Turbo-outsourcing product-to-market plans are written initially to help inventors raise money and find industry helpers long before the inventors are actually ready to approach a turbo-outsourced partner. Inventors need intellectual property protection and some market research before approaching a turbo-outsourcing partner. They also need the support of an industry helper to prove the product can sell in the marketplace. Since turbo-outsourcing is a new concept, investors and potential industry helpers need the plan to understand exactly what you are trying to accomplish. The turbo-outsource plan is also an operational plan that helps the inventor prepare and follow a strategy that has a good chance of resulting in a profitable turbo-outsource deal.

Turbo-outsourcing plans are more involved than licensing plans because they call for targeting both a marketing partner and a manufacturing partner. In licensing, inventors need to find only one partner. Turbo-outsourcing plans also deal with finding partners who can support the others' goals, provide the fastest possible marketing launch, and cover the intricacies of structuring a three-way profit split that provides enough incentive for every partner.

Timing is another key issue in a turbo-outsourcing plan. Licensing candidates often move at a deliberate pace, thoroughly evaluating the inventor's product, whereas turbo-outsourcing partners want a quick boost to their profits. If the deals take too long to develop, partners may want to wait and see whether they can get a better profit margin on another product. There is pressure on the inventor to provide more complete information sooner to cut down on the time required for negotiating contracts and to make a better case that the product will not only sell, but sell quickly. Licensing plans and turbo-outsourcing plans have similarities, but the emphasis is on long-term focus for licensing and shorter-term focus for turbo-outsourcing.

Margins are another major difference between the two plans. Licensing candidates will figure out their own manufacturing costs, so your analysis on product costing can be brief. With turbo-outsourcing, you often pursue the marketing partner first, and you need significant backup to show the 50 to 60 percent margin that will make the deal work. This chapter explains the following concepts.

- Match the plan to resource levels: Focus on the results you can achieve.
- Prepare the marketing plan: Include the key elements for success.

Help Is All Around

Stephanie Heroff loved wearing tops with spaghetti straps in the summer, but she didn't like contending with pesky bra straps that kept peeking out. Frustrated that there weren't any solutions on the market, Heroff decided to create her own solution, which was to sew bra straps to the spaghetti straps and place small hooks on the neck side of the strap to hold a removable bra. She had a tailor make 30 prototypes for her and her friends. Heroff was ready to attack the market when she received rave reviews.

Heroff wasn't sure what to do next. She started by visiting the Minneapolis Apparel Mart and talking to apparel representatives, clothing manufacturers, and clothing stores. After talking to almost a dozen people, she received a lead for a potential manufacturing partner, Private Label Industries of Los Angeles. The company agreed to produce prototypes and to help finalize the product's design in return for part ownership and an agreement that it would be the manufacturer when the product was ready for the market.

Heroff and the manufacturer realized that the product would be expensive to make and that they would need to sell to high-end boutiques to get the price they needed. That required an upscale designer look for the product. Heroff found a designer who was willing to redesign her product for a percentage of the profits.

Heroff's manufacturer was willing to pick up a substantial part of the cost, but not all of it. Heroff's next step was to look for an investor who could also help with sales and distribution. She found an investor with experience in the market, and he took the lead in setting up a network of manufacturer's representatives across the country to sell her product. Heroff and the investor purchased the finished product at a fixed price from the manufacturer and then resold to the market at a price they set, which was 20 to 25 percent higher than the price they paid. Heroff's investment, in addition to time and travel, was the cost of 50 prototypes that she outsourced to a tailor, which depleted her funds. Although Heroff ended up sharing her profits with several part-ners, she secured a good arrangement with her investor whereby she received most of the 20 to 25 percent upcharge. Heroff was able to accomplish her goals in just four months, putting her product on the market much faster than she could have with any other introduction process.

MATCH THE PLAN TO RESOURCE LEVELS: FOCUS ON THE RESULTS YOU CAN ACHIEVE

For companies to get involved in turbo-outsourcing, the deal has to be done quickly and produce a significant financial impact. Putting the right deal together requires delicate balancing of several factors, including high margins, market size, investment costs, and the size of partner companies. Before starting the marketing plan, inventors need to take a realistic view of their product and its potential and then choose the right-size partners.

High Margins

Stephanie Heroff's spaghetti-strap tops could be sold anywhere, from mass merchandisers to high-end boutiques. Heroff's decision to go after high-end stores was made in part because her manufacturing partner was relatively small. But the more important reason was margins. Heroff had numerous people participating in the revenue stream and needed a mar-ket with enough profit to go around. Pricing the product for high-end boutiques offered those higher margins, and it was the right market to tar-get. Virtually every product faces the same situation. Some market chan-nels, typically the ones with large volumes, offer lower revenue per unit to marketers, while other markets offer higher returns.

Chapter 11 (pages 199 to 200) discussed manufacturing costs and margins. To help you decide on the right markets for the margins, prepare a chart similar to the one in Figure 14.1. Find one or two products against which to benchmark your product. Use those figures to determine what your product's price would be in a market of similar products. In Figure 14.1, the benchmark product is a standard spaghetti-strap top. Heroff's

Figure 14.1   Marketing/Margin Comparison:
New-Style Spaghetti Strap

	High-End Boutiques and Department Stores	Midrange Department Stores	Mass Merchandisers
Benchmark product	Standard Top	Standard Top	Standard Top
Benchmark product price	$40.00	$25.00	$15.00
Percent difference	35%	35%	35%
New product price	$54.00	$33.75	$20.35
Total discounts through the distribution channel	55%	55%	58%
Price received by marketer	$29.70	$15.19	$8.54
Cost of upgrade features for higher-end product*	30%	10%	N/A
Manufacturing costs[†]	$12.40	$8.10	$6.45
Margin	58.2%	46.6%	24.4%

* Markets that sell higher-value products may require feature upgrades such as better materials, better packaging, or in some cases additional features.
[†] Manufacturing costs will be lower for higher-volume production.

research showed that people would pay 30 to 35 percent more for her product.

Not all markets will work like the one in the example. Sometimes manufacturing costs fall even more dramatically for larger production, and sometimes partners will accept lower percentages for a bigger market, so don't assume that the highest price per unit will always be your best choice of a target market.

Market Size

Market sizes can vary dramatically. In Heroff's case, the mass merchandisers' market might be 100 times larger than the market served by high-end boutiques. The market you choose will dictate the size of the manufacturing and distribution partners and the size of the investment that your project can afford.

Figure 14.2   Total Profit Comparison: High-End versus Midrange
Market for New-Style Spaghetti Straps for $10 Million Midrange Market

	High-End Market: *$5 Million*	*Midrange Market:* *$10 Million*
Market penetration %	20%	15%
Market sales	$1,000,000	$1,500,000
Margin	58.2%	46.6%
Total margin	$582,000	$699,000

Before finally selecting your target, you might want to consider the
total margin dollars that are available for each market, which you can obtain
by multiplying the total sales by the percent margin (see Figures 14.2 and
14.3). Your partners may be more interested in a market with a lower margin percent if the total margin dollars for the lower-margin market is con-
siderably higher than the total margin dollars for the high-margin market.
In Heroff's example, mass merchandisers clearly don't have enough margin
for a successful turbo-outsource deal. But high-end boutiques/department
stores and midrange department stores could work. Figure 14.2 details the
total profit if the high-end market is $5 million and the midrange depart-
ment store market is $10 million. Figure 14.3 shows the difference if the
midrange department store market is $25 million.

With the midrange market size at $10 million, either market is a rea-
sonable choice, but with a midrange market size of $25 million, most
partners would probably opt for a smaller margin and choose the larger
market: the $25 million department store market.

Figure 14.3   Total Profit Comparison: High-End versus Midrange
Market for New-Style Spaghetti Straps for $25 Million Midrange Market

	High-End Market: *$5 Million*	*Midrange Market:* *$25 Million*
Market penetration %	20%	15%
Market sales	$1,000,000	$3,750,000
Margin	58.2%	46.6%
Total margin	$582,000	$1,747,500

Figure 14.4   Sales versus Investment: High-End versus Midrange Market for New-Style Spaghetti Straps for $25 Million Midrange Market

	High-end market: *$5 Million*	*Midrange Market:* *$25 Million*
Market penetration %	20%	15%
Market sales	$1,000,000	$3,750,000
Margin	58.2%	46.6%
Total margin	$582,000	$1,747,500
Production and equipment costs	$75,000	$100,000

Investment Costs

Most companies will want to recoup their fixed (i.e., plant and equipment) investments within no more than two years. This investment payback schedule is shorter than the more normal three years for other types of investments because turbo-outsource agreements are typically short, usually only two to three years. You won't know exactly what type of payback schedule the manufacturer wants or how it calculates its payback. As a substitute for calculating an exact payback, I've found that manufacturers seem to be content with their investments if annual sales are 10 to 15 times the investment. That means the manufacturer needs revenue of $1 to $1.5 million to justify a $100,000 investment.

Figures 14.3 and 14.4 will help you select the right market. In our example, the investment needed to make $3.7 million worth of units is only 25 percent more than the investment needed to make $1 million worth of units, which makes the midrange market much more attractive.

Size of Partner Companies

Turbo-outsource deals typically call for quick action by partner companies and create a high impact. An inventor's product meets this requirement if the sales level is 20 to 50 percent of the partner's annual sales. If the new product's potential offers less than a 20 percent increase in sales, it may not create enough impact for the company. If the opportunity is greater than 50 percent, the company may not have enough resources to move quickly on the idea.

Chapter 7 (pages 143 to 144) explained how to find out information about company size. If you have two markets, both with a market size and margin that look promising for a turbo-outsource deal, gear your presentation to the market size of the company you are talking to. In the spaghetti-strap example, you would probably present the high-end market only to a company with sales of $2 million per year; you might present both markets if you are talking to a company with $7 million in sales, because both offer enough opportunity. You would probably present only to the midrange department store market if the company's sales are $15 million.

PREPARE THE MARKETING PLAN: INCLUDE THE KEY ELEMENTS FOR SUCCESS

The turbo-outsourcing marketing plan gives you a strategy to follow, and it is useful as both an investor tool and an information source for potential helpers. This is the plan you make to prepare your product for presentations to potential partners. The plan can be from 10 to 20 double-spaced pages and should be focused on generating a quick reaction from potential partners. The key points of a turbo-outsourcing plan are:

- Market opportunity
- The product
- Market size
- Turbo-outsourcing strategy—general
- Inventor's background
- Market distribution channels
- Evidence the market is ready to buy
- Competition/product advantage
- Product manufacturing cost versus retail price
- Turbo-outsourcing strategy—specific
- Target marketing partners (delete this section if you are showing the plan to a potential marketing partner)
- Target manufacturing partners (delete this section if you are showing the plan to a potential manufacturing partner)
- Development complete/required
- Introduction timetable
- Turbo-outsourcing cost estimate
- Revenue/expense split
- Funding request/offer

Market Opportunity

An immediate marketing opportunity that can be acted on quickly drives a turbo-outsourced deal. The opportunity comes from a market need or desire. Heroff's product is a good example; she could show hundreds of pictures of bra straps sliding out from under a spaghetti strap. Created desire also can launch a potential turbo-outsource deal. The new style of Christmas lights that hang down like icicles were an immediate hit because people saw them and wanted them. The market for faux painting supplies sizzled because people saw the new look and wanted it.

This section should contain either a need, shown with pictures, videos, and quotes from users, or a desire, which you can show by quoting people's reactions to the product, especially when they see the product for the first time. I hear from inventors all the time that their idea is a no-brainer, which means that the need is so obvious no one can miss it. That's the type of market need you want to show at the beginning of the plan.

The Product

Include a short product description and a picture. If your product responds to a market need, you should also show why your product is the perfect solution to fill that need. Turbo-outsourcing plans differ from licensing plans in that they are selling an immediate sales impact versus a long-term benefit to the company. The market opportunity and product section of your presentation should convey the message that there is a big immediate opportunity and that you have the perfect product to capitalize on the opportunity.

Market Size

How big is the total market for your type of product? Use industry data if available or estimates from industry personnel. You can also include sales statistics of relevant products. For Heroff's product, total sales of all spaghetti-strap tops would be relevant, as would sales volume of any competitive products.

Turbo-Outsourcing Strategy—General

People who read your plan, both investors and potential partners, may not know what turbo-outsourcing is, so you might want to offer a brief explanation. The accompanying box, "Turbo-Outsourcing Defined," is an

---

Turbo-Outsourcing Defined

Turbo-outsourcing is a new-product introduction process for inventors whereby a phase of the business—marketing and/or manufacturing—is outsourced to a company that invests its resources and capital in the product in return for receiving a percentage of either the product's sales price or profit generated by selling the product. Inventors still maintain ownership of the product and form their own company with turbo-outsourcing, but they do not take on the burden of running a full operating company. The advantage of turbo-outsourcing over licensing is that the inventor maintains control and can benefit from derivative products. Its advantage over starting a traditional company is that it requires far less money and fewer operational headaches. Turbo-outsourcing not only minimizes the cash outflow from the inventor but also provides the inventor with dynamic partners who are spending their time and money to help accelerate the product into the market. A turbo-outsource agreement has the inventor buy from the manufacturer and sell to the marketing partner, or receive a percent of the sales revenue from either the marketing partner or the manufacturer. Turbo-outsourcing does not require both marketing and manufacturing partners; a deal can be made with just one partner, while the inventor picks up the other responsibility.

---

example you could use in your report. Readers have my permission to use this paragraph word for word in their own turbo-outsource plans.

Inventor's Background

Your background should demonstrate that you understand the needs of your target customers, have contacts in the target industry and have the expertise to negotiate turbo-outsourcing agreements. If your experience is weak in one area, title this section "Inventor's and Advisors' Background" and list the qualifications of your industry helpers. If you list advisors, also list the legal and accounting firms you plan to use.

Market Distribution Channels

Your market opportunity as defined earlier should explain the opportunity in terms of end users—why people will want to have your product. This section of the plan should briefly define the distribution channels you could use to sell your product and list one or two channels you plan on penetrating. For example, for the new-style spaghetti-strap tops, the distribution channels include:

- Catalogs
- TV shopping channels
- High-end boutiques
- High-end department stores
- Midrange department stores
- Mass merchandisers
- Beach shops

A brief description of why Heroff chose specific channels might read:

The targeted market channels are high-end boutiques and department stores. These channels were chosen because they have the on-site sales support to explain the product's use, they support higher margins to compensate the three turbo-outsource partners, and there are several marketing partner options available, including manufacturer's representative groups, distributors, and marketers of other high-end products.

Evidence the Market Is Ready to Buy

Since turbo-outsourcing depends on a quick sales start, you need to include evidence that the market is ready. Provisional orders and letters of intent (see Chapter 6, pages 128 to 130), testimonial letters, and industry advisor comments are all ways to show that the market wants your product.

Competition/Product Advantage

Chapter 2 (pages 44 to 46) covered several effective ways to show the features of your competitors' products and illustrate why your product is better. Include here any market research you have supporting your conclusion that the market believes your product is far better than that of a competition.

Product Manufacturing Cost versus Retail Price

A 60 percent margin requires that a product's manufacturing cost be 15 to 20 percent of its retail price. Chapter 11 (pages 199 to 200) covered how to determine your manufacturing costs and retail price. Try to include as much evidence as you can in this section, including actual cost quotes and validation from the distribution channel on your suggested retail price.

Turbo-Outsourcing Strategy—Specific

This section should list your specific strategy, including the following:

- Target end user
- Target distribution channel
- Market size throughout that channel
- Projected sales
- Type of marketing partner (including whether you are going to handle sales and marketing on your own)
- Type of manufacturing partner

Marketing and Sales Activities

Product description: The Streetboard is a three-foot skateboard with just two wheels that gives riders a snowboard type experience.

Marketing activities
- Product literature, videos, and demonstrations will be available on DVDs and on the company web site.
- Two demo/sales teams will display the board at major skateboard events in California and on the East Coast.
- Sales to skateboard shops throughout the country will be through three rep groups, with Extreme Sports covering the East Coast, PJR marketing covering the southern states (through Texas), and Pioneering Sports Products, covering the West Coast. Contacts with all three groups have been made, and they have indicated they will carry the product, subject to their review and acceptance of the final manufactured product. A Midwest rep group is also being sought.
- Samples will be given to top skateboard riders to use when they offer demonstrations at community events. We have identified two new tricks that top riders can perform on Streetboards to encourage their use.

Target Marketing Partners

Delete this section if you are showing the plan to a potential marketing partner. List the top three or four potential marketing partners you have identified. List for each partner any information you have on their size and product line. Also explain any connection you may have already established (e.g., your industry partner has sold to this company for more than 20 years). If you are going to sell the product yourself, present an outline of how you will sell the product. The box titled "Marketing and Sales Activities" offers an example.

Target Manufacturing Partners

Delete this section if you are showing the plan to a potential manufacturing partner. Explain your top three or four potential manufacturing targets, their manufacturing capabilities, products they manufacture, and their annual sales volumes.

Development Complete/Required

Typically, you write this plan in part to help you find investors, or, if you already have investors, to show an orderly plan to develop your product. This and the next sections of the plan will document what you need to do and your timetable to accomplish those goals. Include these development issues in this section:

- *Patent and trademark issues.* Your partners will want you to have intellectual property protection of some sort to protect their investments.
- *Product development, including prototypes and engineering design.* Include development up through your "looks like, acts like" prototype. Your manufacturing partner will probably want to do the engineering documentation.
- *Packaging.* A packaging mock-up, which is a rough prototype package, should be sufficient.
- *Trade show attendance.* You may need to attend several trade shows to meet additional contacts and to have preliminary discussions with possible partners.
- *Association meeting attendance.* Attend these meetings to make contacts with key helpers and potential partners.
- *Meetings with key contacts.* You will need several meetings with contacts as you progress.

Cost Estimates			
	Costs Paid	Costs Unpaid	Total Costs
• Patent and trademark issues	$7,500		$7,500
• Product development and prototypes	4,000	$4,000	8,000
• Packaging mock-up	600		600
• Trade show attendance	800	500	1,300
• Association meeting attendance	400		400
• Meetings with key contacts	800	600	1,400
• Market tests	1,500	1,000	2,500
• Proving the product will sell	500	400	900
• Approaching potential marketing partners		500	500
• Approaching potential manufacturing partners		200	200
• Finalizing negotiations with partners		4,000	4,000
• Product tests by marketing partner			0
• Final approval of production units			0
• Production start		500	500
• Market introduction		1,200	1,200
Totals	$16,100	$12,900	$29,000

- *Market tests.* Describe any tests you've completed and any that you plan to conduct in the future.
- *Efforts to secure proof that the product will sell.* This could include efforts to get testimonial letters, provisional orders, or letters of support from both end users and potential distribution partners. (See Chapter 6, pages 128 to 130.)

Introduction Timetable

The timetable should list each action you plan on taking for the items in your "Development Completed/Required" section. But you also need to add dates for:

- Approaching potential marketing partners
- Approaching potential manufacturing partners

- Finalizing negotiations with partners, which should take 90 to 180 days
- Product tests by marketing partner, if required
- Final approval of production units by all partners
- Production start
- Market introduction date, which should be tied to a major trade show or other industry product-launch event

Turbo-Outsourcing Cost Estimate

Since you may need investors, you should project what your expenses will be for turbo-outsourcing. List all your costs, including ones you've already paid, so you can demonstrate the extent of your financial involvement. For each item in your timetable, list the product entrepreneur's costs.

Revenue/Expense Split

Though you haven't negotiated the deal yet, you should have a split target in mind, and you want to share this with potential investors so they can see how the money will be divided and the kind of return they can expect on their money. Be sure to state that the split is a *target* and not a guarantee.

Turbo-Outsourcing Revenue Split	
Marketing partner	30%
Costs	20%
Profit	10%
Inventor	10%
Costs	3%
Profit	7%
Manufacturing partner	60%
Manufacturing costs (50% margin product)	50%
Profit	10%

Funding Request/Offer

Use this section only if you need money. List here the investment to date, the investment needed now, and what you are personally investing. For example, using our example in the "Cost Estimates" box, an inventor looking for an $8,000 investment to help fund the remaining $12,900 might list the following:

Investments to date	$16,100
Investments required	$12,900
Provided by inventor	$ 4,900
Investment needed	$ 8,000

To follow up on our example, Streetboard Thrill Sports is offering 5 percent of its profit stream (currently estimated to be 7 percent of the total sales revenue from a turbo-outsource agreement) in return for an $8,000 investment.

15

STEP 10B. SELL YOUR DEAL: MOTIVATE COMPANIES TO MOVE QUICKLY

Companies' first choice for long-range profitability is creating and introducing their own sizzling products. That way, they don't split the profits, they don't pay royalties, and they have the freedom to expand their line without having to worry about sharing the revenue with partners. Fortunately for inventors, companies often spend fortunes developing new products that lack true innovation, which leaves them open to talking to inventors and considering licensing opportunities or turbo-outsource deals.

The main advantage to turbo-outsourcing for the marketing partner is that the company can get into the market quickly, for a modest cost, and develop a market position that could help it with future products. Being first to market is valuable to most companies, and they will be interested in any deal if the market is huge and your product's advantage is significant. For manufacturing partners, many of whom struggle to sell their own products, the advantage to a turbo-outsourcing deal is that they are teamed up with a top marketing organization that can increase production volume in underused plants.

I've been asked whether there really is a difference between turbo-outsourcing and licensing. I believe there is a big difference. Licensing puts the entire risk onto the licensing company. Turbo-outsourcing shares the risk, which makes the decision of signing an agreement easier for partners, but it also adds an element of urgency because one party can hold up the deal. Licensing deals take time, and the bane of many inventors is a highly interested licensing prospect that continuously delays signing a deal. Turbo-outsourcing presents a quick action plan, but companies know that their competitors can sign the deal just as quickly as they can. You have double leverage to entice a company to sign an agreement when market opportunity is urgent and when competitors are waiting in the wings. The inventor's overall sales approach is to emphasize that the market for his or her product is hot, and that if this partner is not interested, plenty of others are. An inventor's leverage in signing a turbo-outsource deal is typically several times higher than his or her leverage in signing a licensing deal. This chapter explains these concepts to help you move forward.

- Focus on quick market sales: Set the stage with your opening remarks.
- Explain that the margin loss is small: Illustrate each partners' benefits to the other.
- Target a major player to base-load sales: Structure an irresistible deal.
- Prepare the turbo-outsource presentation: Put it together with sizzle.
- Negotiate the agreements: keep it simple and flexible.

True Middleman

As an inventor, Vijay Malek decided to concentrate on products that conserve space. While looking for product ideas, Malek found that while kids had hundreds of CDs, adults had only a few. He also became aware that many women like to play their favorite CDs while cooking, and these women weren't looking for a cumbersome CD rack. They just wanted a handy rack that would hold 10 to 12 CDs in as small a space as possible. Malek responded to the need by creating Hang 10, a wall-mounted CD rack that holds CDs at an angle and sticks out only three inches. Malek decided that the best way to reach this market was to sell the product where his target customers shopped: the local supermarket. Unfortunately, selling an impulse product at a supermarket is far beyond the capabilities of most inventors.

Malek's solution was to search for a partner company that sold products to supermarkets. He went to the Chicago Housewares Show and walked the aisles looking for the right company. He came across Maverick Ventures, a manufacturer and marketer of housewares products sold in supermarkets, convenience stores, and hardware stores. Malek started to talk to the company, which expressed interest but thought the product's design, pricing, and packaging needed to be optimized for the impulse market. Maverick offered an initial agreement predicated on its final review of the product before production.

With that agreement in hand, Malek was able to get cooperation from a contract manufacturer. The manufacturer was willing to put up the tooling costs, but Malek decided to pay the up-front tooling costs himself in order to earn more money and have the freedom to change manufacturers if this one raised prices or the relationship turned rocky. For Malek, the agreements were perfect. He received an order from Maverick and faxed it to the manufacturer, who also took care of shipping. Malek's only remaining task was to send out invoices.

FOCUS ON QUICK MARKET SALES: SET THE STAGE WITH YOUR OPENING REMARKS

For licensing, you want to start with a big "wow" that showcases your product. For turbo-outsourcing, you want to focus the attention on an immediate marketing need that requires fast action. You want to be the first company in the market. One reason that turbo-outsourcing works for products that aren't on the high end of innovation is that the emphasis is on the market rather than on the product: The goal is to be first to the market. To succeed in creating urgency, you need to use an intriguing teaser when you start your presentation:

> I've been working to develop and introduce a new product idea of mine. The reaction I've received in my market testing with both consumers and retailers has been just tremendous. I realize now I don't have the money to meet the market need, and I don't have the experience to jump into the market fast enough to beat competition. I'm looking for a company to help me sell the product.

This is certainly a much better opening than one I've heard at least 100 times during the past 10 years: "I've tried to sell my product for two years and realize I don't have the experience to launch my own product. My goal now is to license it."

If you can, add a story about a strong market response you've received from someone in the distribution channel. Here's the type of story that works:

> I worked for five weeks trying to get in to see a buyer at Michaels. I don't think I would have even had a chance if it hadn't been for the manager of my local Michaels who called up the buyer personally to

set up an appointment. She kept me waiting 45 minutes, but when I finally saw the buyer she asked me how soon I could deliver 2,000 units. That's when I knew the product was too big for me.

EXPLAIN THAT THE MARGIN LOSS IS SMALL: ILLUSTRATE EACH PARTNER'S BENEFITS TO THE OTHER

You don't want to bring up a three-way split of the profits and try to defend it on your own. More than likely, however, it will come up, and you need to be ready to explain why it isn't a problem. You'll take slightly different approaches with the manufacturer and the marketer, and you need to be able to justify the size of the inventor's share to both parties.

To the Manufacturer

The manufacturer puts up the money and takes about a 10 percent margin on its sales dollars. Your manufacturer contacts may complain that it is too little for too much of the risk and that they could do better introducing their own product. Your response to the manufacturer should be that this deal is far better than being a contract manufacturer and that the only question is whether the opportunity offers greater potential than any others it has on the table.

- *Contract manufacturers.* A contract manufacturer often receives only a 5 to 10 percent profit margin and can lose the business whenever another manufacturer comes along with a better offer. You can offer the manufacturer a guaranteed position as a supplier with a steady 10 percent profit in return for an investment in the production costs of a really hot product.
- *More profit potential.* If the manufacturer has its own product, the question is whether it has the margin, the market appeal, and the strong marketing support that the turbo-outsourced deal offers. If the manufacturer can answer yes, then the manufacturer should pursue its own product. But the manufacturer probably doesn't have a deal in the works or it wouldn't be talking to you.
- *Financial risk.* If the manufacturer thinks it is putting up too much capital, ask whether you should try to have the marketer put up the money. If your manufacturing negotiators say yes, just comment that the marketer will probably insist on a contract manufacturing agreement with the manufacturer, with the right to shop the product around to other manufacturers to receive the best

price. Then ask the negotiators whether they want to surrender that much control to the marketing partner. They will almost always say no.

To the Marketer

Marketers can be conflicted by turbo-outsourcing. On one hand, they do appreciate an immediate market opening. On the other hand, marketers know that their long-term business success depends on being able to establish a strong position in a key market. That position allows marketers to introduce a stream of products and establish a strong line. The turbo-outsource deals compromise that position, as the inventor will try to negotiate rights to a portion of the revenue for derivative products. The marketing company does not want to share future products with you or the manufacturer. The response to this concern is that the length of the deals are short, that the manufacturer is no different than any other contract manufacturer, and that you, the inventor, are willing to sell out your position in the future if the project is a big success.

- *The terms of the agreement are short.* Typical deals are only two to four years, and the marketer isn't obligated to continue with the inventor or manufacturer on future products.
- *It's the same as contract manufacturing.* The terms of manufacturer are not much different than if the marketer wants to outsource the product to a contract manufacturer. The manufacturing partner might make more on production than it would as a contract manufacturer because the marketer can't get competitive bidding. The cost is still reasonable because the manufacturer provides help with product design, engineering documentation, and prototype production.
- *The inventor will sell out in the future.* At the start of the project, no one knows how things will work out, but if the marketer does establish a strong market share, the inventor can explain that he or she would consider relinquishing ownership for a fixed sum in the future.

Regarding the Inventor

The inventor's share of 5 to 10 percent profit based on sales may create concern with either partner. Inventors can justify their share by reiterating that (1) they have generated this profitable opportunity for the company and (2) that their share of revenue could easily be less than the $200,000 to

$500,000 cost to either company to develop a product on its own. If the inventor's share of revenue is more than that, well, then everyone is making a big profit. Finally, the companies are entering this venture with low risk. If the product doesn't sell, inventors are out all their time and money invested. The marketers and manufacturers lose very little if the product fails—and far less than if they fail with products they themselves develop.

TARGET A MAJOR PLAYER TO BASE-LOAD SALES: STRUCTURE AN IRRESISTIBLE DEAL

Inventors will have smooth sailing in signing their deals if they can identify one large base-load account that will cover the up-front costs of production. A major customer could be a large distributor, a retailer, or an industrial user. This is a key reason you want to have industry helpers: They can identify key targets and might be able to help you get a preliminary commitment such as a provisional order or a letter of intent from a major customer. Meeting as many contacts as possible is also the reason you want to attend association meetings and trade shows.

You can provide encouragement to a company to be a base-load customer by offering incentives, which can be either market opportunities (e.g., exclusive agreements) or priced-based discounts (e.g., preferred pricing or co-op advertising). You can also offer combinations of these benefits. While you can't give a total commitment without your partners agreeing, you can tell the major customer that you want to present the possibility of acquiring it as a base-load account in return for the partners offering key incentives. The incentives may lower profits, but it will work in your favor, since you will be providing your partners an almost risk-free deal. Some of the incentives you can offer include private-label deals, short-term exclusive agreements, exclusive co-op ad programs, demonstrations and seminars, staff training, product discounts, and guaranteed preferred pricing.

- *Private-label deals.* You might offer just one customer, whether a dealer or a retailer, a private-label deal with preferred pricing (typically 15 percent less than standard prices) in return for its promotion of your product. Under a private-label agreement, the customer will sell the product under its own label rather than the marketing company's label. Sears Kenmore products are an example of private-label products that are made by major appliance manufacturers like Whirlpool and Maytag. Customers might prefer an exclusive private-label agreement because it will give them an advantage over their competition and because they will receive a bigger discount than companies buying the marketing partner's brand.

- *Short-term exclusive agreements.* A 12- to 18-month exclusive agreement with one major customer offers a market advantage to that customer, and it benefits your manufacturing partner by allowing it time to bring its production up to speed to satisfy the larger market.

- *Exclusive co-op ad programs.* Co-op ad programs refer to the practice of marketers paying some percentage of their sales to their retail customers for the retailers' ads, circulars, and other promotional material up to a total dollar value that is based on a percentage of sales. When you see a sales catalog in your Sunday paper for Toys "R" Us, for example, typically the manufacturers of the toys featured have paid for half the cost of the ad through a co-op advertising program. A company might set up a co-op fund of 6 percent of purchases that can be used to pay for 50 percent of the costs of catalog placements, ads, and mailings. If a customer purchases $1 million of product, the marketer would set aside a fund of $60,000 to pay for 50 percent of the retailers' costs for promoting its product. As an incentive for a base-load purchase agreement, the turbo-outsource partners might offer a 10 percent co-op fund. That not only encourages the customer to sign, but also encourages it to promote your product to end users. Co-op program funds can also be used to help sponsor events, contests, or major presentations at trade shows that feature your product.

- *Demonstrations and seminars.* Some products require, or are greatly helped by, demonstrations, seminars, or other in-store or local events. Potential customers might be swayed by a program where you and your partners do demonstrations only with the major partner for 6 to 12 months.

- *Staff training.* If a trained sales staff at the customer is a big plus, your group could commit to training the key customer first, before training any competitors.

- *Product discounts.* You can offer major discounts of 15 to 20 percent for a large purchase agreement that base-loads your production.

- *Guaranteed preferred pricing.* This guarantees a customer that it will have lower pricing than all competitors for a fixed period of time, which could be one to three years.

PREPARE THE TURBO-OUTSOURCE PRESENTATION: PUT IT TOGETHER WITH SIZZLE

The presentation has similarities to the licensing presentation (see Chapter 10, pages 176 to 180), except it is focused more on the market opportunity than the product. Include these 10 items:

1. Give a short overview.
   - Market opportunity
   - Target market
   - Market size
   - Product description
   - Yearly profit and sales potential
2. List contacts that indicate the market is ready to move now. Use as many contacts as you can.
3. Describe any major customers who are ready to buy now.
4. Demonstrate and show the product. Explain how it will work and function.
5. List the major selling features of the product.
6. Explain why the product perfectly fits the opportunity.
7. Detail any intellectual property protection.
8. Show a projected retail price and manufacturing cost.
9. Provide info on the other partner.
   - Name
   - Size
   - Other products
   - Market success
10. Propose a revenue split. Show the chart you prepared for the revenue split in your turbo-outsourced marketing plan (Chapter 14, page 240).

NEGOTIATE THE AGREEMENTS: KEEP IT SIMPLE AND FLEXIBLE

As an inventor, you should retain a lawyer to help finalize agreements. Nonetheless, you should have knowledge about the contract so you can intelligently discuss terms with your marketing and manufacturing partners. In some agreements you will be taking a commission from the manufacturing partner; in others you will buy from a manufacturer and resell to the marketing partner. A third option is to receive a commission from the marketing company. All these agreements are fairly straightforward and can be executed with a sales/representative agreement. Inventors probably receive more favorable terms and generate better long-term success with a three-way agreement between inventor, manufacturer, and marketer. There is a sample three-way contract at the end of the chapter. The 14 most important items contained in a three-way agreement are as follows:

1. *Responsibilities.* Explain clearly what each party is responsible for. Include items like warehousing, invoicing, and collections.

2. *Profit split/revenue sharing.* This section should explain the flow of revenue and how the money will be divided.

3. *Adjustment procedures.* Manufacturing costs might go up; the product might require more discounts than expected; your group might need to respond to competitive pressures. You need to have a mechanism to readjust the profit and revenue sharing.

4. *Commitment levels.* Though it is difficult to define and hard to enforce, you want to list some type of commitment level from all the partners so they will perceive that their level of commitment is equivalent to that of the others.

5. *Product review/product quality.* Generally you want to allow the product entrepreneur (i.e., the inventor) and the marketer the right to review product quality and the right to review and approve product changes.

6. *Product changes.* All parties should have input into and approve product changes.

7. *Ownership of units.* The agreement should be very clear about who has ownership and responsibility for the product from manufacturing through sales to the end customer.

8. *Funding.* Who will fund start-up costs and continuing operations? This should be spelled out in the agreement.

9. *Term.* How long will the agreement last, and what are the options for continuing the product?

10. *Agreement termination.* Spell out the situation and process for terminating the agreement by one party.

11. *Damages.* Each party's responsibilities should be clearly defined in the agreement. In cases where one party fails to perform, you want that party to be terminated and all rights to the continued manufacturer and sale of the product to revert to the other parties.

12. *Ownership of intellectual property.* The intellectual property rights should always belong to the inventor. You don't want to assign the intellectual property rights to the other parties. You will allow the manufacturer and marketer to use your intellectual property rights as long as the agreement is in force.

13. *Derivative products.* You might discover the need for other products for the market under this agreement. They could be complementary products, product improvements, or product line extensions (see Chapter 13, pages 225 to 226). All parties to the agreement should have the chance to add any derivative products suggested by any of the partners. If any party declines, then the other parties should have the right to introduce the product on their own under a separate agreement.

14. *Dispute resolution.* Write a clause calling for arbitration in the case of disputes.

Sample Turbo-Outsource Agreement

Agreement for Manufacture and Sale of Product A

This Agreement (**Agreement**) is entered into as of this 10th day of March, 2005, by and between John T. Smith (Product Entrepreneur, or **PE**), 2867 Pierce Street, Maple Fill NC 28454; ABC Manufacturing Co. (**Manufacturer**), 7837 Northern Pike, Toledo, OH 43964; and Sporting Promotional Products, (**Marketer**) 5830 Broadway St., Tucson, AZ 85426 to manufacturer and market Product A into the North American market.

Background

PE is the inventor who has created a new product, Product A, and obtained a U.S. patent and trademark and wishes to have the product produced and sold into the North American market. **Manufacturer** has the plant equipment and plant capacity to produce Product A in the desired quantities, and **Manufacturer** is willing to produce Product A for sale into the market. **Marketer** has marketing and sales experience in the Product A market and **Marketer** wants to participate in the marketing and distribution of Product A. The three parties together want to enter into this Agreement to participate together in the launch of Product A into the market and agree as follows:

1. Project Outline

Manufacturer agrees to be prepared to produce Product A in quantities specified in this Agreement and to provide the production capacity, including production equipment and operating capital, required to produce those quantities. **Manufacturer** will sell Product A to **PE** at pricing set per the terms of this Agreement. **PE** will provide product design, quality review, and technical assistance to **Marketer** and **Marketer**'s customers. **PE** will sell the product to **Marketer** at pricing set per the terms of this Agreement. **Marketer** will provide the funding for marketing, sales, and customer service expenses and sell Product A to the distribution channel and end users.

2. Pricing

Manufacturer agrees to set pricing per unit at 10% over its per unit costs. As of the signing of this agreement those costs are $2.20 per unit. **Manufacturer** agrees to raise prices by no more than 5% per year, and those increases should be justified with appropriate documentation to support the cost increase. **Marketer** and **PE** may audit **Manufacturer**'s costs to verify cost increases.

PE agrees to sell Product A to **Marketer** for no more than a 10% markup over his price from **Manufacturer.**

Marketer agrees to mark up Product A for marketing and sales cost plus a fee of 5%, for a total markup of no more than 20% over his price from the **PE. Marketer**'s cost may be audited by **Manufacturer** and **PE** once per year if the **Marketer**'s suggested retail price reflects more than a 20% markup of the **PE** price to the **Marketer.**

3. Pricing Adjustments

Must be agreed to in writing by all parties at least three (3) months prior to the effective date of such increase.

4. Sales Volume

The parties have projected the following sales volumes:

Year 1 (starting July 1, 2005)	1,500,000 units
Year 2 (starting July 1, 2006)	3,000,000 units
Year 3 (starting July 1, 2006)	3,500,000 units

Parties to the agreement will provide their best efforts to fulfill their responsibilities to meet these sales levels.

5. Responsibilities

PE will provide:

- Product design for current Product A and future modifications to Product A
- Periodic product quality review and inspection
- Start-up manufacturing assistance
- Seminars and training at major trade shows and customers
- Staff training at both **Marketer**'s and **Manufacturer**'s facility
- Ongoing presence on key association committees and other trade events
- Payment to **Manufacturer** within 45 days of shipment to **Marketer**'s warehouse
- Funding for all of **PE**'s activities

Manufacturer will provide:

- Production start-up tooling
- Production space and capacity sufficient to produce units called for in sales volume

- Raw goods inventory for production start-up
- Sufficient finished goods inventory space to hold units for truck load shipments to **Marketer**
- Sufficient engineering and quality inspection support
- Every 30 days, a monthly production schedule for the next three months
- Other support, funding, and services required to meet production levels required by Section 4, Sales Volume.

Marketer will provide:

- Marketing and sales support similar to that provided by **Marketer**'s own similar-size product line
- Funding for all marketing and sales activities
- Warehousing for shipments to customers
- Customer service, order entry, billing, and collections for sales to customers
- Technical support, as required
- Every month, sales forecasts for the next 12 months
- Reports to **PE** and **Manufacturer** regarding market feedback on major issues related to product performance and quality
- Payment to **PE** within 35 days of shipments from **Manufacturer** to its warehouse

6. Product Specifications

Final product specifications to be provided by **Manufacturer** and approved and accepted by **PE** and **Marketer.** Specifications to be approved 90 days prior to first production run.

7. First Article/Quarterly Inspection

All parties must approve the initial production units regarding product quality and performance. **PE** and **Marketer** may request additional quarterly reviews for their approval. Inspections and approval may be called for at any time in the case of significant customer complaints.

8. Product Changes

Changes may be suggested by any of the three parties, but must be approved by all three parties prior to implementation.

9. Ownership of Production Units

Manufacturer owns production units until they are shipped from its warehouse to the **Marketer**'s warehouse and the product is paid for. (Product is shipped FOB **Manufacturer**'s plant). **Marketer** takes ownership once the product leaves the **Manufacturer**'s plant. **PE** never takes physical ownership of the product but has ownership from the time he pays for the product until he is paid for the product.

10. Intellectual Property

All intellectual property related to Product A will remain the property of **PE.**

11. Warranty Limitations

Manufacturer is responsible for product quality and warrants production units to meet specifications from Section 6, Product Specifications. Under no circumstances is **Manufacturer** responsible for consequential damages. Warranty claims from **Marketer** to be filed through **PE** to **Manufacturer.**

12. Merchandise Returns

Returns may be made for warranty reasons only. All returns subject to the **Manufacturer**'s standard return policy in Attachment 2.

13. Derivative Products

Derivative products are defined as complementary products, Product A with modifications or additional features, and product line extensions. No party will introduce a derivative product for the period of this agreement and for an additional two-year period after termination of the agreement without first offering to sign an agreement similar to this one with the other two parties. The party presenting the agreement is free to introduce the product on its own if the other parties decline to participate. In the event that only one party declines, the two remaining parties will enter into a mutually acceptable agreement to introduce the product idea.

14. Confidentiality

All parties agree to be bound by the Mutual Confidentiality and Nondisclosure Agreement in Attachment 1. [See Appendix C for sample agreement]. The confidentiality agreement will survive for 24 months after the termination of this Agreement.

15. Company Status

All parties shall act as independent contractors and not as agents, partners, or joint venture partners. Each party is a separate legal entity and none of the parties shall have authority to bind another party to an agreement or expense or incur any other obligations on behalf of the other party.

16. Conflict of Interest

All parties warrant that they are under no obligation to any other entity whereby conflicts of interest are or may be created by entering into this Agreement and that they are free to enter into this Agreement.

17. Term

The term of this Agreement is three (3) years from the effective date of this Agreement. This Agreement can be extended by mutual written consent of all parties for an additional period of 12, 24, or 36 months.

18. Termination

Two of the parties may terminate this Agreement with the third party to this Agreement for failure of that third party to perform its obligations hereunder. The two parities seeking termination must provide a written complaint to the other party explaining why they believe the other party has failed to perform its obligations hereunder and allow that party 30 days to respond to those complaints.

Upon termination of that party, the remaining two parties may enter into a new agreement, find a new third party, or terminate the entire agreement. Termination of this Agreement or termination of any party to this Agreement does not relieve any party of its confidentiality and payment obligations hereunder.

19. Product Ownership Upon Termination

The product ownership at the time of termination will reside with the party that has paid for or is obligated to pay for that product under this agreement in accordance with Section 9 herein.

20. Damages

No party shall be liable to any other party to this Agreement for any consequential, incidental, or indirect damages arising under or out of this Agreement.

21. Dispute Resolution

Parties agree to have disputes settled by a mutually agreed upon arbitrator(s) in the State of Ohio, in accordance with the American Arbitration Association Commercial Disputes Resolution Procedures.

22. Complete Agreement

This agreement represents the entire agreement between the three parties.

23. Assignment

This agreement is not assignable by any party without the consent of the other two parties.

24. Governing Law

This Agreement is governed by the laws of the State of Ohio.

25. Execution

Each individual executing this Agreement on behalf of a party to this Agreement represents that he or she has authority to enter into this Agreement on behalf of such party and that this Agreement is binding on such party.

For Product Entrepreneur

_____

Date

_____

Signature

_____

Printed Name

_____

Title

For Manufacturer

_____

Date

_____

Signature

_____

Printed Name

_____

Title

For Marketer Products

_____

Date

_____

Signature

_____

Printed Name

_____

Title

PART IV

THE LONG-TERM INVESTMENT: BUILDING A COMPANY

16

STEP 6C. PROVE THE CONCEPT: ESTABLISH THAT THE PRODUCT WILL MAKE MONEY

Inventors start their own companies for a variety of reasons, including that their target market is too small to interest a company in a licensing or turbo-outsource arrangement, that they are unable to license their idea, that they want to be an entrepreneur and control their own company, and that they want to maximize the wealth they can create from their idea. However, all of the early steps, up through preparing your business and marketing plan, are similar no matter what strategy you are following. You want a patent, a prototype, and industry helpers for any product introduction strategy. You want to prove the product will sell in the licensing and turbo-outsourcing processes to convince companies to become involved with your product. When you are starting your own company, you need to prove the concept will sell so that you can raise money, and if you don't need to raise money, you should still prove the concept before investing heavily in the project. Otherwise, you just might lose your investment. You may discover early that a product won't sell and save your resources to introduce another product at a later date.

Starting your own company has the potential to create the most wealth for the inventor. But it also forces inventors to raise the most money from investors, because inventors typically don't have the funding resources of a licensee or a turbo-outsource partner. It is common for inventors to need 4 to 10 times more money to introduce their own product than they'd need to pursue either a licensing or turbo-outsourcing agreement. Adding to the fund-raising challenge is that investors require a higher level of proof that the product will sell, because they don't have the same spin-off benefits that a licensee or turbo-outsource partner might have. Investors also don't have anywhere near the market knowledge of the potential partner companies to assess whether a product will sell. Inventors usually need to prove the concept with actual sales results in market tests that closely simulate the conditions of the market at large to convince investors that their product will sell well. This chapter shows how to prove your concept.

- Develop a manufacturing strategy: Cover both short- and long-term options.
- Generate first sales: Show that customers place high value on the product.
- Test during the sales period: Discover how to generate the highest margins.
- Determine your manufacturing costs: Evaluate your profit versus your risk.
- Illustrate future markets: Show rapid growth potential for investors.

One Stage at a Time

Mike Mogadam's friend owned what looked like a successful bar business, but it went broke primarily due to bartender theft. Bartenders either kept the money they charged customers or offered customers free drinks in return for big tips. Mogadam, an electronic engineer, decided he could solve this problem. He invented the Barmate, a wireless point-of-sale system for liquor control at bars and restaurants. The Barmate features a $125 spout that attaches to liquor bottles and pours a set amount into each drink. It also sends a wireless signal to the cash register to record the sale and to a central computer to keep tabs on nightly sales volume and liquor inventory levels.

Mogadam was 32 years old when he started his project, which eventually became a multi-million-dollar company. But at the time he launched the product he had very little money. After receiving positive feedback from bar owners, he decided to proceed on a step-by-step basis to prove his product would sell. Only after gathering his proof would he proceed to raise the money needed to launch his company. Mogadam followed these five stages:

  1. Market research. *This consisted of interviews with bar and restaurant owners and managers to verify the market wanted a better liquor control system.*

2. Prototype development. *Mogadam created a working prototype that he tested in a simulated bar environment to prove the product would work.*

3. Sales proof. *Mogadam exhibited his concept at a New York convention for bar owners and secured several provisional orders to purchase Barmates when Mogadam was able to build and ship them.*

4. Final engineering, beta testing, initial preproduction units for sale. *The cost for this step was $100,000, but Mogadam was able to raise the funds from family, friends, and investors because of his existing provisional orders.*

5. First production run. *After selling his preproduction units, Mogadam was able to secure a $300,000 Small Business Administration (SBA) loan to begin production.*

DEVELOP A MANUFACTURING STRATEGY: COVER BOTH SHORT- AND LONG-TERM OPTIONS

Investors are going to want to understand and evaluate your manufacturing plan. The three stages of production to worry about are units for an initial sales test, units for intermediate sales levels, and units for full production. You may want to build the units yourself or use a U.S. or foreign manufacturer. If you are unsure about which manufacturing strategy to follow, you should be able to get assistance from either your local inventors' club (check out www.uia.usa.com and www.inventorsdigest.com) or from a manufacturing executive at the Service Corps of Retired Executives (SCORE). Find your local contact online at www.sba.gov/gopher/Local-Information/Service-Corps-Of-Retired-Executives/. Inventors should plot out a long-term manufacturing strategy even if they don't need investors. You want to be sure that your product eventually can be produced at 30 percent or less of its perceived retail value. For example, if you have a new outdoor hammock with a perceived value of $30, you want to have a manufacturing process in mind that will produce the product for $9 or less. That will leave you with $6 of profit on every product you sell to retailers. (Retailers will buy the hammock at $15, or 50 percent off the suggested retail price.) I've seen many inventors design a product that doesn't require any tooling investment for the initial sales tests, but unfortunately the design doesn't lend itself to cost-saving measures at higher volumes. When that happens, the inventor won't make any money. Thinking through the entire production scheme helps inventors choose a design and production strategy that will result in the best design for long-term success.

Initial Sales Units

Your initial sales units are needed for a sales test. You need only between 25 and 200 units to prove a product will sell. In some cases, when the product is expensive, inventors may need only a few sales. Mogadam's Barmate in the inventor story is an example where two sales were plenty to show that the product could sell. Inventors want to make their product for the lowest possible total investment, including tooling, materials, setup charges, packaging, and manufacturing costs for the initial units. You want to avoid a significant investment because your product might not sell, or it may need extensive modifications before it is ready to sell. Inventors need to either make the product themselves or engage a contract manufacturer who will typically use temporary tooling or labor-intensive production tactics to avoid big tooling costs. Inventors can also purchase some parts, use parts from other products, and make missing parts themselves and then assemble the product. Inventors who want to use contract manufacturers can often receive in-kind or inexpensive help by using the same tactics discussed in Chapter 3 (pages 62 to 63).

Intermediate Sales Levels

Inventors starting their own business don't usually have the luxury of jumping from a test market to national distribution. Instead, they need to develop a midsize sales base that establishes the product in a market niche. The success of this phase of the business dictates how much money you can raise for a national rollout. Inventors need to show a profit in this phase, but they can get by with a margin of 20 to 30 percent because of a lower level of production. (See Chapter 5, pages 102 to 103, for an explanation of margins.) Either set up your own production or have a contract manufacturer produce the product. Chapter 6 (pages 130 to 131) details how to find a contract manufacturer and receive a firm price quote. You can follow that same strategy again here to receive costs estimates for midsize production runs.

Full Production

Inventors want to know that there is a production method that will eventually produce their product with a margin of at least 40 percent. If inventors can't eventually hit that margin, they will never make much money. Also, investors don't want to fund your project if it will never make enough money to allow the company to grow or to pay back their investment. Since you are probably a start-up company with limited resources, determine the most economical production method for sales of $500,000 to $1 million. That's enough production for overseas sourcing (Chapter 6, pages 130 to 131) or a U.S. production facility with adequate tooling for a low per-piece price. Ensure that the manufacturing costs at that level let you sell the product to the next person in the distribution chain at a 40 percent margin.

GENERATE FIRST SALES: SHOW THAT CUSTOMERS PLACE HIGH VALUE ON THE PRODUCT

Your goal in an initial sales period is to prove to yourself and investors that the product will sell and to conduct market research to fine-tune your product and your package. You must do initial sales with either a "looks like, acts like" product or preproduction units (Chapter 4, pages 91 to 95) in order to get adequate market feedback. Buyers know you are not prepared to sell anything until you have a market-ready product—and they will tell you only that they *might* buy. That doesn't help you—because they also might *not* buy.

Inventors have a successful first-sales period if they sell enough units through normal distribution channels to prove the product can sell. Inventors should try to duplicate their eventual sales plan in the sales period, but sometimes it may be practical to sell a product directly to consumers, bypassing distribution. Inventors can sell through fairs, flea markets, and trade shows; retailers; manufacturers' representatives; mail orders; catalogs; and distributors.

Before you actually start to sell your product you should incorporate your business. Inventors open themselves up to legal liabilities when they sell a product. You may be personally liable if the product should injure someone or some other type of calamity should occur. Incorporating insulates your personal assets from any business claims. Bigger libraries and bookstores typically carry numerous books on incorporating. You can also contact the secretary of state in your home state, whose office will send out the necessary forms and filing instructions. *Entrepreneur* magazine (www.entrepreneur.com) sells booklets showing how, in each state, to incorporate a business without a lawyer. Most incorporations can be completed for less than $400. If you are reluctant to incorporate on your own, ask for help from your accountant or lawyer.

Fairs, Flea Markets, and Trade Shows

Many inventors' first efforts to sell their product comes at consumer shows: home shows, auto shows, sports shows—or at flea markets. While these venues don't simulate your eventual distribution channel, they do provide significant benefits to inventors:

- Creating some revenue to offset costs to date
- Proving end-user demand to help land initial retail stores
- Meeting key contacts in the local market
- Receiving immediate input regarding the product's features and benefits
- Changing the price during a show to gauge the product's perceived value
- Taking orders to justify a tooling investment

Retailers

You can build sales success by putting your product into retail stores in your local geographic area, either by selling the product outright or by offering it on consignment. Small retailers will accept a product for testing, but you can also get your product into bigger stores and chains on a local basis. Often, the manager of a chain store will have the authority to test-market a product from a local vendor. You won't know until you try.

The best situation is if you can convince the retailers to buy your product. Retailers will typically pay 50 percent of your suggested retail price. If a retailer won't purchase the product, you can offer it on consignment, which means the retailer pays only for the units that sell. If retailers do buy, they might ask you to guarantee sales, which means that you will offer a full refund for any units that don't sell.

Inventors doing tests at a larger store may need a Universal Product Code (UPC), also referred to as a *bar code*. You can obtain these for less than $500 from the Uniform Code Council, www.uc-council.org. (Check resources at the back of the book for full contact information.)

Provide the retailer with as many selling aids as possible, including a good package and point-of-purchase materials, which could include a small sign or a display box. Stop back and check with the store owner or manager at least twice a month to see how the product is selling and whether you can do anything to help sales.

Manufacturer's Representatives

While making contacts, you may have run into manufacturer's representatives who sell your type of product to either distributors or retailers. Inventors without sales experience might want to select one representative to help them place the product into several stores. The representative can also help you with packaging and store display materials that will entice both retailers and end users. Expect to pay between 10 and 15 percent commission of your sales revenue to the representative for assisting you.

Online Auctions

Sales by auction can reinforce your price point and establish that the product is something people want. But eBay is not for everyone. People have to be looking for your type of product or no one will find it to buy it. You must use the right search terms to be successful. Start by trying all the search words you can think of that might apply to your product. If a product description (e.g., "window deicer") doesn't get any hits, think of similar products that might meet the same need as your product. For example, if your product is a window deicer for autos, you could search "window scraper."

Once you find several search terms, write your sales copy for eBay, including the search terms in your product description. For the window deicer, the inventor could describe it as the advanced window scraper system. Indeed, eBay has excellent instructions on how to put a product up for sale on its site, or you can contact an eBay shipping depot in your area that can also help you. The eBay shipping stores, which are private businesses, often have credit card processing and other tools to help you take orders. Be sure to include a photo of your product.

Catalogs

To sell to catalogs, inventors need to provide a sales flyer that includes a photo of the product, a suggested retail price, and the catalog discount price, which is 50 percent off the suggested retail price. The beauty of catalogs is that if they elect to include your product in a catalog, you don't need to deliver for four to six months. That gives inventors an order they can use as leverage to arrange financing or production. You can find catalogs by going to the web sites catalogs.google.com or www.shopathome.com.

Once you find a catalog company that seems to fit your product, request an actual sales catalog that the company mails out to its customers. Find products that are similar to yours and then contact the catalog company and ask for the buyer of that product. Once you have the name, send a sales flyer to the buyer and offer to send a sample. Follow up with a phone call after you send in the flyer to see if there is any interest. Also ask the buyer when the next catalog will be printed and when the buyer will finalize his or her product selections for the catalog. Be sure to follow up 30 to 60 days before the buyer's final catalog selections.

You might get a request from the catalog company to share in the cost of printing the catalog. For example, the catalog might ask you for $1,000 to $3,000 to help cover its printing costs. Vendors often pay the majority of the actual cost of printing a catalog. Rather than paying the sum requested by the catalog, offer 10 percent free goods to cover the costs. If the catalog orders 100 units, offer to ship 110 units to defray some of the costs of printing.

Distributors

This part of a consumer sales channel is more difficult to sell to for test sales because distributors have considerable costs in adding a product from a new vendor. But you might be able to sell through a distributor if you have a key helper there. You need to prepare a sales flyer similar to the one you did for the retailer, but you need to have a different pricing structure. You should set your price to the distributor at 44 percent of your suggested retail price. The distributor will raise the price 50 percent, and then the retailer will raise the price another 50 percent. If your product has a suggested retail price of $9.99, your price to the distributor will be $4.40, and the distributor's price to the retailer will be $6.66.

Industrial distributors typically buy products at 40 percent off the end-user price. They are usually easier to sell to than consumer product distributors because they typically have smaller product lines and lower costs to add a new product.

Distributors are an ideal test source because they simulate the larger market, and sales through a distributor are the surest sign that a product will sell. There are several offers you can present to distributors to encourage them to pick up the product:

- Travel with each salesperson, if necessary, to show them how to promote the product.
- Turn over existing accounts to the distributor.
- Grant the distributor a six-month exclusive in its geographic area.
- Run promotions during the next six months in the distributor's market area.
- Handle all product complaints and returns.

TEST DURING THE SALES PERIOD: DISCOVER HOW TO GENERATE THE HIGHEST MARGINS

Your test sales period is designed to prove the product will sell. But inventors can also use the period for testing pricing, packaging, and product benefits. Inventors can find the best combination of the three by changing these elements either at different stores or when the product is sold through different distributor salespeople. This is a tactic you can also use with catalogs. Simply offer different price points to different catalogs and see whether the change in pricing helps or hurts your sales level.

Pricing

Either offer a product at various prices at different stores or offer an instant rebate of 10, 20, 30, and 40 percent at different stores. To use rebates, set your price at the high end based on your market research. Your product might not sell at all at the list price and only minimally with a 10 percent instant rebate, but then sell well with 20 percent or higher rebates. That would indicate the right price is 20 percent less than your high-end price.

Packaging

Packaging is a big cost. A *blister pack,* which is a clear piece of hard plastic surrounding your product, is four to five times more expensive than a shrink-wrapped package. Retailers prefer a smaller package that takes less space, but a small package may not show end users enough benefits to convince them to buy your product. Packaging has less impact in catalogs and for industrial products, and there you should probably go with your lowest-price packaging option.

Product Benefits

What sales information do you want to put on your package? Large companies test many options to find (1) which benefits sell best and (2) what phrasing best communicates those benefits. You should probably test the message on your package with potential end users before the sales tests, but often you will have two or three benefit statements, product names, or catchy phrases that all score well. If possible, try different benefit statements to see which ones produce the best sales results.

DETERMINE YOUR MANUFACTURING COSTS: EVALUATE YOUR PROFIT VERSUS YOUR RISK

If you plan is to use a contract manufacturer, you can get manufacturing quotes in the same manner as discussed in Chapter 6 (pages 130 to 131). If you are going to proceed with manufacturing on your own, you need to establish production and start-up manufacturing costs. Production costs are needed to determine that you can make a profit. You also want to consider your start-up costs versus the amount of profit you can make. Most companies want a two- to three-year payback for start-up costs, which means that you want the profit in your first three years to equal your start-up manufacturing costs.

Production Costs

You want to compare production costs per unit to the product's perceived value. Production costs include:

- Materials
- Labor per unit
- Packaging
- Overhead

You should be able to project the labor, material, and packaging requirements fairly closely if you've made some prototypes or preproduction units. To calculate overhead costs, add up all of your overhead charges and then divide those charges by the number of units you will produce. That calculation provides the overhead cost per unit. For example, consider Sun Flower Plastic, a company that manufactures a plastic container to hold tools and other products in the back of vans or four-wheel drive vehicles. Its monthly overhead might look this:

Rent of manufacturing space	$ 700
Product liability insurance	350
Quality control—⅓ person's time	700
Shipping—¼ person's time	500
Machine depreciation	300
Utilities (electricity, phone, etc.)	300
½ management time	2,500
Scrap and rework	300
Purchasing—¼ person's time	500
Total	**$6,150**

If the company sells 500 units per month, its overhead charge per unit would be $12.30 ($6,150 ÷ 500 = $12.30). The production costs for 500 units would look like this:

Material	$ 2.50
Labor	3.00
Packaging	1.80
Overhead	12.30
Total	**$19.60**

Sun Flower Plastic would need to sell its product for $32.66 to see a 40 percent margin, which means the retail price would be $65.00 retail. If that price is higher than the product's perceived value, you might want to also show the number of units needed to hit the cost that corresponds to your perceived value. If Sun Flower Plastic thinks its retail price should be $40.00, the price paid to Sun Flower would be $20.00 (representing retailers' 50 percent discount), and the manufacturing costs would need to be $12.00 to produce a 40 percent margin. The cost chart that reflects $12.00 per unit in manufacturing costs would call for a production level of 1,308 units per month.

Material	$ 2.50
Labor	3.00
Packaging	1.80
Overhead	4.70
Total	**$12.60**

Start-Up Manufacturing Costs

You need to calculate the start-up manufacturing costs (1) to determine whether you can raise the money and (2) to ensure that the costs can be covered by the profits from the first two to three years of sales. Investors will want to compare these costs to your sales and profit forecasts to determine whether the product is a good investment. Inventors definitely have to pay start-up manufacturing costs if they produce the product themselves, and sometimes they have to pay the costs even if they use a contract manufacturer if it won't agree to amortize those costs. The following items need to be included in start-up manufacturing costs:

- Security deposits, utility fees, building modifications, if any
- Engineering documentation (a package of engineering drawings that are sometimes required by manufacturers)
- Tooling and fixtures, including molds for injection molding or steel castings and fixtures to hold parts in place so they can be machined or assembled
- Three to four months of raw material inventory to produce your product

- Operating cash, which typically requires the cash equivalent to four to six months of sales for a successful product (maybe more if sales are slow)
- Packaging up-front costs, which often run $3,000 to $7,000 for molds, creative materials, and printing plates
- Consignment and demo units (probably at least 5 to 15 units to show to customers and prospects and to give to representatives)

ILLUSTRATE FUTURE MARKETS: SHOW RAPID GROWTH POTENTIAL FOR INVESTORS

Investors want to see that you have a nice product that will start making money quickly. But they also want to see that the product could be the first of many products or could develop significant future sales. When I covered funding presentations in Chapter 3 (pages 69 to 74), the emphasis was on getting money for the initial stages of the business. You want the formal investor presentation to focus on the opportunity that is just ahead. But when you are trying to raise significant cash to start production, you should add to your presentation details of the growth that your product can expect as it develops. You can do this with an extended timeline showing phases of future growth. Figure 16.1 shows the growth phases for a medically proven Arthritic Relief Exercise Band for Knees that is targeted initially to physical therapists.

Preparing a chart of projected future growth gives investors a chance to see that an investment in your product might be a really big winner, exactly what investors are looking for.

Figure 16.1   Growth Strategy—Arthritic Relief Exercise Band for Knees

Phase 1.	Sales to physical therapists and orthopedic surgeons in the United States. Annual volume: 500,000 units per year.
Phase 2.	Expand product line to include shoulder and back relief. Sales to physical therapists and orthopedic surgeons in the United States. Annual volume: 2 million units per year.
Phase 3.	Expand sales internationally. Annual volume: 4 million units per year.
Phase 4.	Introduce consumer products sold through personal trainers and health clubs. Annual volume: 5 million units per year.
Phase 5.	Introduce consumer product to be sold through drugstores and mass merchandisers. Annual volume: 12 to 20 million units per year.

17

STEP 7C. CHOOSE YOUR SALES STRATEGY: DETERMINE HOW TO BECOME A SIGNIFICANT MARKET FORCE

The licensing and turbo-outsourcing introduction paths focus on selecting a company with marketing and sales know-how that will then sell your product to distribution and end users. When you start your own company, *you* are the one who sells to distribution and end users, and you need to develop a sales strategy to do that. All sales strategies revolve first and foremost around your distribution strategy, which relates to how your product reaches the end user. Distribution ranges from selling directly to consumers or industrial users to selling through wholesalers, who sell to distributors, who then sell to retailers, who finally sell to end users. Your distribution channel dictates, at least in part, the proper packaging, pricing, promotional programs, and sales and customer service support that your company needs.

Selling through distribution channels is usually much more difficult than selling directly to consumers simply because distribution channels have to perform several administrative tasks to bring your product on board and because they have more to lose if the product doesn't sell or doesn't perform as promised, especially if the inventor goes out of business. Buyers in the distribution channels are knowledgeable about the market, and inventors need to be on their toes to sell to them.

A sales strategy needs to build momentum before the market thinks the product won't succeed. Distribution channel buyers will think your product is failing if you can't report new market success every time you call on them. Buyers believe that a great product will sell, even if that buyer didn't buy the product the first time around. If a buyer turns you down, your only chance of succeeding on a second call is by pointing to some success in the market. Without a success story, the buyer might believe the product doesn't have sales potential. This chapter explores these concepts.

- Discover all your distribution options: Choose distribution that encourages small companies.
- Offer incentives to bring the right salesperson on board: Give up a percentage to leverage big increases.
- Focus on your top three choices: Dedicate the effort needed to close major accounts.
- Develop a sales plan to penetrate accounts: Build momentum in the market.

Stage Strategy Brings Success

When Dale Carsel and Bob Schneider landed a job to paint a large home, they noticed that the owner had decided to wallpaper about two-thirds of the wall space. They suggested to the owner that instead of wallpapering, he might consider faux finishing, *the art of painting with a sponge, rag, or other applicator to simulate the appearance of wallpaper. The owner agreed to try faux finishing on one wall, so Carsel and Schneider cut a pattern out of a six-by six-inch sponge and finished the wall. When the owner loved the look, Carsel and Schneider thought they had a product idea—precut faux painting sponges—that could sell in the market.*

Carsel and Schneider started their sales efforts by testing their Sponge Prince product line at eight Sherwin-Williams paint stores in the Ohio area. Sherwin-Williams offers discounts to professional painters, and that is where many professional painters buy supplies. The product started selling well, but the inventors hit the jackpot when a buyer for Jo-Ann Fabrics spotted the Sponge Prince while redecorating her own home. She tried selling the product out of a few of her stores, and after successful testing, the product went into 60 Jo-Ann Fabrics stores nationwide. Using the same test-first sales strategy, Carsel and Schneider were able to place the Sponge Prince in 22 Home Depot stores in the Ohio area.

The inventors wanted a next-phase sales expansion that was in line with their resources, so they went after the home shopping TV market next. They approached QVC, showed a video of the product in use, detailed their success at paint and home-improvement stores, and sold their concept to QVC. The product went on the air and garnered $60,000 to $70,000 in sales with every eight-minute showing. Market momentum was clearly building *for Carsel and Schneider, but they began to realize that doing the selling themselves was time-consuming and expensive. They wanted a better way to generate more sales.*

Their thoughts first turned to distributors, but before they launched that strategy, they noticed that Valspar, a major paint supplier to home-improvement stores, carried a line of glazing paints being promoted for use in faux finishing. The inventors approached Valspar about selling the Sponge Prince as a complement to their glazing paint. A short test demonstrated that combining the products helped both companies' sales, and Carsel and Schneider were off to the races.

DISCOVER ALL YOUR DISTRIBUTION OPTIONS: CHOOSE DISTRIBUTION THAT ENCOURAGES SMALL COMPANIES

Inventors don't have the resources to promote or offer product support to many of the larger distribution channels. The bigger distribution channels are also reluctant to buy from an inventor because they worry the inventor will go out of business. Buyers have told me that they wait until the inventor calls on them a third or fourth time before buying, just so they can be sure the inventor has staying power. While inventors have trouble approaching the biggest channels first, they typically have many more distribution options than they believe. By being creative, they often will be able to find just the right distribution channel waiting for them.

Distribution Channel Options

I've listed here some of the channels you might be able to use depending on your product. By no means is this list complete. If you watch closely, you will see products sold in an almost unlimited number of places in your daily life. Many of the items on the following list are just the first tier of many distribution channels. For example, you might have a flying airplane toy that has a suggested retail price of $3.99. You could sell the product, through distributors, to convenience stores, gas stations, hobby shops, toy stores, drugstores, mass merchandisers, supermarkets, and fund-raising groups. You would need a different type of distributor for every market, and each retailer would represent a different market channel.

This partial list is just to help you think of various channels you might be able to use. Make a complete list for your product before going on to the next section, which helps you evaluate which channel will work best for your product.

- Sell direct. You or your sales force can sell directly to users. Commonly used for industrial or commercial products.
- Sell through manufacturer's representatives, who may sell directly to users, to distributors, or to retailers.
- Sell through dealers, such as Patterson Dental, which sells supplies to dentists. Dealers are common in professional markets (doctors, dentists, chiropractors, accountants) and also for for products needing high support. ATV vehicles and power equipment are often sold through dealers, who typically offer both installation and service support.
- Sell through distributors to large retail chains, specialty stores, or mass merchandisers like Target. Bicycle accessories are almost all sold through distributors that carry a whole line of bike products, which makes purchasing much easier for bike shops.
- Sell through promotional products firms, also called *advertising specialty companies,* that offer special premium products that companies can give to customers. High-end executive gifts are sold through promotional products companies; so are pens, rulers, and all kinds of other gadgets companies hand out through their salespeople.
- Sell through private-label agreements with larger companies. In a private-label agreement, you sell a product to another company, which then puts the product in its own packaging and sells the product under its own brand name.
- Sell through an alliance with companies that sell complementary products. Several companies might package their products together to sell as a complete product line. The companies might have a common customer service and sales group, with each member of the alliance paying a portion of the expenses; or one company might provide customer service and sales and then charge a fee to the other companies. The alliance could sell through distributor's or manufacturer's representatives or through the direct sales efforts of all the partners.
- Sell products yourself, at trade shows, fairs, or flea markets.
- Sell through mail order catalogs.
- Set up your own site on the Internet or sell through eBay.
- Sell through clubs or organizations. You can sell exercise equipment through health clubs, golf equipment through golf clubs, and bridge-scoring products through card clubs.
- Sell through a larger company that sells to your target market. This is a common tactic with industrial products when your product complements another company's products.

- Sell through fund-raising groups. Schools, scouts, and other organizations are always looking for products they can sell to raise money.
- Sell through professional offices. Chiropractors, physical therapists, speech therapists, and similar groups will offer products related to their business.
- Sell through TV shopping networks. The big three are QVC, Home Shopping Network, and ShopNBC.
- Sell through rack-jobber distribution networks to drugstores, convenience stores, and small retailers. Rack jobbers buy shelf space from a store, stock it with their own merchandise, and then collect money from the retailer after a product is sold.
- Try direct response sales through radio or TV ads.
- Sell through magazine ads. This tactic is effective if your market is small and has a trade magazine. A product for model railroaders, for instance, might do well in a magazine ad.

Scoring Distribution Channel Options

Choosing the right distribution channel depends on four main factors: (1) whether the channel is open to inventors, (2) the size and profitability of the channel compared to the inventor's costs and ability to supply it, (3) the effort required by the inventor to sell through that channel compared to his or her resources, and (4) whether the channel can provide sufficient sales to support the product. TV shopping channels are often an ideal way for inventors to distribute a product because they actively look for new inventor products, can sell $50,000 to $100,000 worth every time the product is featured (a substantial volume at an affordable cost), and the only support required is a day for filming the spot. Not every distribution channel is so easy to evaluate. The following list contains the items you should consider as you evaluate potential networks. Then Figure 17.1 offers an example of distribution channel analysis for a piece of sports equipment—a new type of elliptical trainer.

- *Is the market open to inventors?* Markets with many small vendors are the easiest ones for inventors to sell.
- *Does the channel want another product?* Sometimes one of your competitors dominates a market and the channel is anxious to have another supplier. Or a competitor gives poor service, or its product doesn't work well enough. In all these cases the distribution channel will bend its normal procedures to take on a small supplier.

Figure 17.1   Distribution Channel Analysis—Easy Joint Elliptical Trainer

Product description: The elliptical trainer includes flexible five-inch rubber bands that attach to the trainer and wrap round the user's knees to provide relief for people with arthritis or injured knees. The trainer also provides increased resistance for better training for endurance runners.

Distribution channel options

A. Mail order catalogs
B. Health clubs through distributors
C. Physical therapists direct
D. Home health stores through distributors
E. Physical therapists through medical equipment distributors
F. Sporting goods stores
G. Other manufacturers to physical therapists or medical distributors

	A	B	C	D	E	F	G
Is the market open?	Yes	No	Yes	Yes	Yes	No	Yes
Does the channel want another product?	No	No	?	?	?	No	?
Is the market size large enough for a two- to three-year payback?	No	Yes	Yes	Yes	Yes	Yes	Yes
Does the discount structure allow a 40% margin?	Yes	No	Yes	Yes	No	Yes	No
Can the inventor finance required inventory?	Yes	Yes	Yes	Yes	Yes	No	No
Can the inventor meet the design and packaging requirements of the channel?	Yes	No*	Yes	Yes	Yes	No[†]	Yes
Can the inventor meet the channel's promotional requirements?	Yes	Yes	Yes	Yes	Yes	No	Yes
Can the channel provide the sales support customers require?	No	Yes	Yes	Yes	Yes	No	Yes
Can the channel provide the support the product requires?	No	Yes	Yes	Yes	Yes	No	Yes

* Health clubs will require a more rugged construction with high-quality materials.
[†] Sporting goods stores require more elaborate packaging and easier installation than the inventor can provide.

Analysis: Distribution channels C, D, and E, which are selling the product through distributors or direct to physical therapists or home health stores, appear to be the best options.

- *Is the size of the market in line with your start-up costs?* You need to be able to produce profits per year that equal about one-half to one-third of your start-up investment. Some distribution channels may be too small to justify the expense needed to launch your product.

- *Does the discount structure allow you a 40 percent margin?* Some distribution channels require several levels of discounts (e.g., selling to distributors who sell to rack jobbers who sell to retailers). The inventor may only get 20 percent of the suggested retail price in this type of channel. Unless inventors' costs are low, they won't make money selling into any channel with many discounts.

- *Can you support the inventory required?* A channel may require weekly deliveries or just-in-time shipments. If their product comes in many sizes or colors, inventors will need heavy inventory to be able to react quickly to orders.

- *Can you meet the design and packaging characteristics of the channel?* Some channels require an upscale product finish or upscale materials, which may require more substantial tooling or start-up manufacturing investments. Other channels may require testing approvals or other regulatory certifications that could be expensive.

- *Can you meet the promotional costs of the channel?* Some channels, particularly ones that are dominated by large retailers, expect not only large co-op advertising programs, but also direct-to-consumer advertising. Those channels will ask about an inventor's promotion program, and they are unlikely to buy if you don't have one.

- *Can the channel provide the sales support customers require?* Some products need demonstrations or explanations from salespeople, technical service, installation support, or ongoing maintenance and service. You want to ensure that the distribution channel you choose provides the service your product requires.

- *Can the channel provide the stimulus your product requires?* You might have a product that no one has heard of—for example, an aquarium window, which is a four-inch fish tank used to replace interior windows in office buildings. When the product is first introduced, no one will have heard of it. The inventor will need a sales channel that can let the market know about the product and convince people to buy it. In this case, a perfect distribution channel might be interior decorators.

OFFER INCENTIVES TO BRING THE RIGHT SALESPERSON ON BOARD: GIVE UP A PERCENTAGE TO LEVERAGE BIG INCREASES

My first job with inventors was with the company founded by John Naughton, who invented the first reclining dental chair. He designed the chair and then made 10 test units. Once he perfected the design, he asked dental dealers for the name of the best five salespeople in the industry. One man constantly came out on top. Naughton offered the salesperson a minority ownership position to become his national sales manager. He accepted, and Naughton's company quickly rose to more than $20 million in sales.

I'd say at least 25 percent of the successful inventors I interview for my articles in *Entrepreneur* magazine either hire (offering generous commission packages) or become partners with a top marketing and sales professional in their chosen market. Many inventors understandably wait to look for a top sales and marketing professional until they have tried to sell the product themselves. The risk in trying it yourself is that if you are not successful, the product will lose momentum in the market and your sales professional will have trouble selling to prospects that have already turned you down. You will probably need to offer 15 to 20 percent of the company to attract a top professional. That may appear to be a heavy "penalty," but the sales professional will probably sell 5 to 10 times the volume most inventors can sell on their own, and having a sales professional on board will help inventors raise more money.

FOCUS ON YOUR TOP THREE CHOICES: DEDICATE THE EFFORT NEEDED TO CLOSE MAJOR ACCOUNTS

Selling a product to a small customer is almost as much, if not just as much, effort as selling to a big account. While inventors may have done sales testing in small stores, once they are ready to go into the larger market they are better off concentrating on landing one or two large accounts to base-load their business before trying to sell to smaller customers in the market. Inventors should target their big accounts early in their sales efforts because many of the tactics used to land that business, such as exclusive agreements, in-store demonstrations, or joint promotional programs, are most attractive to the big customer when you have only a few accounts. The six steps that follow should help.

1. Start by selecting the two or three top target accounts. The best companies are ones that are aggressive in the markets, use heavy

promotion, and introduce new ideas. Read trade magazines and talk to your industry contacts to determine your best targets.

2. Study those target companies and look for a shelf area, demonstration, or promotion similar to what you think will work for your product. If your top target is a retailer, visit the stores, evaluate the store layout, and decide on the location in the store that would draw the most sales for your product. Also look into past promotions, in-store demonstrations, sales flyers, classes, and anything else the targeted company might do that would fit with your business.

3. Choose the market target that has run programs, has shelf space, or fits your product best. Then decide where in the store or catalog your product would fit best. Take digital pictures of shelves where you would want your product to go and then have your product transposed into the picture so it appears that it's already in the store. Take sales flyers of store promotions and substitute your product for one on the flyer. Photograph yourself doing a demonstration of your product and then have the picture digitally placed into the store's layout as though you have already done store demonstrations. All of these digital substitutions can be done with Adobe Photoshop or other software programs. Art schools have people who can do this, or hire a graphic artist (look in the Yellow Pages).

4. Prepare a brief portfolio for the buyer with your product information, focus group and market test results, any testimonials you might have, and a list of your industry helpers and advisors.

5. Set up an appointment with the buyer. Resist sending information by snail mail or e-mail. You will have a much better chance with a formal presentation. If the buyer resists setting an appointment, send a cover letter with this information only:
   - You have a new product to meet a desire or need. Don't say what the product is.
   - In market tests you have outsold competitor products. List products that the target customer sells as the competitors you have outsold in test stores.
   - You are in a position to produce a certain number of units per month.
   - The target customer is your first choice for distribution and you are willing to work on an exclusive basis for an introductory period.
   - You have several promotional programs in mind similar to ones the target customer has already used with great success.
   - You would like a chance to present your product in person and

explain how you can cooperate with the target to create excitement in its store or business.

6. Deliver a convincing presentation. A flip chart easel presentation is probably best since the buyer may not give you enough time to set up for a laptop presentation. An 18- by 24-inch easel works best. You can typically buy easels at office supply or art stores. Include these items in the presentation:

   - A picture of the product on a store shelf, if going to a retailer or distributor, or a product in use if you are selling to an end user. Remember, retail and distributor buyers are concerned about whether the product will sell, so concentrate on the product's sales potential rather than on its features.
   - A picture of the product in its package. On this sheet also highlight the competitor products your product outsold in tests.
   - Suggested retail prices, plus the price to the company you are talking to.
   - Need or desire that your product meets. Also include some brief results from focus groups (e.g., 80 percent of focus group participants rated the product as a top-three purchase choice).
   - A chart with a picture of the target's store or logo with the statement, "[target customer's name] is my first choice." Then under it write "for exclusives and special promotional campaigns."
   - Show your layouts of the product on the store shelf or in various promotional flyers where you digitally substituted your product.
   - Highlight your advisors and helpers and state your monthly production volume capacity.
   - Close with a picture of your product and target customer's logo with the statement that you want to work together to develop exciting promotional opportunities.

You want to convey that you are willing to be flexible and creative to develop a program that will work for the customer and that you are willing to do this on an exclusive basis for six months to a year if the company will give you support and commitment to promote the product. Then you can ask for a commitment: "I'd like to work out a program to put 15 units into every store." "Would you be willing to do a 10-store test?" Make it a call to action.

You should also be prepared to answer this question for the company: "Why did you choose me as your top prospect?" Answer by reviewing the steps you used in your selection process. Include these remarks:

- You started by looking for prospects that had a brand-name image with your target customer group.
- You made a list of three to five companies with strong marketing organizations.
- You evaluated each company based on its fit with your product and the support it could offer the target customers.
- Finally, you decided the buyer's company was the best fit for your product because it carries the right mix of products and provides the service target customers want and need.

DEVELOP A SALES PLAN TO PENETRATE ACCOUNTS: BUILD MOMENTUM IN THE MARKET

I have found that inventors tend to use a scattered approach to selling their product. They put everything out to everyone and just hope something happens. That rarely works. Inventors need to make an intense effort and many calls to land business, and you can't do that without a plan that focuses on a select number of sales targets at any given point in time. Once you make a major sales effort to your first targets, you can then move on to your second set of targets. Figure 17.2 shows a sample action plan of the actual strategy used for the Java-Log, a fireplace starter log made out of coffee grounds. Plan your sales targets for two years out, and match your target to the resources you have for both sales calls and production capacity. Make certain you have the money and ability to produce the products needed by your target customers. You will inevitably be forced to make changes to your plan, but don't panic too early and switch gears. Remember, buyers you talk to have had many inventors who made one call and then disappeared. Buyers want to see and talk to an inventor at least three or four times before committing to a purchase.

Many inventors don't think a sales plan like the one in Figure 17.2 is ambitious enough, but in fact it is very ambitious. However, it calls for a totally different perspective. The goal is not how many prospects you can call on. The goal is how many people you can meet and talk to at your target stores. At the Home Hardware stores the Java-Log inventors talked to buyers, store managers, and chief executives. They attended the same functions as Home Hardware people; they communicated test results; they used the contacts of community people they knew—bankers, politicians, economic development people—to help them land the account. Concentrate your efforts on in-depth calling, setting up special promotion programs and providing every bit of service you can to land your prospect accounts.

Figure 17.2   Sample Timeline for Action

Sales Action Plan
Robustion Products, St. Laurent, Quebec, Canada
For the Java-Log

Product description: The Java-Log is a fireplace log made from recycled coffee grounds. The product sells for $2.50 per log and burns hotter than wood or rolled paper logs.

Target distribution: Hardware stores where competitive rolled paper products are sold.

Base-load target account: Home Hardware, a major hardware chain in Canada with centralized buying.

[Comment: The inventor of Java-Log had to set up a collection system to obtain used coffee grounds from coffee stores and had limited financial resources. Selling to a Canadian hardware chain provided Robustion Products an optimum market size for its first two years of business.]

Sales plan action timeline

Date	Action
Summer 2001	Initiate calls with three Canadian hardware chains to propose a sales test in the Montreal area for the fall/winter 2001 season.
September 2001	Finalize an agreement to run a test with one Canadian hardware store, with Home Hardware being the preferred chain due to its nationwide Canadian coverage.
Fall 2001	Sales test complete in a small number of Home Hardware stores.
Summer 2002	Sign an exclusive deal for nationwide Canadian distribution for the Java-Log with Home Hardware stores.
Fall 2002	Initiate Internet sales for Java-Log.
Spring 2003	Secure three manufacturer's representatives. One for Eastern Canada, one for Western Canada, and one for New England for fall/winter 2003–2004 season to sell to individual hardware stores and attend buying shows for hardware chains.
Summer 2003	Secure at least 10 Home Depot test sites in Canada for the fall/winter 2003–2004 season.
Summer 2004	Secure five additional manufacturer's representatives for complete coverage across the northern half of the United States
Summer 2004	Add all Canadian Home Depot stores and secure a test market of 10 to 15 Home Depot stores in New England.
Fall 2004	Arrange for a test market at a local Montreal area supermarket chain.

18

STEP 8C. PRESERVE YOUR CAPITAL: STRUCTURE DEALS TO KEEP CONTROL

New product introductions are a risky business, and much of the risk comes from the high cost of producing and selling products. Licensing and turbo-outsourcing cut those risks by sharing the burden with partner companies. You can do the same when you are introducing a product on your own by receiving financial help from investors, vendors, and customers.

The timing of financial help, whether it comes from vendors or investors, is important, because the value of a share of stock can skyrocket as a product achieves market success. An inventor might sell a share for 10 to 25 cents if he or she is raising money for a patent or prototype. That same share might be worth $1 after a successful sales test, and it might be worth $5 once you start getting orders in the market. So although an inventor may want lots of money in the bank, waiting until it's absolutely necessary allows the inventor to sell shares for the highest possible price—and also to retain a controlling interest in his or her company.

You should follow the advice in Chapter 3 (pages 56 to 61) to bring in industry helpers and other investors early on for a low price per share, but you want to limit the amount of money you take in at that time. You can get $1,000 to $2,000 from people to help launch your business while still owning the vast majority of the shares. But you should use the many tactics in this chapter to keep your sale of shares to outsiders as low as possible. Chapter 3 (pages 61 to 67) covered an overall funding plan that phases in the sell of stock throughout the introduction process. This chapter explains how to minimize the stock you actually have to sell in that funding process.

- Offer early deals with buyback clauses: Save control of your company.
- Provide options to buy stock at a later date: Sweeten the deal for early investors.
- Sell vendors on long-term benefits: Offer loyalty in return for concessions.
- Learn all the tactics for stretching the dollar: Use both sales and purchasing tactics.
- Structure short-term financial support from investors: Obtain financial backing with minimal loss of ownership.
- Look for private-label or OEM agreements to back loans: Avoid diluting your ownership position.

Offering Shares Keeps the Project Moving

Joe Robertson loved his swimming pool, but he quickly tired of the drudgery of cleaning the pool filter. His filter was three feet long and had to be thoroughly rinsed with a hose every day. The job took 30 minutes. One day, Robertson was cleaning a paint roller and he noticed how easy it was when water pressure spun the paint roller during cleaning. He went to work immediately to develop a holder that would let his pool filter spin, too. After a few false starts, Robertson had a very crude prototype of his product, the Spin Clean, ready. He wanted a professional-looking prototype, and he solicited some quotes from prototype shops, but they were all too expensive.

Robertson went looking for a partner who could help design and build a professional-looking prototype. He found a mechanical engineer, Dave Dudley, who agreed to help in return for part ownership. Dudley pinpointed several problems in Robertson's initial design, corrected those errors, and finalized an initial production design.

Dudley produced the first prototype by machining parts out of plastic, which was time-consuming and expensive, but the prototype helped Robertson and Dudley perfect the Spin Clean's design. Then the partners were ready to do some in-store product testing. They needed to make a small production run, and Dudley was convinced a mold was the only way to get "looks like, works like" preproduction test units. When the original mold estimates came in at $20,000, Robertson and Dudley headed for their local inventors' club to *see if someone could suggest a low-cost solution. There they met Ben Ridge, a silicone-mold expert (www.reproduce100s.com), who offered to make a temporary mold that could produce enough products for a test in seven pool supply stores. Ridge offered to be a partner, but Robertson decided to pay for his services to avoid further diluting his ownership position.*

With a successful test, Robertson was able to land a 2,500-unit order from Leslie's Pool Market, a chain with 500 stores. The temporary mold was not able to handle that type of production. But the partners, with Ridge's help, found a manufacturer who, based on the purchase order from Leslie's, was willing to fund the tooling and wait for payment until Leslie's paid Robertson and Dudley.

OFFER EARLY DEALS WITH BUYBACK CLAUSES: SAVE CONTROL OF YOUR COMPANY

Prototypes, engineering work, and patents are all expensive, and they all occur when the shares of your product have the lowest value. You might have to give up 25 percent or more of your ownership if you don't have many of your own financial resources. But you can use a simple tactic to help you buy back those shares. When you sell shares or exchange ownership for work in progress, do it with a provision that you can buy back the shares within 24 months at two to four times the value of the shares at the time of issue. For example, let's say you need $3,000 to help pay for a patent. In return for the $3,000 you offer a 15 percent share in your product, which might represent 30,000 shares (at 10 cents per share) compared to your own 170,000 shares. With a buyback clause, you have the option of buying back the investor's shares for $9,000 (if the buyback clause designates three times the original investment).

This is an effective tool for an inventor because the product might have a successful initial sales period, a provisional order from a big customer, or even an actual order within two years. The stock might then be worth $1 to $2 per share. The inventor could buy back the 30,000 shares from the original investor by selling just 1,500 to 3,000 shares at the higher price, and the original investor gets a good return on his or her investment. If your investors want to hold onto shares, you can designate the buy back offer for 50 or 75 percent of the shares at two to four times the investor's original investment. The early investor would keep his or her shares if your product starts slower than expected and you can't buy back the shares.

PROVIDE OPTIONS TO BUY STOCK AT A LATER DATE: SWEETEN THE DEAL FOR EARLY INVESTORS

Inventors want to take on investment slowly, but some investors, especially experienced start-up investors and industry helpers, aren't anxious to invest only $1,000. That investment is so small, some investors might not be willing to take the time to investigate your idea. The same situation exists for your industry helpers. They might think their profit potential is too small to justify spending the time to help you.

One way to avoid this problem is to offer the investors and industry helpers future options in exchange for their initial investment, at a higher price, based on achieving certain milestones. Offering future investment opportunities helps to motivate both investors and industry helpers to believe your product could eventually provide a big payoff. An example of executing this tactic would be to initially sell 10,000 shares of stock for $0.10 a share, or $1,000. With that purchase the investor or helper would also have the option to purchase 10,000 shares at $2,500 when the inventor makes a preproduction run for market tests, 10,000 shares for $10,000 when the product goes into production runs in excess of 5,000 units, and 10,000 shares for $20,000 when the product exceeds $30,000 in sales for three consecutive months. Be sure to put a time limit on these options. For example, investors and helpers might have 30 days to execute their options once the investor sends them a written notice that the product has achieved a milestone that activates an option. This tactic provides the inventor flexibility to bring on investments while maintaining as much ownership of the product as possible.

SELL VENDORS ON LONG-TERM BENEFITS: OFFER LOYALTY IN RETURN FOR CONCESSIONS

Vendors or partner companies, particularly manufacturing partners, are always a great source of funding, especially because you often don't need to give up any shares of your company. If you are not going to manufacture the product yourself, the number one source of funding for your venture can be your contract manufacturer. Chapter 11 (pages 197 to 199) discussed all the advantages manufacturers gain by producing a "hot-selling" inventor product. The very same situation exists for manufacturers who are making your product on a contract basis. You can often get a contract manufacturer to pick up or amortize some of the costs if you can convince the company of your product's potential and commit to giving the manufacturer production orders for one to two years. You can use a presentation similar to the one discussed in Chapter 13 (pages 217 to 219) when you request any of the following:

- *Amortized tooling and start-up costs.* When a manufacturer amortizes costs it takes all of the start-up costs and then prorates the charge over a certain number of units. For example if the start-up costs are $25,000, the amortized costs might be $0.25 per unit. This is a big cost savings to the inventor, but you will need to convince the manufacturer that you can sell 100,000 units. If the manufacturer wants a reward for its risk, you might need to offer to pay the amortized costs per unit for 25 to 50 percent more units than required to cover the costs. In the preceding example you might agree to pay the extra $0.25 per unit for 125,000 or 150,000 units rather than the 100,000 units that would cover the tooling costs. That extra charge may seem expensive, but it is usually preferable to giving up shares in the company by taking on additional investments.

- *Engineering support and product improvements.* This support is often available at no charge from the manufacturer since the manufacturer will consider it as sales costs to land new business. Engineers at the company might have suggestions that can lower your product's costs or improve its performance. They might be able to help you find better sourcing for components, and they can often help you do the engineering documentation you might need for regulatory approvals or to meet the demands of large customers. Inventors should always ask for an engineering review of the product from the manufacturer's engineers. You aren't obligated to take their suggestions, but you might find that their suggestions are extremely helpful, both to achieve lower prices and to produce a more durable product.

- *Extended terms.* The worst situation for inventors is when manufacturers request 100 percent down payment, and the best situation is when manufacturers agree to be paid after the inventor is paid. This is a major issue. Four to six months is the typical time that elapses between a manufacturer's purchase of material and the manufacturer's receipt of payment. If you are paying for everything up front, you need operating cash equal to three to four months of sales, which could easily double or triple the investment you need to launch your company.

  If the manufacturer won't be flexible because it is worried that you won't be able to pay, you might offer a guarantee to the manufacturer from your investors in order to avoid selling too many shares. For example, let's say the manufacturer wants up to $100,000 in guarantees to cover nonpayment, either by the inventor's customers or by the inventor, before the manufacturer will accept delaying receipt of payments until the inventor is paid.

That way the manufacturer will still be paid even if your customer doesn't pay you. You could have your investors provide this guarantee return for $10,000 to $20,000 worth of stock. In effect, they get the extra stock for accepting the risk of guaranteeing payment to the manufacturer if a customer doesn't pay you. Your success with this tactic depends on the investors believing in your product and having the financial wherewithal to cover the guarantee.

LEARN ALL THE TACTICS FOR STRETCHING THE DOLLAR: USE BOTH SALES AND PURCHASING TACTICS

If you are manufacturing the product yourself, you will have a range of vendors that sell products to you with whom you will want to negotiate for a number of favorable terms. Even if you are using a contract manufacturer, you will have other bills you will need to pay, including packaging charges, freight charges, legal and accounting fees, and a host of other fees where you might be able to stretch your dollar. Vendors are not your only source for operating funds; you can also cut your need for operating capital by means of the terms you offer to your customers, such as requiring down payments and offering discounts for prompt payment. You can also use funding or loans from banks or other financial groups to help fund your business so that you don't have to sell more shares.

The following list is a good starting point for ways to eke out operating cash without taking on additional investors. You should also visit your local Small Business Development Center for advice on other tactics and to find out what other programs might be available in your state to help you preserve cash. Go to www.sba.gov/sbdc, which has a link to a complete list of SBDC sites in the United States.

- *Using orders to borrow money.* If you have a large order and you can't afford to fund it, often you can get an investor's family member or friend to furnish the money in return for receiving interest. If you have an order for $20,000 and need $10,000 to produce it, try to borrow the money with the promise of paying back the $10,000 plus some additional amount in interest when you get paid. You might offer a 10 percent interest rate for what will end up being a four- to six-month loan. This option is worthwhile only if you are making a minimum of 30 to 40 percent profit on your product. That way you can afford to pay back the loan and still have a profit left over to finance future sales. If your margins are lower than 30 percent, you will end up making very little on the order and will just have to borrow again when the next big order comes in. With a low margin, you are better off getting an investment of

$10,000 and giving up shares so you don't constantly have to go through the hassle of borrowing money on every order.

- *Selling products for cash.* One reason inventors can profit from Internet sites and trade show attendance is that they can sell products and be paid immediately. Selling some portion of your sales for cash helps you finance future growth. You can also offer a discount to retailers or distributors for cash on delivery (COD) purchases. You might need to offer a 5 to 10 percent discount, but the customer might help you out if you explain you are a new company with tight cash flow.

- *Selling receivables.* Some inventors don't like to offer COD terms. It makes them appear financially unstable. Instead they will sell their receivables, which is also called *factoring.* A receivable is an invoice with an amount due. If you ship $10,000 worth of products to a customer, you will generate an invoice for $10,000. That is money you expect to get paid, and it is referred to in industry as a *receivable.* If customers are financially sound, receivables can be sold for 90 to 95 percent of their face value. You can find factoring companies by doing an Internet search (try the keywords "factoring companies" or "buying receivables"). Factoring companies are listed in the Yellow Pages of your phone book as *Factors.*

- *Asking for down payments.* Inventors can ask for a 25 to 50 percent down payment, especially if their product is made to order for a customer. Inventors can also ask for a down payment on a private-label order or for an order accompanied by a special request such as special colors or unique packaging. Customers will worry about your financial status if you ask for a down payment for routine retail or distributor orders, but you can ask for a down payment if you've been working with those retailers or distributors through the introduction process and they understand you are an underfinanced inventor/entrepreneur.

- *Receiving an advance from distributors in return for an exclusive.* Distributors might be willing to pay an advance on their purchases to help you start production—provided the product is something they want in the market. This arrangement can work either as an advance on the first order or as an advance that is paid off with a 10 to 20 percent discount on purchases. For example, if the distributor gives a $10,000 advance, it will receive a 10 percent discount on all purchases until the advance is paid off, which means a 10 percent discount on its first $100,000 of purchases.

    This strategy is difficult to implement when you are selling your standard product. But it is a fabulous option when the distributor or retailer tells you: "I really like your idea but I feel it needs a few changes." Rather than running off and making the product changes, offer this response. "Thanks for your input. Maybe we can take your idea and make it pay off for both our companies. For a small advance, I could make those changes, and in return for the advance, I could offer an exclusive agreement to you for one year. Is that something you'd like to pursue?"

You can use this same strategy when you talk to a company in another market that thinks the product needs a few modifications for its market. This project might be more involved than a distributor advance. A request for product modifications can be answered with a request for codevelopment funds or an advance. "We can produce a market-ready product. You can provide a development fund to produce models and prototypes for testing, and in return I'll commit to not selling to any of your direct competitors."

- *Extended credit.* I discussed extending credit to the manufacturer. You can use the same tactics with all of your vendors. If you purchase $10,000 worth of products per month with 60-day terms (which means you pay the vendor in 60 days rather than the standard 30 days), you will need $10,000 less in operating capital. I've found that you'll have the best results if you tell vendors in advance that you will pay them in 60 days. Otherwise they might start to worry that you won't pay them at all and cut off your credit to you and ask for cash on delivery (COD) terms.
- *Cash discount terms.* A common payment term on invoices is 3 percent 10, net 30. The 3 percent 10 means that customers can get a 3 percent discount on the invoice if they pay within 10 days. The net 30 means that payment is due 30 days after the invoice is issued. Customers with strong cash positions often take the 3 percent discount, because that is a much better deal than leaving money in a bank. The early discount can cut into your operating cash needs, but some companies pay in 30 days and still take the 3 percent 10 terms. If companies do that, simply remove the 3 percent 10 terms from their future invoices.

STRUCTURE SHORT-TERM FINANCIAL SUPPORT FROM INVESTORS: OBTAIN FINANCIAL BACKING WITH MINIMAL LOSS OF OWNERSHIP

Inventors face many legal considerations when they have 10 or more investors. You should consult with an attorney from the moment you start to raise money to be sure you are not violating any state or federal laws.

Once you approach 10 investors, you may be required to issue a formal private-placement stock offering. *Private placement* is the term for stock that is not sold publicly (as an over-the-counter stock or on one of the stock exchanges), but sold only by the company or through its broker. Even if you don't need a private-placement document, you may be governed by regulations regarding accredited (investors with more than $200,000 in annual income and $1 million in assets) and nonaccredited investors. The legal fees for preparing private-placement fund-raising documentation can run anywhere from $15,000 to $100,000 and take anywhere from 30 to 90 days.

Inventors have a problem when they are ready to launch their product after a successful market test. They need to raise money for the launch, including paying for legal fees, at a moment when their shares have a relatively low value. Another problem is that inventors don't want to lose market momentum, and fund-raising can take 90 to 120 days. Inventors need quick capital, and the legal requirements can significantly delay a market introduction. Bridge loans are the typical tool used to allow inventors to launch their product and still sell shares for maximum value. A bridge loan usually is in place for 90 to 270 days and provides capital for launching the product with the understanding that the inventor will launch a fund-raising campaign to repay the loan at some designated interest rate, often 10 to 12 percent. In addition, the investor gets a certain number of options to buy stock at the existing stock price when the bridge loan is executed. The number of option shares is equal to anywhere from 5 to 20 percent of the loan.

For example, consider an inventor who needs a bridge loan of $100,000 to launch his product. His product currently has finished a test run, and the inventor has determined each share is worth $1 and that after the product launch the share will be worth $3. A bridge loan benefits the inventor, as he might be able to launch the product and sell stock for $3 a share rather than selling the stock for $1 before the product launch. The offer to a bridge financier would be to:

- Borrow $100,000 until $100,000 is secured in a fund-raising campaign
- Pay 10 percent annual interest on the loan until it is repaid
- Grant options to buy 10,000 shares of stock at $1 per share

If your company succeeds, the bridge financier gets 10 percent interest, all his money back, plus an option to buy 10,000 shares of stock for a $1. Since those shares will soon be worth $3, the financier's option on 10,000 shares for $1 would be worth $20,000 (i.e., the $30,000 the stock is worth at $3 less the $10,000 the investor would need to pay to acquire the shares). If you fail, the bridge financier loses his money. The advantage of this strategy is that the inventor gets cash to keep moving forward without a delay and that he needs to sell far fewer shares to raise the capital needed.

People who do bridge financing are sophisticated investors, and you will need to show that your idea has a great chance to succeed and that you have either a pool of willing investors to draw from or a private-placement broker who has agreed to take on the sale of your stock. Your attorney may know of bridge financiers and brokers who handle private placements. Some brokers who handle private placements are investment bankers, and others are smaller regional stock brokerage firms. If your lawyer can't help you, talk to the people at your local entrepreneurs' club. You can locate the clubs in your area, as well as potential private-placement brokers and bridge financiers, at your local Small Business Development Center (www.sba.gov/sbdc has a link to U.S. SBDC sites).

LOOK FOR PRIVATE-LABEL OR OEM AGREEMENTS TO BACK LOANS: AVOID DILUTING YOUR OWNERSHIP POSITION

The advantage of a bank loan over an investment is that the inventor doesn't offer shares of the company. The disadvantage of a bank loan is that you have to pay the loan plus interest over a certain time period. Inventors typically have trouble getting bank loans because they are brand-new businesses without any firm guarantee of success. One way to offer enough evidence of success is to secure one large customer, offer that customer a special arrangement, and use its purchase order or contract to secure the loan. The three most common methods for obtaining a big order are private label, OEM, and exclusive distribution and retail agreements (discussed in Chapter 17, pages 273 to 275).

Private-Label Agreements

A private-label agreement is one in which your product is sold under another company's name and in that company's package. Private-label agreements are not necessarily exclusive agreements; inventors can have a private-label agreement and still sell the product to other customers them-selves. Most private-label agreements call for the product to be slightly different, either with more upscale materials, different color schemes, or slightly different features. But the product doesn't necessarily have to be different. Follow these six steps to find a private label prospect.

1. *Find prospect companies.* The three best types of prospects are com-panies that already sell private-label products, companies that

have broad product lines; and companies with complementary products. You can find companies that provide private-label products by reading trade magazines or talking to people in the industry at association meetings. Companies with broad product lines often use private-label products to fill voids in their line or just to have enough products to dominate shelf space at a retailer. You can find companies with broad product lines at trade shows or by reading trade magazine ads. Complementary products, which are products that work together to meet a need, almost always sell better together. For example, a company with a better spackling spatula will probably double its sales if it is sold with a better feather sanding device for smoothing out walls after spackling. The two products used in combination provide an easy-to-use wall repair kit that will be more appealing to retailers and consumers than either product alone.

2. *Prioritize your prospects.* The best prospects are those with strong complementary products, as your product will help the company sell more of its other products. The second choice is companies that already private-label, and the third choice is companies with broad product lines. Choose the bigger companies with a good credit rating, as an agreement with them offers the best chance to land a bank loan. Check out the companies' credit scores in a *Dun and Bradstreet Company Directory,* found at larger local libraries, or visit the web site smallbusiness.dnb.com.

3. *Produce a mock-up package with the target customer's logo to present to the company.* Look at other packages from the target company before preparing your package to see whether the company has a certain look or style to its package.

4. *Set your price.* A private-label agreement works only if you make a profit from each sale, first to pay back the bank loan and second to help fund the rest of your business. But you can't set your price too high or the product will end up overpriced for the market. Set your price 20 percent above your manufacturing costs. You can't go lower or you just won't make any money. If that price results in a retail price that is too high, a private-label agreement probably isn't a good choice for you.

5. *Learn the names of the sales and marketing managers of your target companies.* You can usually find this on the companies' web sites, in their annual reports, or just by calling them. Contact individuals and set up an appointment. By far the best strategy is to set up three or four appointments with different prospects at a trade show. Sales and marketing people are easier to meet at trade shows, and you will save on travel expenses.

6. *Prepare an easel and computer presentation.* Don't make the presentation too long—five to seven minutes is best. Show these points in your presentation.
   - Why the product is needed. Problems the market has or desires of end users.
   - Positive focus group results or some other type of market testing information. Keep it short, with two or three bullet points. Include the suggested retail price point indicated by the research.
   - Picture of the product. You should also be ready to present the prototype.
   - Picture of the product in that company's package.
   - Price at which you are prepared to sell the product.

OEM Agreements

OEM is an acronym for *original equipment manufacturer,* the term used when you sell a product to a manufacturer for use on the products that it resells. Martin Connolly, as an example, created a new-style racing wheel, the Rev-X, which he sold through his company Spinergy to bike shops around the country. He also sold the product to bike manufacturers that used the wheel on the bikes sold to end users and bike shops. The sale to bike manufacturers is considered an OEM sale, since it is provided to a company that is making and selling new (also referred to as *original*) equipment. OEM sales to big companies can provide a base of business for the inventor to use as leverage in obtaining a bank loan. Follow these six steps to proceed with an OEM sale.

1. *Decide whether your product is an OEM candidate.* Your product has to be incorporated into another company's product, and only some inventions fit this category. Other inventions are stand-alone products and are not candidates for an OEM sale.
2. *Prepare a list of candidates.* Once you decide on the type of company that can use your product, go to the trade association or trade magazine web sites to find a list of companies that could use the product. Use *Gales' Source of Publications and Broadcast Media* to find trade magazines and *Gales' Source of Associations,* available at larger libraries, to find associations if you can't find them on an Internet search.
3. *Prepare an analysis of how your product is better than one the company is using now.* If your product offers a new feature, explain how your product improves the OEM's product. If possible, do focus group tests with your industry helpers or with end users

to substantiate that your product provides improved performance of the target company's products.

4. *Set the price.* You need the same 20 percent profit discussed in the private-label agreement action plan.

5. *Find contact names of salespeople, regional managers, and marketing people.* Contact them at a trade show or arrange for an appointment. These contacts won't be able to make the purchasing decision, but you'll need their support to make a presentation to the company.

6. *Prepare an easel and computer presentation.* Emphasize the following with slides or pages:
   - Show a picture of your product by itself.
   - List the product's key benefits.
   - Illustrate briefly any market research results, especially results stating how people believed your product improved the OEM's product.
   - Explain how you think the OEM could incorporate your product into its own product.
   - List the key benefits of the OEM incorporating your product into its own product.
   - State your product's target price.

19

STEP 9C. DEVELOP A BUSINESS PLAN: CREATING HIGH VALUE FOR YOUR COMPANY

Stories of bootstrap entrepreneurs are revered legends in American culture. Starting out with no money, never borrowing a penny, and still creating a multi-million-dollar business is still a goal of many inventors today. These inventors are not about to do a business plan and raise money. Unfortunately, bootstrapping fails far more often than it succeeds, and inventors are better off forgetting about bootstrapping and instead planning on raising money right from the start. You need to raise money because windows of market opportunities might exist for only six months to a year, and inventors need to move fast to succeed; often, investments in tooling and fixtures are required to produce products at the right price points; today's consumers demand upscale product appearances that require a manufacturing investment; and inventors need inventory and operating cash if they plan to sell to large companies.

The number one reason for raising money is that market momentum is essential for success. You need to look like a player in the market; you need to be able to support large orders; and you need to participate in trade shows to develop a stream of business. If you don't look like a player, people assume you won't last, and both small and large customers will be reluctant to buy from you.

Inventors need a business plan to raise money for their start-up company. The plan I recommend is a hybrid of a fund-raising business plan and an operations plan, which offers elements of both. I believe this approach is needed because inventors often don't have their own management experience, nor do they have it on their team, and that experience is what banks and investors look for when they evaluate companies for a loan or investment. Inventors need to compensate for the lack of management experience by showing that they have carefully considered the operations plans and cash flow requirements of their business.

Business plans are offer more details than turbo-outsourcing and licensing plans. Those plans focus primarily on the product and the market opportunity. When you start your own company, most bankers and investors will look first at whether you have the management skills to control expenses, produce products at a profitable cost point, and create a steady flow of sales. Investors believe that inventors without those skills will probably fail no matter how much their product is needed. Although the plan will feature the product and the opportunity, inventors need to demonstrate in their plan that they will successfully manage their company. This chapter helps the inventor with these concepts.

- Understand the three-year payback: Generate funds for the right size product launch.
- Deliver what the reader wants: Explain three points to entice investors.
- Prepare the business plan: Include key elements for success.

Stage Growth Works Best

Wayne Willert is a building and roofing contractor who realized that standard gutter bolts (the steel bolts that hold gutters to the frame of a house) were not the best solution for attaching gutters. The problem Willert recognized is that driving the steel bolt into an aluminum gutter produces a wicking effect in the aluminum that creates a weak bond. The obvious solution was to use aluminum bolts to hold up the gutter. That solution had been tried before, but the torque required to push the bolt into the wood fascia of a house was too high and the aluminum bolts would bend or break.

Willert felt the solution would be to design a bolt that required far less force to penetrate the wood, was resistant to breaking, and offered firm holding power in the wood fascia of the house. Willert tested his Gutter-Bolt on several projects with good results. Then he had several other contractors try the Gutter-Bolt, also with success. After that, he was able to sell his product at a home show and in a local hardware store. Willert then hired a contract manufacturer to make a production run, and he was ready to go.

Willert's introduction strategy called for starting with low-volume production and sales to local hardware stores and then to increase production and expand sales, first regionally and then nationally, to independent hardware stores, to chain hardware stores, and to distributors that serve the professional contractor market. But before Willert could get started, a rack jobber approached Willert. The rack jobber had shelf space at Home Depot and promised huge sales, though at a lower margin. Willert was tempted but turned down the offer because he wasn't able to finance the big order and because he worried that he would never make much money at the lower margin. Instead, Willert stuck to his original plan. He started with direct sales to independent hardware stores, which represent two-thirds of his sales. These sales without a distributor had a higher margin and allowed Willert to finance improved tooling to lower his manufacturing costs. Once costs were lower, Willert added Allied Building Products Corporation, a distributor to the construction trade; Hardware Wholesalers, Inc., a distributor to retail hardware stores; and the Do It Best Corporation, a supplier to Do It Best hardware stores.

The Gutter-Bolt is a success today because Willert coordinated his plan for production and sales. He understood the profits available to him from each market and focused on markets that would provide the pricing he needed based on his manufacturing costs. Willert's plan allowed him to stay on a course to establish his successful profitable company.

UNDERSTAND THE THREE-YEAR PAYBACK: GENERATE FUNDS FOR THE RIGHT-SIZE PRODUCT LAUNCH

A business plan for inventors isn't simply a matter of figuring how much money you need and then writing a plan to raise that money. Investors and banks typically want to see that an inventor-managed company will be able to earn its total investment back in two to three years—that is, not just the bank's money but *all* the money needed to launch the product. This means if you need $300,000 to launch your company, you need $300,000 of profits after three years of sales.

Inventor business plans I see often have two years of losses, or they show the inventor working part-time on the product and not drawing a salary for several years. Those types of plans won't work for sophisticated investors and banks. That doesn't sound like a successful company. You must work full-time, you must have your salary and all other costs listed in the plan, and you must have a sales plan to produce profits within six to nine months, or you probably won't be able to raise money.

Before starting their plan, inventors need to evaluate the right business that will give them a three-year payback. Figure 19.1 evaluates the d-skin, a plastic disc that you lay on a CD or DVD to prevent it from being scratched.

In small markets the product sells at a wholesale price of $0.50 and in large markets at a wholesale price of $0.25. You won't be able to predict your exact profit margin until you have completed a full-scale financial analysis for your company. As a substitute, though, I've found that you can estimate profits at 5 percent of sales and be in the ballpark. For example, a $300,000 investment will require sales of $6 million over three years to hit the goal.

In many cases, this evaluation will reveal that the inventor isn't yet ready for a business plan because the initial market won't produce a three-year payback. Inventors need to switch to a market that will support a three-year payback. If inventors don't have contacts in that market, they should obtain them before writing the plan. The market-size profit evaluation requires you to estimate market size (see Chapter 3, pages 70 to 71) and manufacturing costs at different sales levels (see Chapter 1, pages 26 to 28). It also calls for you to estimate your market share or your sales levels.

The most believable way to estimate your sales is by citing sales of other inventor products on the market or by estimating your sales at 5 and 10 percent of the total market. The 5 and 10 percent assumptions won't be accurate but should give you a range of sales you could hit. To find the numbers of other inventors' products, find inventors with products at trade shows, in trade magazine publicity releases, and by asking your

Figure 19.1   Market Size and Profit Evaluation for the d-skin

Targeted Customers	Computer Gamers and Gadget Lovers	Company Technology Departments	Small to Midsize Businesses through Office Supply Stores	Market to all through Big Retailers Like Best Buy
Market explanation	Sold through magazines, Internet sites, and computer gaming stores	Sold through office supply distributors that sell directly to large companies	Sales to office supplies to protect backup files and software discs	Sold for computer users, music and DVD users
Production volume	1,000,000	3,000,000	10,000,000	25,000,000
Start-up costs	$125,000	$125,000	$500,000	$500,000
Sales volume	$500,000	$1,500,000	$2,500,000	$6,250,000
Three-year profits @5% of sales	$75,000	$225,000	$375,000	$937,500
Three-year payback	No	Yes	No	Yes

contacts. Call the inventor company, explain you are an inventor selling to the same market, and reveal that you are trying to estimate sales for a business plan. At least half of the inventors will give you some indication of their sales level.

DELIVER WHAT THE READER WANTS: EXPLAIN THREE POINTS TO ENTICE INVESTORS

There is an old adage that states "Nothing sells success like success." There is no doubt that investors and banks want to help fund companies if they can sense success and market momentum. To oblige them, you have to demonstrate that your product has had successful market tests, that you have strong management skills, and that other people are investing in the company.

Sales to Date for Market Testing

Investors and other funding sources are skeptical when entrepreneurs state that they "sold $45,000 last year but will sell $2 million next year" if only they get the funding. That sales jump is too big. A market test, however, is designed to sell only a small amount to prove that the product will sell, to find out what packaging and promotion works best, and to iron out production problems. A jump from $45,000 in a *market test* to $2 million in sales is far more believable.

I believe that inventors appear to be more cautious and better managers when they state that their first sales period was market testing. It is prudent to make sure a product will sell before investing large amounts of money in a product launch. Investors value prudence.

Strong Management Team

To an investor, you're not a strong manager until you've successfully taken a product to market. Since most new product inventors haven't done that, they need to rely on the support of others to show management. You need to list your industry helpers as partners, and you need to list your contacts at consulting groups such as the Small Business Development Centers (SDBCs) or other local small-business help groups. Find people to assist you and include them in your plan. If at all possible, try to get at least some of the advisors to invest money in your project.

You also need to be sure you have advisors or industry helpers with engineering or manufacturing expertise. Manufacturing costs and start-up costs are difficult to predict, and even established companies with strong management make big mistakes. I've been on projects where the estimates of both have been off 50 to 100 percent. Investors will be skeptical of any costs you present in a plan unless you have people with strong engineering or manufacturing backgrounds on your team. If you don't have that, you may need to use a contract manufacturer to begin production simply because investors will have more confidence in its estimates of costs.

Strong Equity Position from Investors and Self-Funding

Unfortunately, inventors often don't try to raise money until they are totally broke. That leaves them in a vulnerable position, as investors will want too much of the company, plus it makes the inventors look like they can't manage their business. For the best success, try not to raise more than 80 percent of the money at any given point in time from professional investors or banks. Raise the rest from your own funds, your industry helpers, or your friends and families. Figure 19.2 shows how an inventor can demonstrate an orderly financial plan in which he or she brings equity to the venture from a circle of supporters.

Figure 19.2   Funding History

Activity Funded	From Inventor	From Family and Friends	From Industry Helpers	From Contract Manufacturer	From Independent Investors
Preliminary stages, including patents and prototypes	$8,000	$4,000	$3,000	$2,000 in-kind support	$0
Initial sales tests	$2,000	$1,000	$1,000	$2,000 in-kind help	$0
First production run	$2,000	$4,000	$1,000	$4,000 temporary tooling	$4,000
Initial marketing campaign	$1,000	$1,000	$1,000	$0	$1,000
Money required for market expansion	$1,000	$3,000	$10,000	$15,000 tooling amortization	$40,000

PREPARE THE BUSINESS PLAN: INCLUDE KEY ELEMENTS FOR SUCCESS

Business plans vary in format, but the one I propose includes traditional fund-raising elements, plus operation plan data that is not included in all plans. Depending on your operations and marketing efforts, you may be able to delete some parts of the plan. For example, if you are using a contract manufacturer you don't need to worry about a bill of materials. Customize the format to fit your business. The operational plan data is needed by the inventor to plot his or her strategy, plus it helps to have the data in the plan to overcome concern that investors may have about the inventor's management experience. The outline for the business plan is followed by a discussion of each section of the plan.

BUSINESS PLAN OUTLINE

1. Executive Summary
2. The Product
    a. Description
    b. Intellectual property
    c. Key benefits
    d. Competition
    e. Target customer evaluations
    f. Pricing versus competition
    g. Development status
3. The Market
    a. Target customers
    b. Target dstribution channel
    c. Market size
    d. Key contacts
4. Market Test Results
    a. End-user focus group studies
    b. Summary of key industry contacts' comments
    c. Market sales test results
5. Sales and Marketing Activities
    a. Distribution plan
    b. Major targeted customers
    c. Partnerships and alliances
    d. Promotional plan

    e. External sales team

    f. Internal sales team

    g. Key contacts

6. Manufacturing Overview

    a. Production methods to date

    b. Future production process

    c. Proposed investment

    d. Bill of materials

7. Engineering Team

8. Management Team

9. Action Timeline

10. Funding Required

11. Equity Position

12. Equity Offer

13. Income statements, Balance Sheets, and Cash Flow Statements

EXPLANATION OF BUSINESS PLAN ELEMENTS

Executive Summary

Keep this section short, no more than two pages, and one page is even better. Explain the following:

- What you are doing (you're introducting product X to a market)
- What your sales proposition is (why people will buy your product)
- Why you feel your product will be successful (you sold X dollars worth of product during your initial market test)
- How much money you need
- Your projected sales and profits for three years

Here is a sample executive summary for a tire-cutting product.

ETC Corporation has introduced a tire-cutting device that separates tire treads and sidewalls. The result is that old tires are easier to store and ship and therefore tires with high-quality tread can be recycled. Twenty-five units were sold at $99 each through a tire equipment distribution during an initial market test; ETC requires an additional 85,000 for manufacturing tooling and marketing expenses to sell the product nationally. Sales and profits are expected to be:

	Sales	**Profits**
Year 1	$150,000	$25,000
Year 2	$275,000	$75,000
Year 3	$450,000	$125,000

The Product

If possible, show a picture of your product along with a picture of the product in use or on shelf space.

Description

A short product description, one paragraph is usually enough, plus a description of why you developed the idea, which should be a short description of the need you observed that generated the concept or an experience that made you think the idea was worth pursuing.

Intellectual Property

State any patents or trademarks you have or have applied for. If a patent hasn't been issued yet, state the date the patent was applied for.

Key Benefits

It is important in this section not just to state the benefits, but also to show that your product is a 35 to 40 percent or more improvement over other products in the market. You need to translate your features into a big market advantage. An example is "a new-style diaper bag with eight see-through pockets so moms can find items easily." That statement isn't strong enough. You need to state that "five out of 10 moms found the new diaper bag cut in half the time needed to find items."

Competition

List only the three or four major competitors. These can be products similar to yours or products that people use for meeting the same need. For example, Tekno Bubbles, a party product that produces glow-in-the-dark bubbles, does not have any direct competition. Competition would be other products that people might buy for party intrigue. Do a features-and-benefits comparison and explain why your product is better. Try to position your product as a major advancement over competition. If possible, list the sales numbers for the competitive products, which will reinforce the market potential of your product.

Pricing versus Competition

List your pricing versus the competition, both for end users and to the distribution channel.

Target-Customer Evaluations

Show here any test results you have from focus groups, or list favorable comments you've received from end users who prefer your product to competitors' products.

Development Status

Is your product completely developed, or do you need to make product improvements, changes in design or materials, or change the production method?

The Market

The profit potential of markets varies tremendously. Some markets are growing, customers have passion and commitment, and the use of products is evolving, so there are many opportunities for new products. The gourmet cooking market is an example of a strong market. Gourmet cooks have passion; they spend lots of money on cooking tools; and new trends, new styles, and new dishes provide constant product opportunities for entrepreneurs. Other markets are not so lucky. The pipe wrench market elicits few changes, little passion, and not many product opportunities. You want to illustrate that your target market is one with high profit potential.

Target Customers

Start by stating which end-user customers you have targeted. Next cover these items:

- *Importance of the overall market.* Explain why the activity your product is involved in is important. For a gourmet cooking product, you need to discuss how important gourmet cooking is to target customers and how much money they spend on gourmet cooking products.
- *Importance of your product in the overall market.* Explain why your product is important in the overall market. In the case of a gourmet product, explain why the product is important in the field of gourmet cooking.

Target Distribution Channel

Explain what distribution channel you plan to use, from your internal sales force to the final end user—everyone involved in the channel. List also any key customers in the channel, including manufacturer's sales agents, distributors, and retailers.

Market Size

State how big the channel is and the total volume of products that moves through it. You can possibly get this data from trade associations or trade magazines. If you can't, list the sales data of other products in the channel, which you should be able to get from companies' annual reports or salespeople.

Key Contacts

List any key contacts or key companies in the market. You want to show here that you have either talked to or visited with these contacts, or that you have a way to meet them through other contacts.

Market Test Results

End-User Focus Group Studies

Include a short summary of any focus groups, including how many people listed your product as a top-three purchase choice, how people perceived the product's price, and which other products were evaluated.

Summary of Key Industry Contacts' Comments

It is helpful if you can list favorable contacts from at least three or four people in the market or distribution channel.

Market Sales Test Results

List the stores or customers that you've sold to and the sales results. If possible, compare your product's sales to sales of other products that are nearby on a shelf. Plan readers won't know whether selling five units of your product in a month is good or bad without some frame of reference (e.g., sales of other products).

Sales and Marketing Activities

Distribution Plan

Explain which companies in the distribution channel you are going to approach, what you've done to contact them to date, and how you plan on signing or selling to those companies. You should include a table of the major potential distribution customers and when you plan to contact them. Make sure here that you have sufficient staff or outside sales agents to call on the customers (a minimum of four to five calls) often enough to land an order.

Major Targeted Customers

List major customers you've targeted as potential base-load customers (see Chapter 17, pages 278 to 282).

Partnerships and Alliances

Explain any partnership or alliances you might have signed, or are attempting to sign, that will facilitate sales.

Promotional Plan

This includes trade shows you will be attending, advertising or direct mail campaigns, Internet promotion programs or events, seminars, and any other activities you've planned. This section should also discuss your Internet strategy, whether you will have your own web page or plan to sell through other Internet sites or eBay.

External Sales Team

Detail in this section how you will call on accounts, including inventor calls, calls with your industry helpers, use of manufacturer's representatives, or the use of your own sales team.

Internal Sales Team

This would include how you will handle Internet sales, incoming calls from consumers, and customer service. If your product requires technical service, you should also list here how you will handle that.

Key Contacts

This should be a listing of the key market contacts you have already made and how they will help your sales efforts. For example, you might list the name of the sales manager you know at a major distributor and indicate that the manager has stated that the distributor will carry your product and run joint promotions with you.

Manufacturing Overview

Production Methods to Date

In many cases inventors have produced products with low-volume production methods and have had high costs. Investors might see those costs and think you won't be able to make a profit. This short section shows a progression in your business and that your costs will be lower in the future. State the name and location of your manufacturer if you used one.

Future Production Process

Include an explanation of the production process, whether you will be adding tooling and fixturing, and the name of the manufacturer that you will be using. This section should also mention whether you have an overseas manufacturer and whether you are using an outsourcing broker to control quality. If these don't apply, explain how you plan to ensure that the products produced will meet your specifications. This is an important point, because overseas shipments are made with a letter of credit. That means you deposit the money to purchase the product in a bank, and when the manufacturer ships the product the money is withdrawn from the account. You might not see the product for 10 to 30 days after you pay for it. Without careful quality checks, you could easily receive products you won't be able to sell but have already paid for.

Proposed Investment

State what investments you need to start low-cost manufacturing, including tooling and fixtures, travel to vendors, and initial inventory purchases.

Bill of Materials (BOM)

If you are going to produce the product yourself, include a bill of materials, which is a listing of all the parts in the product, the vendor(s) for each part, and the unit costs. The BOM will end up showing your total material costs. (See Chapter 6, pages 130 to 131, for a sample.)

Engineering Team

Inventors often learn a great deal about making their product, but if they are not engineers, they need to show some engineering backup in case problems arise that are beyond their expertise. The engineering team could consist of acquaintances who will help you when needed, an engineering firm you hire, or engineers at a contract manufacturer. List only the people you can rely on when needed, and include a short description of their background.

Management Team

This includes people who are full-time, your advisors and helpers, and your accounting and legal support. I can't emphasis enough how important management is in an investor's evaluation. You need to list thorough information about key people on your management team, their work history, and the products they have been involved with in the past. The accompanying box shows a sample management summary for John Johnson, who is an industry helper for a C&R Circulation, a company introducing a whole-house air exchanger, which circulates outside air into a new house periodically to counteract the effects of stale air in new houses with very tight construction.

Industry Helper Background

John Johnson, Sales Manager, Midwest Heating and Ventilation Supplies, a distributor of heating and ventilating supplies to Heating and Ventilation Contractors in seven Midwest states. Johnson sells to approximately 250 heating and air-conditioning contractors.

1998–2004 Sales Manager, Midwest Heating and Ventilation
1994–1998 Salesman, Midwest Heating and Ventilation
1988–1994 Salesman, S&H Heating and Air-Conditioning, a Peoria, Illinois contractor
1980–1988 Installer, S&H Heating and Air-Conditioning

Johnson has been involved as a distributor with the introduction of more than 20 major new products, including whole-house humidifiers, mold and fungus vent controls, more efficient furnaces, and stale air monitoring systems. He has also been involved in the launch of the two major air-exchange systems on the market today, one from Carrier and one from Honeywell.

Action Timeline

This is a timeline for 12 to 24 months showing major marketing, manufacturing, and promotional activities. This is not typical for most business plans, but I've found it inspires confidence in investors, especially in cases where an inventor has thin management experience. In some cases, you might want to list an even longer timeline if the product shows tremendous growth potential. The accompanying box shows an action timeline for a new-style cell phone headset, Good Vibrations, which picks up sound vibrations from the user's head to make that person easier to understand. (Talking creates noise vibrations through bones that can be used to accentuate the voice signal in a cell phone, thus making this technology possible.)

Funding Required

You should provide a list that specifies in some detail how you plan on spending the money. You don't need to show here how you will spend each dollar, but you should provide an overview that will raise readers' confidence that you are spending the money wisely. Break the list into major categories, such as marketing, manufacturing, and administrative programs.

**Action Timeline for Good Vibrations—
Improved Cell Phone Headset**

July 2005   Finish fund-raising round for $500,000 for first-
                   phase market expansion, including high-end
                   and cell phone accessory catalogs and major
                   department stores.

August 2005   Order packaging artwork.
                   Contract with an overseas sourcing agent.

September 2005   Approve overseas contract manufacturer.
                   Negotiate favorable terms regarding start-up man-
                   ufacturing costs and payment terms.
                   Finalize sales agreements with the Hello Direct and
                   New Products International catalogs, Bookstone
                   catalogs and stores, and the web stores at
                   www.sun-rise.com, e-corporate gifts.com, and
                   ceo.allroud-shopping.com.

October 2005   Approve preproduction units from manufacturer.
                   Place first order for 30,000 units with manufac-
                   turer.
                   Order packaging for 100,000 units.

November 2005   Finalize details of order from Nieman Marcus.
                   Add two sales agents for sales to high-end depart-
                   ment stores.
                   Obtain first 25 units for major publicity campaign
                   to key magazines and newspapers.

December 2005   Secure orders from major vendors for February
                   delivery.
                   Perform first article (*first article* refers to the first
                   units produced) inspection.
                   Continue publicity program.

January 2006   Take delivery of initial production run.

February 2006   Initiate product shipment to first-phase customers
                   (high-end and cell phone accessory catalogs and
                   department stores).

March 2006   Exhibit at three major electronics products trade
                   shows per year, the first is in March.

May 2006   Order second 30,000 units for first-phase market.
                   Initiate second round of financing of $1,000,000 to
                   expand into the second phase of market expan-
                   sion, which includes a private-label contract

                                                              (Continued)

	with a major cell phone supplier (e.g., Verizon or RadioShack) and sales to major office supply store chains.
June 2006	Obtain pricing and start-up costs for producing 250,000 units per order. Start sales process for private label contracts with Verizon or RadioShack for Christmas 2006 season. Initiate sales process for major office retailers: Office Max, Office Depot, and Staples.
July 2006	Finalize agreements for fall delivery to second-phase customers. Finalize any product design changes required by private-label suppliers.
August 2006	Finish second financing round for $1,000,000. Order 750,000 units from manufacturer, 250,000 with delivery in late September, 250,000 with delivery in mid-October, and 250,000 with delivery in early November.

Funding Required

Promotional programs	$25,000
Literature	
Web site development	
Point-of-purchase displays	
Attendance at three trade shows	
Publicity campaign	
Manufacturing expenses	$45,000
Inventory to support sales	
Packaging equipment	
Tooling and fixtures	
Inspection equipment	
Administrative expenses	$20,000
Legal and accounting fees	
Rent deposit	
Computers and other office equipment	
Company letterhead, other supplies	
Operating cash	$40,000
Total	$130,000

Equity Position

This section should list all the stock owned in your company, including the stock you own without investing, also called *founder's shares*, and the stock you plan on selling with this business plan. You also want to multiply total stock times share price for a capitalization structure. Consult with your attorney before committing to paper the Funding Required, Equity Position, and Equity Offer sections of your plan. Depending on the legal restrictions on your fund-raising, these three sections may instead need to be put into a private placement memorandum or a formal stock offer that your attorney will prepare. In case you use other formal documents with your stock sale offer, your business plan would stipulate that it is not an offer to buy. Your attorney will know the exact language required by your state. Equity position information can be short and sweet, but you should list the actual shares of anyone who owns more than 5 percent of the company.

Equity Position

Number of Shares	
Founder's stock	
Jerry Matthews—inventor	250,000
Stock sold for $0.20 per share	
Sold from Jan. 1, 2004 through May 30, 2004	
Jerry Matthews	40,000
Ray Matthews—inventor's father	20,000
Tim Donnelly	20,000
Four others	20,000
Stock sold at $0.75 share	
Sold from Oct. 1, 2004, through Dec. 15, 2004	
Ray Matthews	5,000
Tim Donnelly	5,000
John Darvin	20,000
Eight others	16,000
Stock to be sold at $2 per share	65,000
Total shares	461,000
Total capitalization after sale of stock	$922,000

Figure 19.3 Typical Financial Statements

Income Statement

	Year 1	Year 2	Year 3	Year 4	Year 5
Revenue					
Product revenue	228,000	675,000	1,050,000	1,400,000	1,700,000
Total revenues	**228,000**	**675,000**	**1,050,000**	**1,400,000**	**1,700,000**
Total cost of sales	136,800	405,000	630,000	840,000	1,020,000
Gross profit	**91,200**	**270,000**	**420,000**	**560,000**	**680,000**
Operating expenses					
Employee expenses					
Operational payroll	65,000	165,000	185,000	225,000	245,000
Payroll taxes and benefits	15,600	39,600	44,400	54,000	58,800
Total employee expenses	**80,600**	**204,600**	**229,400**	**279,000**	**303,800**
Marketing and sales expenses					
Marketing expenses	15,000	25,000	35,000	35,000	40,000
Travel and entertainment	5,000	18,000	24,000	24,000	24,000
Total marketing expenses	**20,000**	**43,000**	**59,000**	**59,000**	**64,000**
Total web site and technology expenses	10,000	10,000	10,000	10,000	10,000
Total general and administrative	15,000	25,000	35,000	35,000	35,000
Total operating expenses	**125,600**	**282,600**	**333,400**	**383,000**	**412,800**
Net operating income (EBITDA)*	**(34,400)**	**(12,600)**	**86,600**	**177,000**	**267,200**
Financial expenses					
Depreciation	8,000	8,000	8,000	16,000	16,000
Pretax net profit (loss)	**(42,400)**	**(20,600)**	**78,600**	**161,000**	**252,000**
Income taxes	0	0	0	15,250	44,250
Net income (loss)	**(42,400)**	**(20,600)**	**70,600**	**145,750**	**207,750**
Cumulative net profit (loss)	**(42,400)**	**(63,000)**	**18,600**	**156,350**	**364,100**

(continued)

* EBITA is earnings before interest, taxes, and amortization. *Amortization* in a financial document is a term for writing off your equipment expense. If a piece of equipment costs $1,000,000 and has a 10-year life, you would amortize the tooling costs at $100,000 per year.

Figure 19.3 *Continued*

	Balance Sheet				
	Year 1	*Year 2*	*Year 3*	*Year 4*	*Year 5*
Assets					
Current assets					
Cash	82,000	37,400	39,000	97,300	449,400
Accounts receivable	18,000	60,000	90,000	120,000	150,000
Total current assets	**100,000**	**97,400**	**129,000**	**217,300**	**599,400**
Property and equipment (Net of depreciation)	72,000	64,000	56,000	120,000	104,000
Total assets	**172,000**	**161,400**	**185,000**	**337,300**	**713,400**
Liabilities and stockholders' equity					
Liabilities					
Current liabilities					
Accounts payable	9,000	27,000	40,000	52,000	70,000
Total current liabilities	**9,000**	**27,000**	**40,000**	**52,000**	**70,000**
Total liabilities	**9,000**	**27,000**	**40,000**	**52,000**	**70,000**
Stockholders' equity[†]					
Paid-in capital	240,000	240,000	240,000	240,000	240,000
Retained earnings	(77,000)	(105,600)	(95,000)	45,000	403,400
Total stockholders' equity	**163,000**	**134,400**	**145,000**	**285,000**	**643,400**
Total liability and stockholders' equity	**172,000**	**161,000**	**185,000**	**237,000**	**713,400**

[†] Stockholders' equity is the current value of the companys' assets less its liabilities. Paid-in capital is the total cash money that has been invested in the company. Retained earnings equals the difference between the current valuation and the money paid into the company. A negative retained earnings indicates a company has been losing money.

Figure 19.3 *Continued*

Cash Flow Statement	Year 1	Year 2	Year 3	Year 4	Year 5
Revenues	**228,000**	**675,000**	**1,050,000**	**1,400,000**	**1,700,000**
Cash inflows					
Collection of accounts receivable	216,600	641,250	994,500	1,330,000	1,615,000
Proceeds from sale of stock	140,000	0	0	0	0
Total cash inflows	**356,600**	**641,250**	**994,500**	**1,330,000**	**1,615,000**
Cash outflows					
Payments on accounts payable	249,280	653,220	915,230	1,161,800	1,361,160
Payments for deposits	0	0	0	0	0
Payments to purchase equipment	80,000	0	0	80,000	
Income tax payments	0	0	0	15,250	44,250
Total cash outflows	**329,280**	**653,220**	**915,230**	**1,257,050**	**1,405,410**
Net cash flows	**27,320**	**(11,970)**	**79,270**	**72,950**	**209,590**
Cash, beginning of period	**14,500**	**41,820**	**29,850**	**109,120**	**182,070**
Cash, end of period	**41,820**	**29,850**	**109,120**	**182,070**	**391,660**

Equity Offer

This section simply states your offer: You are selling 65,000 shares of stock in 2,500-share increments for $2 per share. Again, use the exact language your attorney gives you for your offer.

Income Statements, Balance Sheets, and Cash Flow Statements

Typical income statements are for either three or five years. You should offer a detailed income statement and a detailed cash flow statement in your plan. (See Figure 19.3 for sample statements.) Typically, SBDCs (www.sba.gov/SBDC/) will help you do these statements; they have the experience and software to do them more quickly than you can do them on your own.

20

STEP 10C. SELL YOUR PRODUCT: MOTIVATE CUSTOMERS AND DISTRIBUTION

Chapter 2 discussed how to pick target customers who would not only value your product, but also pay a profitable price for it. Chapter 17 dealt with choosing a distribution channel that is the right size and provides the right support for your product. Part of the reason we choose target customers and distribution channels early in the process is so that the product is designed with the features, packaging, and pricing that the target customer and distribution channel require. The final step is to actually motivate those parties to either buy or carry your product.

Motivation is more difficult for inventors than it is for an established company. Distribution resists one-product vendors because of the expense of adding a vendor, the concern that the inventor company might go out of business, and the uncertainty about the inventor company's customer service and support for handling problems. Industrial and commercial end users are wary of inventor companies for the same reasons. Consumers, as a rule, prefer to buy products from companies they know and have learned to trust. Fortunately, markets are always open to truly novel products that customers want. To overcome market resistance, inventors need to have their package and promotional material connect with customers in a big way, and they must learn how to use promotions and alliances to entice the distribution channel to take a chance on their product.

Much of this chapter concentrates on selling to the distribution channel. For most products, distribution channels are a much harder sell than end users. They have more costs and risks in taking on a new product, and they have probably lost money in the past when new products failed. Even though end users may want the product, it won't sell if you don't have it in stores or other outlets where end users can find it. Thus, although inventors need to be able show that end users will be motivated to buy, they should expect to spend most of their time convincing distribution to carry their product. This chapter shows you how.

- Create sales and promotional material: Discover the message that sells.
- Stage your sales to generate momentum: Focus your first efforts on easier-to-sell channels.
- Develop an arsenal of promotional tactics: Ensure your early sales customers enjoy success.
- Forge alliances to build credibility: Select tactics that will encourage steady activity

Climb to the Top with Distribution

Carl Vanderschuit was playing around with some LED lights one Halloween night when he noticed an eerie effect as he looked through a drink at one of the lights. Vanderschuit immediately thought that putting an LED light in a freezable cube for drinks was a great idea. His Litecubes could be dropped in a glass for an instant light show—the perfect party item, Vanderschuit thought, for anyone looking for a great conversation starter. It took Vanderschuit some time to develop the prototype and resolve problems with having the LED light come on only when it was in a drink, but after considerable tinkering, he had a product ready to sell.

Vanderschuit ran into immediate resistance from retailers, so he switched targets and made his first sales through inventor-friendly catalogs and online retailers such as Solutions, Ship the Web, and Grill Lover's Catalog. Vanderschuit kept trying retailers without success until he noticed a line of bar products in Renovation Hardware, which seemed like an ideal fit for the Litecubes. Vanderschuit made a presentation to the company and landed an order to place his product in 100 stores.

Even with that success, Vanderschuit wasn't able to land more retailers, so he decided to pursue another inventor-friendly distribution channel, the advertising specialty market, which sells products to companies that give promotional products to their customers. Pens with company logos are an example of an advertising specialty item. Vanderschuit attended the Advertising Specialty Industries (ASI) Show and the Promotional Product Association (PPAI)

Expo. There Vanderschuit hit pay dirt. Several distributors placed orders for 10,000 Litecubes, which sell for $9.99 to $14.99 for a set of four. The distributors planned on selling the Litecubes to companies who would give them away at events and parties.

Vanderschuit was still blocked out of retailers, who didn't think the Litecubes' expected volume would justify the expense of adding a new vendor. Vanderschuit finally solved that problem by cutting his manufacturing costs to the point where he could add a master distributor for drugstores and grocery stores. A master distributor sells to other local or regional distributors who then sell to the retailer. With the master distributor in place, Vanderschuit was finally able to generate nationwide retail sales.

CREATE SALES AND PROMOTIONAL MATERIAL: DISCOVER THE MESSAGE THAT SELLS

The first requirement for selling to a distribution channel is to have a product that end users will purchase when they see it on a shelf or, better yet, that they'll come into the store and ask for. The inventors need packaging, sales, and promotional material that strikes a chord with end users and motivates them to read the package and then buy the product. The inventor's job is to find benefits, slogans, and visuals that grab the consumer's attention. To find the message that sells, you need to understand the target customer's goals, buying behavior, and self-image, configure a crucial product benefit, create a company look and an arresting visual, and then come up with a clever tagline.

- *Understand customer's goals.* Customers' goals vary depending on the product: to perform a certain function, to support a major interest, to create some fun and surprise, or to enhance the customer's self-image. Functional goals solve a need the customer has, such as washing windows. Supporting a major interest could be buying products for a hobby or avocation or, in the case of a business, buying products so that the company appears to be a technology leader. Buying products for fun or surprise might include items like the Litecubes, a game, or any other product that entertains us. Products that support your self-image include high-end briefcases, high-tech cell phone headsets, L.L. Bean clothes, or off-road vehicles.
- *Understand customer's buying behavior.* There are four types of buying behaviors your customers might exhibit: maximizing, judicial, low-cost, and minimizing. *Maximizing consumers* buy the best product they can afford—the fanciest cell phone, the most innovative

barbecue grill, or the most exotic computer monitor. *Judicial buyers* weigh the features and benefits of a product versus its cost. *Low-cost buyers* shop for the lowest-priced products, and *minimizing buyers* buy as little as possible and only when they absolutely have to.

- *Understand customer's self-image.* Self-image is a huge motivator for most purchases. Here are some of the self-images people may have:

Adventurous	Technologically savvy	High achiever
Cutting-edge	Party animal	Good taste
Intelligent	Family-oriented	Romantic
Outdoorsperson	Unconventional	Financially savvy

- *Configure a crucial product benefit.* This benefit has to coordinate well with the customer's goals, buying behavior, and self-image. For example, consider the advanced cell phone headset that uses vibrations from your cheekbone to send a clearer voice signal to the cellular network. There are several target customer groups, but consider only two for the purpose of illustration: *salespeople*, who use the cell phone to talk to customers, and *teenagers* who use the phone to talk to friends. Consider the difference in goals, buying behavior, and self-image of the two groups.

Characteristics	*Salespeople*	*Teenagers*
Goals	Functional	Functional and fun
Buying behavior	Judicial	Maximizing
Self-image	Professional	Trendy and fun

The overriding benefit to salespeople is clearly that customers will hear them perfectly. This functional benefit is expressed in a name like Crystal Clear Headsets. For teenagers, the feature is the same: People can hear the caller. But that is not the benefit that entices teenagers to buy. The benefit is owning the newest, trendiest, most cutting-edge product on the market. A name like Good Vibrations fits that image, which could be enhanced with a designer-headset look rather than the functional-design look that salespeople prefer. For teenagers, the fact that the headset lets people hear better simply lends credence that the headset is cutting-edge.

- *Create a company look.* This refers to the overall packaging, logo, and design. The look needs to match the customers and the chief product benefit. For instance, our Crystal Clear headset for salespeople would have traditional blue, green, or brown rectangular packaging and literature that reflects that Crystal Clear is a product for performance. For teenagers, the look has to be modern, with bright colors and an unusual package—possibly in the shape of a headset. The company's logos should also reflect the differences in the target customer groups.

- *Create an arresting visual.* The visual has to tie in with the customer's goals and motivations. For salespeople, the visual includes writing an order in their car. That is their goal. For our teenagers, the visual might be a teenager holding the phone outward while three teenagers gather around to listen in, which shows that the caller is being heard loud and clear.
- *Develop a clever tagline.* The tagline also supports the customer goals and image. For the salesperson, the tagline might be: "Let customers finally hear your perfect message." For the teenager, the message might be: "Lie back and relax, they'll still hear you" or "when you really want to whisper."

Most inventors decide to get professional help with their packaging and promotional ideas. You'll get a much better result if you work on these seven points first before seeking professional help. Offering this information to your vendor will produce better materials and will help you know whether the package and promotional material will connect with your target customers.

STAGE YOUR SALES TO GENERATE MOMENTUM: FOCUS YOUR FIRST EFFORTS ON EASIER-TO-SELL CHANNELS

While reading Chapter 17 you should have determined the distribution channels that best suit your product, your market, and your financial capabilities. At this point, you want to decide which markets to approach first in order to set up an orderly sales path that matches your sales to your production capabilities. Inventors want to build a sales base with easy-to-make sales to create revenue and profits as well as to generate sales momentum for pursuing larger markets later.

Chapter 16 discussed the benefits of landing a large customer, either an OEM or a private-label deal, to secure bank loans and provide a faster launch to your company. That is an option to keep open at all times, but usually you can't sell big potential customers until you have had some initial sales success. Not all inventors will be able to land a big customer, and they will need to follow a staged market-penetration strategy that starts by targeting easier-to-penetrate distribution channels or markets. If you do land a big customer, you might have the resources to boost production, but I still recommend you follow a staged process for the rest of your customers.

Managing a high-growth business is challenging for inventors unless they have done it before or have an experienced manager on their team.

The Litecubes inventor story earlier in the chapter is typical of inventors using a staged introduction process. Vanderschuit started with the easier-to-sell channels, such as catalogs and advertising specialty distributors, to build up sales volume. Then he pursued larger but more difficult markets—regional retailers and distributors. The staged introduction process builds momentum in one sales channel and then you can move on to the next channel using your initial success to land bigger orders.

Initial Sales Targets

- *Fairs, flea markets, and shows.* Home shows, garden shows, and boat shows as well as state and country fairs and large flea markets are all outlets where you can sell your product and generate revenue and sales momentum. These venues also give you lots of customer feedback that you can use later to help close bigger deals. If possible at shows, compare your sales to similar products being sold by other vendors. You want to be able to tell people that not only did you sell 300 units at a fair, you sold as many units as product A and three times the number of product B.

- *Small local retail chains or local companies.* While retailers in general are difficult to sell to, local retailers and small chains are often willing to help a local inventor they know. Inventors can also provide extra services to local retailers, including in-store demonstrations every Saturday, liberal return policies, in-store displays, and promotion of the product in the local media, which will help drive business to the local chain. Inventors can also sell to individual stores, but the volume at each store is so small that it's difficult to generate enough business to support the inventor.

- *Catalogs.* Catalogs are a great starting point for inventors because they frequently buy from inventors and offer a nice-sized order, neither too big nor too small. Inventors can sell directly to catalogs—and at a slight premium, which protects inventors' margins during start-up production. The best spot I've found on the web for finding catalogs is Dir.Yahoo.com/Business_and_Economy/Shopping_and_Services/Retailer/directories/Catalogs.

- *Internet sales.* Internet sales work only if you have a dedicated group of users that will search out your product. For example, if you have a product for mountain climbers, there will probably be Internet sites that target customers visit frequently and where you can post information about your web site and your product. You should investigate the community sites for your target customers first, before spending too much money on a web site. If the right types of community sites exist, start up a web site and then spend at least four hours per week doing online postings and promotions.

- *TV sales.* QVC (www.QVC.com), Home Shopping Network (www .HSN.com), and ShopNBC (www.shopnbc.com) all have active programs to find new products from inventors. Check their web sites frequently, as all have fairs or inventor days when inventors can present their products. Check out Appendix D for additional information on TV shopping channels.

Second-Phase Sales Targets

Once you have some initial sales success you'll want to branch out to bigger markets to establish more market momentum and generate more cash. Once you finish a second-phase selling into intermediate-size markets, you should be ready to sell to virtually all markets. Here are some possible targets.

- *Manufacturer's sales agents.* These agents (also called *representatives*) are a good choice for inventors because they will work on commission and you need to pay them only when their customers pay you. The agents are already calling on a set of customers, which could be users, distributors, or retailers, and a good sales agent could pick up business for you. Agents are particularly effective if they call on buying groups in an industry. A buying group is an organization that buys products from manufacturers for small retailers. The retailers sign up with the buying group in order to obtain volume discounts. Some buying groups may buy for 200 to 500 stores. You can often find a list of agents on the web site of your market's association, or check out www.manaonline.org. Another good source for finding representatives is www.douglaspublication.com, which sells reference books for a variety of markets, including distributors, rack jobbers, buying groups, master distributors, and manufacturer's representatives. The books are expensive, $220 to $400, but are available in resource sections of large libraries.
- *Regional distributors.* Once you have established some success at a local chain you can often land a regional distributor who will promote your product to other retailers in your region. You increase your chances of landing a distributor if you promise active local publicity and in-store promotions.

- *Regional store chains.* Inventors can target larger regional chains and still offer publicity and support. These stores can also be sold through manufacturer's sales agents or distributors.
- *Private-label agreements.* A private-label agreement could actually be a very large sale for the inventor. Normally, the inventor can't afford to produce enough product for a large order, but in this case the private-label customer might be willing to help fund an increase in production. This is still the best time to consider a private-label agreement because private-label manufacturers prefer to start with a product that is not yet readily available. Chapter 18 (pages 292 to 294) covered how to find prospects for a private-label agreement.
- *Small national chains.* These chains often try to market themselves as having unique, innovative merchandise not available from larger retailers. They often won't buy unless you have had some market success first, but they are an excellent venue for launching your products into the national market. If you decide to use manufacturer's representatives or distributors, be sure to find out what other products they sell to the small national chains you've targeted. If they don't have an established sales relationship, you may want to sell those chains on you own.

DEVELOP AN ARSENAL OF PROMOTIONAL TACTICS: ENSURE YOUR EARLY SALES CUSTOMERS ENJOY SUCCESS

Market momentum is key to successfully introducing a product, and inventors need to do everything in their power to help every retailer, distributor, or manufacturer's sales agent succeed. Inventors have a tough time recovering their momentum once companies in the distribution channel start dropping their product. I've listed here some promotions and sales tactics you may want or need to use. Some may be expensive, and you may end up losing money at a store, but if you don't invest in the customer's early success you might lose that customer forever.

- *Consignment sales.* With a consignment sale, you put the product into a retail store with the understanding that the retailer will buy each product only after its sells. In effect, you *consign* the product to the retailer rather than sell it. This is obviously not desirable, but it is something a majority of inventors are forced to do to generate their initial sales.
- *Guaranteed sales.* When you guarantee a sale, you promise to take back any unsold units and issue a full refund to the distributor or

retailer. Many big retailers require all sales to be guaranteed, even if you are an established successful company.

- *Space charges.* Catalogs may request that inventors help pay for a portion of the printing and mailing costs of the catalog before they will handle your product. You don't want to make an up-front payment, as you can't be sure how much product the catalog company will sell. You can counteroffer 10 to 15 percent free goods on each shipment to cover the space charges. With a 10 percent free-goods offer you would ship $1,000 of free goods with every $10,000 shipment.

- *Slotting allowances.* Some retailers will charge you to have premium space in their store. This tactic is especially popular with mass merchandisers and grocery stores. But you can use this tactic on your initial sales targets, too. Visit the store and decide what would be an ideal spot to feature your product. Then you can offer the retailer free goods, which are products you give the retailer free if the retailer will place your product in the desired location.

- *Co-op advertising programs.* These programs offer retailers anywhere from 5 to 15 percent of your sales to feature your product in their advertising. A 15 percent co-op advertising program that will pay up to 50 percent of the cost of advertising works like this: The inventor company sets aside 15 percent of all the revenue from a customer to pay for a co-op advertising program. When the retailer runs an ad featuring the inventor's product, it sends a copy of the ad and a cost for featuring the product to the inventor company. The inventor company then pays 50 percent of the cost of the ad from the 15 percent of revenue that the customer has set aside for that purpose. If 50 percent of the cost of the ad is greater than the money set aside, the inventor would pay whatever money remained.

- *30-60-90-day billing.* Billing refers to the period allowed for payment. For example, 30-day billing, also called *30-day terms*, indicates the bill is due in 30 days. Rather than asking for 30-day billing, you can ask for a third of the invoice to be paid in 30 days, a third to be paid in 60 days, and a third in 90 days. This tactic is useful when a retailer wants to order only four or five products, which might not be enough to make an effective display. Asking for an order three times larger with extended billing will help the retailer order sufficient products to create the sales presence you want in the store.

- *In-store demonstrations.* Saturday demonstration in stores, showing exactly how the product works, is something that is good for both a retailer and you. Offer a demonstration, at least at your first stores, if a demonstration is an effective sales tool for your product. You can often sell in one day the same number of products it will take the store one or two months to sell.

- *In-store demonstration models.* Offer a free product to use as a demonstrator if people need to feel and touch your product before they buy.

- *In-store displays.* In-store displays include anything from 8½ × 11 sales sheets hanging by the product to big stand-up displays that holds dozens of products. In-store displays attract attention and greatly enhance sales. They are expensive, but they are a wise tool to use at your early stores. The overall costs will be low since you are only selling to a few stores, and the sales boost they produce will help your initial sales campaign. You can check the Yellow Pages for store displays companies who can put together low-cost displays for you.

- *Events.* Bicycle shops sponsor bike races, industrial suppliers bring in guest speakers for their best customers, and hardware stores sponsor seminars on how to build gazebos. Depending on your product, you might be able to put together an event for your retailers—a fishing seminar, for example, is a great tactic for fishing products. You don't necessarily need to pay for the event, because the retailer will probably be willing to do that, but you can coordinate the activity to make the event happen.

- *Sampling.* Every Friday at most supermarkets you will witness many people giving away free samples of a new or existing product. Not all products lend themselves to sampling, but sampling often works for food products and inexpensive consumer items.

- *Volume discounts.* You need to be sure that the store has enough of your product for an effective display. Earlier, I mentioned 30-60-90-day billing as a way to encourage customers to buy enough stock. Discounts at certain price points give incentives to the retailer to place a larger order. If you feel a retailer needs to buy 20 units for a good display, offer a discount for 20 units. Rather than a straight discount, you might offer four free products with every order of 20 to help get more of your product into the hands of retailers.

FORGE ALLIANCES TO BUILD CREDIBILITY: SELECT TACTICS THAT WILL ENCOURAGE STEADY ACTIVITY

Much of the early sales resistance to your product arises from credibility problems. Potential customers are worried that your business might be short-lived. One way to overcome that is by forging alliances with established companies to build credibility. These alliances can be loose arrangements, such as offering discounts on each other's products, or more complex, such as joining together to offer effective demonstrations or seminars at stores and trade shows. Or they can be more formal arrangements where the two companies package their products similarly and work together to form a separate sales organization that promotes both companies' products. The best alliances for inventors are ones where they team up with a much larger customer. The inventor of the Medi-Seal, a sticker that goes into a bike helmet with the rider's name, contact information, and any urgent medical information, tried unsuccessfully to get his product into bike stores. Then he agreed to provide the product to Trek, which included it as a feature on its bike helmets. Once stores started bringing the product in through an alliance, the inventor was able to place his product into their stores, too. Any company that sells to the same target customer group is a candidate for an alliance of some sort. I've listed some of the more common alliance agreements that inventors can use to help establish credibility in the market.

- Groups of businesses selling to the same target customer can form an alliance for merchandising products to retailers, conducting seminars, hosting trade show booths, running contests, or selling complete solutions to key targeted customers.

- Inventors can sign a marketing agreement to have their products sold through larger companies, either through private-label arrangements or under the inventor company's label, offering the product as complementary product. For example, an inventor of a new rivet could have a rivet-gun manufacturer include a sample of his product, packaged in the inventor company's package, with every rivet gun it sells.

- Small manufacturers with innovative products often sign short-term exclusive distribution agreements with distributors, manufacturers' representatives, catalogs, or retailers in return for extra promotional efforts from the distributor, representative, catalog, or retailer.

- Sign research agreements with university professors and well-known individuals. For example, if a company needs research done, have a university professor supervise the research, prepare the paper, and then present the paper at major trade shows. This enhances a research report's credibility and helps promote a company's cutting-edge technology image.

- Use joint sponsorships with trade associations or magazines. Sponsor classes, seminars, web pages, and other marketing activities.

You may even provide free services in order to be connected with an association marketing activity. This tactic increases credibility, gives a company access to a large number of potential customers, and helps the company stay on top of current market trends.

- Try developing advisory councils with key suppliers, distributors, or customers. The councils can be specific to a company's product or more involved in industrywide advice, and can be sponsored by more than one company. For example, the Natural Gas Vehicle Association has a marketing advisory committee on how to increase the use of natural-gas vehicles. If your product is sold to natural-gas-vehicle manufacturers, you can become a part of that committee. You'd gain credibility with your target customer group plus you'd probably meet many customer contacts.

- Share office space, administrative help, warehouse space, and marketing leads with a business serving your same target market in the same town. This is done typically to save costs, but being in a combined, larger office also enhances a company's credibility, especially if you also combine marketing and sales efforts.

- Combine with other companies for a demonstration of a new technology or an improved manufacturing system. Combining forces allows companies to see a fully working system, which attracts more interest than a demonstration by one company, and also builds credibility for all the companies involved. This is especially effective if your product is part of a new trend. Scrapbook product companies, many of which are inventor-started companies, could join forces to provide Saturday demonstrations at Michaels, the big craft store chain, to promote the entire scrapbook market.

- Offer to use a store or retailer as a demonstration site for your product. For example, if you sell solar products, install one of your products in the retailer's location. That enhances your product, and it helps the retailer sell more products.

- Offer to put on motivational seminars or demonstrations during the lunch hour at large companies that have many employees in your target market. For example, an inventor with a mileage gauge for bikes could offer to join with bike manufacturers in seminars on setting up individual bike-training fitness programs. The inventor of the mileage gauge could then use participation at these events to sell products to bike retailers in the area.

- Combine with other companies to offer a full selection of products to retailers or distributors. For example, an inventor company with an improved tool for automotive exhaust repair could combine with another tool manufacture to offer a full line of automotive exhaust tools that could be sold to chains like Midas or Car-X.

- Form an alliance with similar businesses that serve the same target customer group and offer cross-promotions, whereby each company helps promote products of the other company. An example of a cross-promotion is when two companies offer each other's coupons and/or promotional brochures in their products and do joint mailings to retailers, distributors, and catalogs.

- Form a partnership with companies selling products to the same personality group that appeals to your company's products or service. For example, an inventor with high-end toddler clothes for girls could have trouble breaking into the juvenile store market because retailers aren't sure where to place the product or how to create an appealing store display for just one high-end product. The inventor could overcome this by combining with three or four other companies who sell different high-end toddler products to provide enough products for retailers to create a display that would appeal to maximizing moms looking for that special look for their children.

- Join together with other businesses targeting the same customer group to publish newsletters or other materials of interest to people in the target group. Joining together will result in a better newsletter, and mailing to everyone's customers will expose each business to new prospects.

- You can combine with other businesses, associations, and groups to start a club or an Internet chat room related to your business. This gets your name out in front of potential customers. This strategy works extremely well when you have a passionate, small customer group (e.g., selling repair tools for black-powder gun enthusiasts).

Appendix A

THE GO-NO-GO DECISIONS

I originally proposed the five-point go-no-go decision matrix in 1992 in my first book, *How to Bring a Product to Market for Less than $5,000.* (John Wiley & Sons, 1992). My goal was to offer an easy-to-use guide that would help people decide whether their idea had a chance to make money. That matrix proved very popular, and I heard it repeated at seminars for inventors and during invention club presentations. I received comments from inventors who were looking for more detail, as they were unsure how to evaluate their product against some of the criteria, especially whether a product is easy to distribute. In my second invention book, *Bringing Your Product to Market* (John Wiley & Sons, 1997), I introduced a slightly more comprehensive 12-point go-no-go decision matrix. The second decision matrix was as popular as the first. I don't emphasize the go-no-go decision matrix in this edition primarily because the market has changed and companies are more receptive to licensing and turbo-outsourcing. That receptiveness has allowed inventors to skirt many of the issues raised by the go-no-go matrix, and my emphasis in this book has been how to find the invention path that works for your product. Because the matrix is so popular I've decided to include it in this appendix so new readers to my books can use it when deciding which ideas they might want to pursue. You have by far the best chance to introduce successful ideas when you can answer yes to each go-no-go question.

ORIGINAL FIVE-POINT GO-NO-GO DECISION MATRIX

1. Is the product easy to distribute?
2. Is the technology simple?
3. Is the product perceived to be unique?
4. Is the benefit obvious?
5. Can the product be sold for three to five times its manufacturing cost?

Your product needs to meet all five criteria if you are going to introduce the product yourself. It needs to meet only the last three criteria if you are going to use licensing or turbo-outsourcing to introduce your product.

EXPANDED 12-POINT GO-NO-GO DECISION MATRIX

1. Can potential customers quickly understand your customer benefit?
2. Is your product clearly different from others in the market?
3. Does the product have a benefit people want?
4. Can the product be packaged effectively, in terms of both communicating benefits to end users and meeting the requirements of the distribution channel?
5. Is the market open to one-product inventor companies?
6. Does the distribution network exist with product-support costs that you can afford?
7. Are your customers easy to target?
8. Can you afford to make your models, prototypes, and initial production runs?
9. Can you find a contract manufacturer that's willing to absorb some of the start-up manufacturing costs?
10. Can you find market insiders to help you?
11. Does your product have a perceived value that's at least four times its manufacturing cost?
12. Is the market size of the distribution network large enough to justify your time and expense?

Inventors planning to introduce their own product need to answer yes to every one of the go-no-go decisions. Inventors looking to use a licensing or turbo-outsource strategy need to answer yes to only items 1 through 4, 7, 8, 10, and 11.

Appendix B

CHECKLISTS BEFORE STARTING THE INTRODUCTION PROCESS

Inventors who succeed typically have careful preparation to be sure they are ready when they are finally in front of the right contacts, whether it be customers, investors, potential licensees, or potential turbo-outsource partners. As a ready reference point, this appendix contains checklists for success for all three invention introduction approaches: licensing, turbo-outsourcing, and starting your own company. It also contains additional checklists if you're starting your own company: financial considerations, sales and marketing support, administrative tasks, and manufacturing considerations. The checklists provide a ready reference point for inventors so they can double-check that they're ready for the market.

CHECKLIST 1: THE SUCCESS FACTORS FOR LICENSING

	Ready	
	Yes	No

Required

1. Does your product target a desirable customer group?   _____ _____

2. Can you show that the market has a strong need or desire for your product?   _____ _____

3. Do you have intellectual property protection?   _____ _____

4. Have you been able to make a high-quality prototype?   _____ _____

5. Have you found potential licensees for which your product has considerable appeal because the product:
   - Fits with a new market trend or application?   _____ _____
   - Allows the licensee to offer a complete solution?   _____ _____
   - Offers benefits to the distribution channel?   _____ _____

6. Are you able to show that the product's perceived value is four to five times its manufacturing costs?   _____ _____

7. Can you create a powerful demonstration for opening a presentation?   _____ _____

8. Have you prepared a strong licensing presentation?   _____ _____

Helpful to Have

9. Does the product have a strong "wow" factor?   _____ _____

10. Do you have key industry helpers or supporters?   _____ _____

11. Do you have provisional orders or other proof of market demand?   _____ _____

12. Do you have a target introduction date and a compelling reason for introducing a product by that date (e.g., a major industry event)?   _____ _____

CHECKLIST 2: THE SUCCESS FACTORS FOR TURBO-OUTSOURCING

	Ready	
	Yes	No

Required

1. Do you target an easy-to-identify, desirable customer group? _____ _____

2. Can you demonstrate that the product has a fast-start market opening with strong end-user support? _____ _____

3. Are there manufacturers that could be in production within six months? _____ _____

4. Does the product have a 50 to 60 percent margin? _____ _____

5. Can you show that you offer crucial support to enhance the product's success? _____ _____

6. Do you have memorandums of understanding (MOUs) and statements of confidentiality and nonuse ready? _____ _____

7. Do you have enough confidence in your business skills to negotiate the turbo-outsourcing process? _____ _____

8. Have you located a list of potential marketing and manufacturing partners? _____ _____

9. Have you prepared a turbo-outsourcing presentation? _____ _____

Helpful to Have

10. Do you have industry helpers as partners or advisors? _____ _____

11. Do you have intellectual property protection? _____ _____

12. Have you produced a "looks like, works like" prototype? _____ _____

CHECKLIST 3: THE SUCCESS FACTORS FOR STARTING YOUR OWN COMPANY

	Ready	
	Yes	No

Required

1. Does the target customer group think that your product meets an important need? _____ _____

2. Do customers understand your benefit immediately? _____ _____

3. Have you located an easy-to-reach target market? _____ _____

4. Have you located a contract manufacturer or an advisor with experience to help with your manufacturing? _____ _____

5. Is your product's perceived value four to five times your manufacturing cost? _____ _____

6. Have you found enough money to support your prototypes and an initial production run, and do you have access to additional funds? _____ _____

7. Does your product package motivate potential buyers to pick up your product and look at it? _____ _____

8. Have you prepared a business action plan? _____ _____

Helpful to Have

9. Do you have an advisory group of experienced industry professionals? _____ _____

10. Do you have firm orders, or the promise of orders, from established companies in the market? _____ _____

11. Do you have strong intellectual property protection, including patents and trademarks? _____ _____

CHECKLIST 4: FINANCIAL CONSIDERATIONS FOR STARTING YOUR OWN COMPANY

	Ready	
	Yes	No
1. Do you have enough money on hand to survive the first six months?	____	____
2. Do you have a monthly budget to follow?	____	____
3. Have you negotiated terms and lines of credit with suppliers?	____	____
4. Do your documents, including board minutes, clearly state the number of shares owned by each shareholder?	____	____
5. Do you have a detailed list of personal obligations related to the business (credit card debts, personal guarantees, etc.), and have you shared that list with potential investors?	____	____

CHECKLIST 5: SALES AND MARKETING CONSIDERATIONS FOR STARTING YOUR OWN COMPANY

	Ready	
	Yes	No
1. Have you prepared easy-to-understand price sheets?	____	____
2. Do you have a promotional flyer for mailing or to use on sales calls?	____	____
3. Do you have samples to distribute to salespeople?	____	____
4. Have you prepared a list of target customers to approach in your first 60 days?	____	____
5. If required, do you have point-of-purchase displays?	____	____
6. Have you decided whether you'll put units out on consignment or offer guaranteed sales?	____	____
7. Have you set your delivery terms (e.g., three weeks)?	____	____

8. Have you developed a sales procedure and sales script for your representatives to follow? _____ _____

9. Do you have testimonials from satisfied users? _____ _____

CHECKLIST 6: ADMINISTRATIVE CONSIDERATIONS FOR STARTING YOUR OWN COMPANY

Meet with your local Small Business Development Center (SBDC) if you have any concerns on completing these tasks (go to www.sbaonline.gov).

	Ready	
	Yes	No
1. Have you created a legal structure for your firm and registered its operation with your state?	_____	_____
2. Do you have all the necessary licenses and permits? (Check with your local city hall.)	_____	_____
3. Do you have any required general liability, product liability, and unemployment insurance?	_____	_____
4. Have you set up a bookkeeping system to record sales, income expenses, accounts receivables, and accounts payable?	_____	_____
5. Have you determined how to handle payroll records, tax reports, and tax payments?	_____	_____
6. Have your started your corporation properly? Do you hold periodic meetings with your board of directors or officers and take minutes of these meetings?	_____	_____
7. Do you know what financial reports you need to prepare for your investors?	_____	_____
8. Do you have necessary forms to hire new employees?	_____	_____

CHECKLIST 7: MANUFACTURING CONSIDERATIONS FOR STARTING YOUR OWN COMPANY

	Ready	
	Yes	No

1. Have you established performance requirements and detailed specifications for the product and all of its components? ＿＿ ＿＿

2. Do you have firm commitments on price and availability of raw materials, processing hardware, and required components? ＿＿ ＿＿

3. Do you have a contract with a manufacturer to produce your product, or is your own facility operational? ＿＿ ＿＿

4. Have you confirmed your manufacturing procedure by doing a small production run? ＿＿ ＿＿

5. Have you arranged for sufficient storage space for both raw materials and finished goods? ＿＿ ＿＿

6. Do you have quality control inspection procedures in place? ＿＿ ＿＿

7. Have you clarified with your vendors who is responsible for handling quality problems? ＿＿ ＿＿

Appendix C

SAMPLE DOCUMENTS

The following is a sample statement of confidentiality for use with focus groups.

Statement of Confidentiality and Nonuse

I _____ of Address

_____ (hereafter called "Recipient")

do hereby agree to the following conditions regarding the confiden-

tial information received during the evaluation of products from

_____ _____ [*inventor's name*]

(hereafter called the "Discloser") of (company name, if applicable)

_____ Address: _____.

Invention or product name:

_____

Description:

_____

Conditions:

The Recipient agrees that he/she is reviewing the product idea presented by the Discloser only for the purpose of providing market research about the product. The Recipient agrees not to use any exclusive information obtained from the Discloser unless Recipient receives written permission to do so from the Disclosure.

Information will not be considered confidential if, due to no fault or effort of the Recipient, the information is in the public domain as a result of written publication, trade show attendance, offer to sell through sales literature, or any other effort that results in the information being placed in the public domain.

We the undersigned do hereby agree to abide by the conditions of this agreement.

_____   _____
Recipient signature   Discloser signature

_____   _____
Date   Date

The following is a sample statement of confidentiality and nonuse that can be used with memorandums of understanding or with companies before licensing, turbo-outsourcing, or contract manufacturing discussions.

Statement of Confidentiality and Nonuse

For two individuals

This Agreement (the "Agreement") is made and entered into as of ___insert date___ by and between ___your name___ residing at ___your full address___ and ___the other party's name___ residing at ___other party's full address___.

(or)

For an individual and a corporation

This Agreement (the "Agreement") is made and entered into as of ___insert date___ ("Effective Date") by and between ___your name___ of ___your full address___ and ___company name___ a ___insert type of legal entity, for example, partnership, company, sole proprietorship___ with its principal place of business locate at ___insert company's full address___

[Then the following]

Whereas, ___your name___ is the owner of certain intellectual and confidential property (Confidential Property) concerning a ___list your product description___ and the technical know-how related thereto; and improvements thereto and

Whereas, ___name of other party___ desires to receive said confidential property for the purpose of evaluating the idea and to consider entering into a contractual arrangement with ___other party's name___ concerning the Confidential Property, and

Whereas, _____your name_____ is willing to provide _____other party's name_____ with said Confidential Property for the stated evaluation purposes under the terms stated herein,

Therefore, it is hereby agreed as follows:

1. _____your name_____ will disclose the Confidential Property to _____other party's name_____.

2. _____other party's name_____ agrees to receive the Confidential Property under the terms stated herein and that it shall not use or disclose the Confidential Property except for evaluation purposes as set forth herein.

3. _____other party's name_____ acknowledges that such Confidential Property shall remain the property of _____your name_____. _____other party's name_____ shall not disclose that it possesses confidential property.

[*Note:* Number 4 is relevant only if the other party is a company; if not relevant, the numbering of the following paragraphs need to be revised.]

4. _____other party's name_____ shall maintain said Confidential Property confidential within its organization and disclose same only to those employees who are directly involved in the evaluation contemplated under this Agreement, but then only to those employees who have signed a similar agreement with _____other party's name_____, with similar provisions, and to withhold knowledge of said Confidential Property from all other persons. _____other party's name_____ shall comply with all in-house rules concerning the protection of its own confidential proprietary information and shall apply said rules to the protection of this Confidential Property, and shall treat the Confidential Property with no less care than it treats its own confidential property.

5. _____other party's name_____ shall provide secure storage for the Confidential Property.

6. _____other party's name_____ shall not disclose, use, or commercialize, or cause or permit to be disclosed, used, or commercialized, any Confidential Property, without the express written permission of _____your name_____.

7. _____other party's name_____shall keep a record of the names and addresses of those persons to whom the Confidential Property has been made known. _____other party's name_____ shall notify all persons to whom the confidential property has been made known of the obligations under this Agreement. _____other party's name_____ shall keep a record of the persons who leave their employ or terminate their relationship with _____other party's name_____ with knowledge of the Confidential Property and shall advise them of their continuing obligations as provided for in the agreement that they had previously signed with _____other party's name_____ with respect to this Agreement.

8. _____other party's name_____ agrees not to use any ideas, improvements, or concepts relating to the Confidential Property emanating therefrom or any information obtained through testing or other methods of evaluation which shall be in its relationship to and arising from this Agreement which is the property of_____your name_____.

9. Nothing in this Agreement shall be construed to create or imply the existence of a license agreement herein between _____your name_____ and _____other party's name_____ or to grant to _____other party's name_____ any rights other than to evaluate the Confidential Property.

10. _____other party's name_____ shall evaluate the Confidential Property within one hundred twenty (120) days from the date herein. Upon completion of the evaluation, should _____other party's name_____ elect not to extend this Agreement or enter into another agreement, then _____other party's name_____ shall return the Confidential Property to _____your name_____ and shall destroy all notes, documents, records, and copies made, in any form, during the evaluation. The obligations of _____other party's name_____ set forth in this Agreement related to the Confidential Property shall survive the termination of this Agreement.

11. The term "Confidential Property" shall not include written information that is in the public domain in published documents or written information, that was previously developed by _____other party's name_____, as evidenced in written documents.

12. The benefits of this Agreement may not be assigned or otherwise transferred by _____other party's name_____ without the written approval of_____your name_____.

13. This Agreement shall be governed by and construed in accordance with the laws of the State of _____.

IN WITNESS THEREOF, the parties hereto have caused this Agreement to be executed as of the Effective Date first set forth above.

Dated: _____   _____
                              Your name

Dated: _____   _____
                              Other party's name

The following is a sample three-way confidentiality agreement for turbo-outsourcing agreements.

Mutual Confidentiality and Nondisclosure Agreement

This Agreement is made and entered into as of _____ (the "Effective Date") by and between _____ (name of first party **FP**), a _____ (type of legal entity, such as corporation, partnership, or sole proprietorship), located at _____ (first party's complete address), _____ (name of second party **SP**), a _____ (type of legal entity, such as corporation, partnership, or sole proprietorship), located at _____ (second party's complete address), and _____ (name of third party **TP**), a _____ (type of legal entity, such as corporation, partnership, or sole proprietorship), located at _____ (third party's complete address).

Whereas **FP, SP,** and **TP** have entered into negotiations concerning the potential manufacture, sale, and distribution of Product A, during which certain confidential and proprietary information may be exchanged solely for the purpose of evaluating the potential of Product A and deciding the form and terms of a Proposed Business Agreement, individually or collectively referred to as party or parties herein.

Whereas the parties wish to protect, pursuant to this agreement, and in continuation with any subsequent agreement, such information.

Now therefore the parties agree to be legally bound as follows.

1. This agreement shall apply to all confidential information disclosed on behalf of one party to the other parties, including, without limitation, each party's employees, agents, consultants,

officers, directors, attorneys, accountants, financial advisors, or other similar representations, collectively "Related Parties."

2. The parties acknowledge and agree that "Confidential Information" in whatever form disclosed, including without limitation, electronic, written, visual, audible, or oral, and available to any party, includes without limitation: (i) information concerning any of a party's clients or vendors, (ii) information referring to, discussing, or in any way related to a party's business condition, strategies or initiatives, systems, processes, or policies, (iii) know-how, trade secrets, tools, products, procedures, methods, techniques, algorithms, designs, specifications, computer source code, or other proprietary technology or systems: and/or (iv) any other information that a reasonable person would conclude is intended to remain confidential due to the nature of the circumstances under which it is disclosed, or that a party designates as confidential.

3. Each party acknowledges that, in connection with the Proposed Business Agreement, each party may provide Confidential Information to another party in confidence and solely for purpose of negotiating, or otherwise discussing, the Proposed Business Agreement. Each party represents that it will treat all Confidential Information of the other parties as confidential and secret, and that which one party has disclosed or permitted access to, the party receiving such Confidential Information will not disclose or permit access to such Confidential Information except as permitted under this Agreement. Each party

acknowledges and agrees that (i) a party is granted only a limited right of use of Confidential Information and that the party granting such use is not granting any interest in the Confidential Information; (ii) this Agreement shall not effect any transfer of right, title, or interest in any Confidential Information; (iii) a party shall not assert any right, title, or interest in any Confidential Information of the other party; and (iv) neither party grants any license under any patents, trademarks, service marks, or copyrights under this Agreement.

4. Notwithstanding anything in this Agreement to the contrary, the amount, type, and items of Confidential Information disclosed by a party shall be solely within the discretion of the disclosing party, and a party may refuse to disclose information if it believes that it is not in its best interest to do so.

5. Each party agrees: (i) to protect any and all Confidential Information from unauthorized use or disclosure with at least the same degree of care such party uses to protect its own confidential information of similar nature; (ii) to use the Confidential Information only for the purpose(s) expressly stated in and in accordance with the terms of this agreement; (iii) not to copy or reproduce any Confidential Information in any form, except to the extent contemplated by this Agreement: (iv) not to disclose to or otherwise permit any third person or entity access to any Confidential Information without the prior written consent of the party owning such Confidential Information; (v) to limit disclosure of Confidential Information to its Related Parties who

are necessary for and involved in that party's performance of its obligations under this Agreement; (vi) to ensure that any of its Related Parties who receive or obtain Confidential Information are advised of the nature of the Confidential Information and of the obligations such party has undertaken with respect to such information under this Agreement and agrees to comply with these obligations. Each party further agrees to assist the other party in identifying any access, disclosure, or use of Confidential Information in a manner inconsistent with the provisions of this Agreement.

6. Information of a party shall not be deemed Confidential Information if (i) it is already, or otherwise becomes, known by the public through no fault of the receiving party or its Related Parties; (ii) it is lawfully received from a third party having the right to disseminate the information without restriction on disclosure; (iii) it is in the possession of the Receiving Party or its Related Parties prior to disclosure of it by the Disclosing Party or its Related Parties; (iv) it is disclosed pursuant to the lawful requirement or formal request of a governmental agency; or (v) it is voluntarily furnished to others by the party owning such Confidential Information without restriction on disclosure.

7. Upon a disclosing party's request for termination of negotiations or discussions, the receiving party shall voluntary surrender all Confidential Information to the disclosing party that is in the receiving party's possession, custody, or control.

8. The receiving party acknowledges and agrees that neither the disclosing party nor its Related Parties has made or will make any representations concerning the accuracy or completeness of the Confidential Information, and that neither the disclosing party nor any Related Party shall have any liability to the receiving party resulting from the receiving party's authorized use of Confidential Information.

9. The receiving party shall not use the names, trade names, service marks, trademarks, trade dress, or logos of the disclosing party in publicity releases, advertising, or any other external communications or publics disclosures without the disclosing party's prior written consent.

10. The Agreement is effective as of the Effective Date and shall continue in full force and effect for a period of one (1) year or such longer time as mutually agree to in writing by all the parties. In addition, the rights and obligations under this Agreement shall survive the termination of this Agreement for a period of two (2) years.

11. In evaluating, negotiating, or discussing the Proposed Business Agreement, or in performing its obligations under any agreement to consummate the agreement, each party shall act solely in the capacity of an independent contractor and not as an agent, employee, or representative of the other party or any Related Parties. Consequently, each party will not have, and will not make any statement or take any action that might cause any third party to believe the other party has, the authority to

transact any business, enter any agreement, or in any way bind or make any commitment on the behalf of the first party or any Related Parties unless expressly authorized in writing by a duly authorized officer of the first party.

12. No delay or omission by a party to exercise any right occurring upon noncompliance or default by the other party with respect to any of the terms of this Agreement shall impair any such right or be construed to be a waiver thereof. A waiver by a party of any of the provisions of this Agreement shall not be construed to be a waiver of any succeeding breach thereof or any other provision.

13. This Agreement shall be construed in accordance with the laws of the State of _____ (list a state as agreed to by the parties).

14. Any dispute claim or controversy arising out of or relating to this Agreement shall be fully and finally resolved by arbitrations in accordance with the rules of the American Arbitration Association.

15. This Agreement constitutes the entire Agreement between the parties with respect to its subject matter, and there are no understandings or agreements relative to that subject matter other than those that are explicitly expressed herein.

16. The parties understand and agree that the rights and obligations under this Agreement may be sold, assigned, or transferred by either party only upon written consent of a duly authorized officer from each party.

17. Nothing in this Agreement shall obligate either of the parties to consummate the Proposed Business Agreement or otherwise enter into any business relationship. Each party claims and reserves the right, in its sole discretion and judgment, to terminate all negotiations and discussions with the other.

In Witness whereof, the parties have caused the Agreement to be executed by their duly authorized officers as set forth below.

First party name	Second party name
By: _____	By: _____
Name: _____	Name: _____
Title: _____	Title: _____

Third party name

By: _____

Name: _____

Title: _____

Appendix D

WEB ADDRESSES FOR INVENTOR STORIES

Inventors are listed in the order in which they appear in the book.

Dan Tribastone, inventor of the Omni-Jug, storage container for fluids used in orthopedic surgery.
www.entrepreneur.com/article/0,4621,299050,00.html

Kelly Greene, inventor of the SwimCords, which allow swimmers to exercise in a small pool area by swimming in place.
www.entrepreneur.com/article/0,4621,289536,00.html

Ross Youngs, inventor of the UniKeep three-ring binder.
www.entrepreneur.com/article/0,4621,314282,00.html

Dan Schlueter and **Russell Schlueter,** creators of a new type of kitty litter.
www.entrepreneur.com/article/0,4621,300831,00.html

Stephanie Kellar, inventor of a new-style, nonpinching eyelash curler.
www.entrepreneur.com/article/0,4621,299768,00.html

Bob Olodort, inventor of the Stowaway Keyboard, a full-size folding portable keyboard for use with personal digital assistants (PDAs).
www.entrepreneur.com/article/0,4621,311092,00.html

Joanne Johnson, Marcel Sbrollini, and **Rod Sprules,** founders of Robustion Products, which sells the Java-Log, a fireplace log made of coffee grounds.
www.entrepreneur.com/article/0,4621,316080,00.html

Marlene Carlson, inventor of Puzzle Toe shoes for toddlers.
www.entrepreneur.com/article/0,4621,311587,00.html

Michael Karyo, product entrepreneur who introduced silicone cookware.
www.entrepreneur.com/article/0,4621,316812,00.html

Kristin Penta, started Fun Cosmetics Inc., which sells Penta's new
cosmetic creations for teenage girls.
www.entrepreneur.com/article/0,4621,271099,00.html

James and Anthony Tiscione, product creators of the Auto Card
Manager, a convenient credit card holder.
www.entrepreneur.com/article/0,4621,306830,00.html

Vic Pella, creator of four millennium-2000 novelty products that
launched in the spring of 1999.
www.entrepreneur.com/article/0,4621,230513,00.html

Jack Panzarella, creator of under-car-mounted neon lights to showcase
"hot" cars.
www.entrepreneur.com/article/0,4621,232590,00.html

Bob Evans, creator of the V-shaped Force Fins for divers, which he
parlayed into 20 years of product innovation.
www.entrepreneur.com/article/0,4621,309533,00.html

Devee Govrik, creator of the Junk Drawer Organizer.
www.entrepreneur.com/article/0,4621,227945,00.html

Karen Alvarez, creator of the Baby Strap, which holds babies securely in
shopping carts.
www.babycomfort.com/ent.html

Candace Vanice, creator of fat-free french fires.
www.entrepreneur.com/article/0,4621,231151,00.html

Jason Lee and **Patrick McConnell,** inventors of the MountainBoard,
which is a snowboard on all-terrain wheels for riding down
mountains in the summer.
www.entrepreneur.com/article/0,4621,276092,00.html

Tim Abbot, creator of garden edging that doubles as a hose for easy
watering.
www.nd.edu/~cba/011221/press/2004/09_hayes_entrepreneurship
.shtml

Fred Fink, inventor of a new automotive tool to hold up a car hood once
the hood springs fail.
www.entrepreneur.com/article/0,4621,229266,00.html

Stanley Hochfield, inventor of the GustBuster golf umbrellas, which can
withstand winds of more than 60 miles an hour without damage.
www.travelite.org/issues/2000sp/gustbuster.html

Mary Ellroy, founder of Gamebird LLC in Norwalk, Connecticut, and a
prolific toy and game inventor; creator of the Great States game.
www.entrepreneur.com/article/0,4621,308047,00.html

Cassie Quinn, creator of a more versatile diaper bag.
www.entrepreneur.com/article/0,4621,229919,00.html

Gary Kellmann, creator of the Hair Holder Holder, a device for holding
hair products, as well as several products targeted specifically to
preteen girls.
www.entrepreneur.com/article/0,4621,230025,00.html

Nathaniel Weiss, inventor of the G-Vox Interactive Music System, which
transposes notes being played by a musician into a music score on a
computer.
www.entrepreneur.com/mag/article/0,1539,231845,00.html

Stephanie Heroff, inventor of the spaghetti-strap summer top with
sewn-in bra straps.
www.entrepreneur.com/article/0,4621,281306,00.html

Vijay Malek, creator of storage products, including Hang 10, a wall holder
for up to 10 CDs, which is sold in supermarkets and drugstores.
www.entrepreneur.com/mag/article/0,1539,230908,00.html

Mike Mogadam, inventor of Barmate, a liquor-control system for bars
and restaurants.
www.entrepreneur.com/article/print/0,2361,230081,00.html

Dale Carsel and **Bob Schneider,** creators of the Sponge Prince, a faux
finishing pattern sponge.
www.entrepreneur.com/article/0,4621,290431,00.html

Joe Robertson and **Dave Dudley,** inventors of the Spin Clean, a system
designed to quickly clean pool filters.
www.entrepreneur.com/article/0,4621,291290,00.html

Wayne Willert, creator of the Gutter-Bolt, an aluminum bolt that doesn't
bend or break when hammered into a home's wood fascia.
www.entrepreneur.com/article/0,4621,315722,00.html

Carl Vanderschuit, inventor of Litecubes, freezable cubes with an
enclosed LED light and battery.
www.entrepreneur.com/article/0,4621,302504,00.html

Go to www.dondebelak.com for a list of more than 50 inventor stories that have not been featured in this book.

GLOSSARY

accredited investors: Investors who make more than $200,000 annually for their previous two years and have expectation of making $200,000 the following year, or those who have assets worth more than $1 million. Nonaccredited investors don't meet either of these requirements.

amortize: To turn a large payment into a series of smaller payments. For example, if a $10,000 tooling charge is amortized into the cost of 100,000 production parts, $0.10 extra, referred to as a *per-unit surcharge,* will be charged on every part until 100,000 units are produced.

back orders: Orders that are not shipped on time. For example, if normal delivery is two weeks and an order can't be shipped for eight weeks, then the order would be identified as a back order.

bill of materials: A document that shows all of the parts and materials in a product, usually by sub assemblies.

blister pack: A piece of clear hard, molded plastic that is glued to a paperboard backing. A popular package especially for small products as the product is easy to see but still protected from damage or theft.

brand name: Any proprietary product or company name. Examples are Pillsbury, Betty Crocker, Mr. Coffee, Toro, and Sony.

branding: A strategy marketers use to make their name known to end users, through advertising and promotion, by prominent placement of the product's name on the product and package, or by developing a unified look in the company's product line.

bridge financing: Provides funding to a company while a company is in the process of raising money. Typically, a loan will be repaid with interest, with the possibility of a bonus of stock warrants or options. The loan is repaid once the fund-raising round is complete.

buying groups: Organizations that buy products for many small retailers. They are able to negotiate better pricing and terms by pooling their retail client's buying power. They typically buy for anywhere from 250 to 500 stores.

cannibalizing: The practice of taking one product apart so that its parts can be used to make another product.

card pack: A package containing 15 to 120 postcards that advertise products or services to be mailed to a targeted list of potential customers.

cavity: A part of a mold that can produce one part. Injection-molded parts are typically produced from two-, four-, or six-cavity molds, which means that two, four, or six products can be manufactured at once.

claims: The part of a patent that defines the boundaries of a product's patent protections.

clip art: Pictures or drawings of people, places, or events that can be cut out and used for sales flyers or promotional libraries. Books of clip art are available at art and office supply stores or online. You can locate many clip art services on the Internet by entering the term "clip art" into any Internet search engine.

consignment: Giving a product at no charge to a store, sales representative, or dealer, with the understanding that the product will either be returned at a later date or paid for when it is sold.

contract manufacturer: A manufacturer that agrees to make another manufacturer's, marketer's, or inventor's product for a fee.

co-op advertising: A promotional program in which manufacturers and retailers or distributors split the costs of ads, mailings, or catalogs that promote the manufacturer's products. A co-op advertising allowance is the percentage of a customer's purchase that a manufacturer will pay toward the costs of ads, mailing, or catalogs. For instance, when a manufacturer offers a 10 percent co-op advertising allowance, it will pay a dollar amount equal to 10 percent of the retailer's purchases for ads and other promotions.

copy: All the words used in an ad, on a package, or with promotional display.

copyright: The legal right granted to exclusively publish, distribute, sell, and produce an artistic work, which in some cases can include a product's artistic look.

direct mail: Any type of promotion in which materials are mailed or delivered to homes, apartments, or businesses.

distributor: A company that buys products from suppliers and later resells them to retailers, other companies, or consumers. A distributor owns the products it sells, in contrast to a manufacturer's representative, who never buys the product.

due diligence: A thorough evaluation of a company completed by an investor or venture capitalist prior to deciding whether to invest in a company.

factoring: The practice of selling receivables for immediate cash. For example, if a manufacturer ships a $20,000 order to a customer, that manufacture issues an invoice, which means it is owed money or expects to receive money for the shipment, which is why an invoice is called a *receivable*. If the manufacturer needs immediate cash, it will sell the receivable to a factoring company, usually a commercial finance company. The charge for factoring ranges from 4 to 10 percent of the value of the receivable.

first to invent: As of 2004, U.S. patent law is based on the first-to-invent concept. In the case of several people applying for similar patents, the person who can document that he or she had the idea first will be awarded the patent. Most of the rest of the world uses a first-to-patent system, which means the patent goes to the party who applies first. There is a strong push from companies in the United States to switch to a first-to-patent system, but to date those efforts have been unsuccessful.

focus group: A market research term for a group of 5 to 15 people brought together for the purpose of evaluating a product, a marketing strategy, various packages, or any other aspect of a company's product design or marketing programs.

four-color artwork: Another term for full-color artwork. Printing is done with only black, yellow, red, and blue ink. All other colors are produced by combining these four basic colors. One-color artwork means only one color of ink is used. Four-color artwork is expensive because it requires a color separation process (which turns a photograph into four printing plates, one for each color ink) and a large printing press.

guaranteed sales: A manufacturer's or distributor's commitment to issue a credit for any unsold and returned merchandise.

incremental costs: The actual extra spending a company has when doing a project. If a manufacturer who makes a prototype for you has a model maker on staff, incremental costs will be for only materials used, since the manufacturer is already paying the model-maker's salary.

injection molding: A common method for producing small to midsized plastic parts. An injection-molding machine shoots molten plastic into a mold, cures it so that it becomes solid, and then pops the part out of the mold. Ideal for high-volume, automated production. The process has high start-up costs because of expensive tooling charges.

in-kind investments: Investments consisting of free service or materials rather than cash. Examples are free rent, working without pay, or a manufacturer allowing an inventor to use its prototype shop.

intellectual property: A product of the intellect that can be exclusively owned by a person or company, who can then restrict others from using that property. In the United States, patents, trademarks, and copyrights are the only types of intellectual property allowed by law.

invention: A new device, method, or process that has resulted from study or experimentation.

job shop: A company that doesn't have any of its own products but instead produces products for other manufacturers, marketers, and inventors. Job shops are similar to contract manufacturers, the only difference being that contract manufacturers will usually have some of their own products.

lead time: How long it will take to deliver a product. If you are producing your product overseas, you might have a 14- to 16-week lead; if you produce in the United States, your lead time might be 2 to 4 weeks.

letter of credit: A statement from a bank that it will transfer money to a supplier's bank once a shipment has been received. Sometimes required by overseas suppliers before they will ship products. Before a letter of credit will be issued, a marketer or inventor needs either a line of credit with a bank or an escrow account equal to the amount of the letter of credit.

license: A contract arrangement in which an inventor agrees to allow a manufacturer to produce his or her idea in return for a *royalty* (a predetermined share of the manufacturer's sales dollars). A 5 percent royalty based on sales will give an inventor an amount equal to 5 percent of a company's net sales of the inventor's product.

manufacturer's representative: Also called a *sales agent*. A person who acts as a sales representative for several manufacturers, never taking possession of the product but instead funneling orders to the manufacturers in return for a commission (usually 5 to 15 percent). Companies whose sales are too low to justify having their own sales force use manufacturer's representatives.

margins: Gross margins are the percentage of gross profit that a company makes on every sales dollar before taking into account administrative, sales, marketing, and general expenses. Gross profit margin is equal to the selling price minus the manufacturing cost divided by the selling price times 100 percent. Net margin is the selling price minus all costs (manufacturing, marketing, administrative, etc.) divided by the selling price:

$$\text{Gross margin} = \frac{\text{selling price} - \text{manufacturing cost} \times 100\%}{\text{selling price}}$$

markup: The percentage by which a retailer or distributor increases the price of a product. If a retailer buys a product for \$1 and sells the product for \$2, the product has a 100 percent markup.

$$\text{Markup} = \frac{\text{dollar increase in the product's price by retailer or distributor} \times 100\%}{\text{purchase price paid by the retailer or distributor}}$$

mock-up: A crude model of a product that helps an inventor visualize what the final product might look like. Often made out of cardboard, papier-mâché, or another easily shaped material.

model: A representation of what the product will be like (usually structurally sound and functionally similar to a production unit). A model is different from a prototype in that it will not be quite like the final product; It may have different materials, a different size, or a different feature. A prototype is very close to, if not exactly like, the final product.

original equipment manufacture (OEM): Companies that produce their own products from components, some of which may be supplied by inventors. An automotive manufacturer like GM is an OEM. An inventor who supplies a mechanism for tilt steering wheels is an OEM supplier because his or her product is sold only to the OEM, not to the to end users.

option: A right to buy shares of a company at a specified price. Options often have a time period associated with them, but it can be long, sometimes from three to five years.

outsourced company: Before the days of the Internet, called a *virtual company*. A company that outsources most if not all of its functions, including manufacturing, R&D, customer service, and sometimes sales and marketing.

overhead: Any expense that occurs regularly—rent, administrative salaries, utilities, telephone, and Internet fees. Also referred to as *fixed costs*.

patents: An exclusive right granted by the government to inventors to protect their invention. *Utility patents* are related to how a product is built and works. *Design patents* are related to how a product looks, and a *process patent* is related to how a product is produced (e.g., chemical or pharmaceutical processes).

payback period: The time it takes to produce profits equal to or greater than the money invested. If an inventor and his or her investors spend $50,000 to launch a product and they produce $50,000 worth of profits in 18 months, then the product has an 18-month payback period.

per-unit surcharge: Often used with amortization agreements. A charge by which a contract manufacturer recovers tooling or other costs. If a manufacturer has absorbed $10,000 in up-front setup costs, those costs might be recovered by charging a $0.25 per unit surcharge over and above the product's manufacturing cost.

point-of-purchase display: A display that either holds your product or is placed near your product to catch customers' attention and sell the benefits of the product.

positioning: A marketing term that relates to the practice of adding features and benefits to a product so that target customers will perceive it in a certain way, such as technologically advanced or as a value leader.

private-label agreement: A manufacturer's production of an item that is then sold under another company's name. For example, manufacturers that make the products sold under the Sears brand name are producing a private-label product.

prior art: Describes previous patents or products that are somewhat similar to yours. If you create a new style of coffeemaker, all previous coffeemakers would be considered prior art.

private-placement memorandum: A legal document used by small companies raising money and often required by law when companies have more than 10 nonaccredited investors.

pro forma: A projected income and cash flow statement. Most loan documents require an income and cash flow statement projected at least 12 months into the future.

promotional allowance: A type of price discount that pays for a customer's promotional programs. A 10 percent promotional allowance, for instance, gives a retailer reimbursement for its promotional costs for a particular product equal to 10 percent of the retailer's purchases of that product.

prototypes: A sample of what a product will look like once its produced. Prototypes are usually manufactured with a different technique than the one that will be used to manufacture the final product.

public domain: When an idea becomes known to the public it is said to be in the public domain, and it loses its confidential status. Selling the product, publishing press releases, and attending trade shows are means of placing a product into the public domain.

rack jobber: A distributor who contracts with stores to furnish all of a certain type of product, such as hair care products, nails and screws, stationery products, or toys. Rack jobbers typically can put whatever products they want on their shelf space, but they agree to charge the store only for what is sold. Rack jobbers may need to pay the retailer to rent space for its products.

receivables: The money that is owed by customers to a manufacturer, marketer, or distributor.

right of first refusal: A contract term that offers one party to a contract the right to match any offer from another person or company to the other party in the contract. For example, a company might have the right to match a license agreement from another company in return for a $20,000 advance.

royalty: A payment made to an inventor or a company with a product or technology in return for the right to produce that product.

slotting allowance: A payment to a store that a store might require before offering shelf space to the marketer or manufacturer.

subscription agreement: A formal document whereby a private company sells stock to investors. The agreement must comply with security agreements for formal stock offerings. Use a lawyer to draw up formal agreements when you sell stock.

temporary tooling: Tooling that is expected to last for only a short production run.

terms: A period of days after which a payment is due. For example, "30-day term" means payment is due for a product or service 30 days after the product is shipped or the service provided.

trade dress: Refers to the look of a product or its package. Competitors are not allowed to have a product that violates another's trade dress, which means that the product looks enough like the other product or package to confuse buyers.

trade secret: A secret method of producing something that is not patented but instead is protected by employees signing confidentiality agreements and by limiting access to the secret process.

trademark: A protected name or symbol identifying a company or product, officially licensed to the owner and manufacturer.

turnover: How long it takes a store to sell its inventory. If a store sells out of a product in two months, then the product has a two-month turnover.

wholesale price: The price at which a product is sold to distributors.

RESOURCES

AGREEMENTS

www.allbusiness.com. Site contains sample business agreements, letters of intent, term sheets, employment forms, and many other useful forms.
www.legalforms.com, www.findlegalforms.com, www.lawdepot.com, www .amerilawyer.com, www.findlaw.com. Sites with legal forms, including stock sales agreements.

BOOKS, GENERAL

Why Didn't I Think of That: Bizarre Origins of Ingenious Inventions We Couldn't Live Without by Allyn Freeman and Bob Golden (John Wiley & Sons, 1997), www.wiley.com. This book covers the origins of 50, mostly famous, inventions from the Barbie doll to the Singer sewing machine. They all started with rather humble beginnings from everyday people.
The Deviant's Advantage: How Fringe Ideas Create Mass Markets by Ryan Matthews and Watts Wacker (Crown Business, 2002) Read this book anytime you start thinking a lone, underfinanced inventor can't make a difference.

BUSINESS ASSISTANCE

www.sba.gov/sbdc/. Locations of local Small Business Development Centers (SBDCs). Offers a listing of all the SBDC centers in the United States.

www.smallbusiness.dnb.com, the web site for Dun and Bradstreet credit reports, and www.knowx.com/db/search.jsp are both sites with information on the credit ratings of most companies.

www.sbaonline.gov/gopher/Local-Information/Service-Corps-of-Retired-Executives. Site lists local chapters of Service Corps of Retired Executives (SCORE) throughout the country.

BUSINESS INFORMATION

Almanac of Business and Industrial Financial Ratios by Leo Troy (Aspen Publications, 2002), www.aspenpublishers.com. Book provides lists of operating ratios for different types of businesses. Book is helpful guide to what other businesses make as a percentage of sales of similar products. Helps inventors understand some of the costs, such as scrap, bad debt, and administrative expenses, that they might otherwise overlook.

www.business.com. A good site for all types of business searches, including product category searches and financial and product line information about numerous companies.

www.findarticles.com, www.magportal.com, and www.newspaperarchives.com. All are web sites you can use to locate magazine and newspaper articles.

Gale's Source of Publications and Broadcast Media. This reference book is available at most larger libraries. It has an index of trade magazines, by category, so you can find the trade magazine for the industry related to your product idea.

Gale's Book of Associations. Available at many larger libraries, this is the reference source for finding trade associations for your industry.

www.trainingdialo.com/quicksolutions/4916.html. This is a web site for Thompson Dialog and is by far the best site I've found for generating company information quickly and easily. A little difficult to use at first, but once you have the routine down you can find company information in one to two minutes. Excellent site.

Other business information sites: www.hoover.com, www.bemis.com, and dir.yahoo.com/Business_and_Economy/Directory/Company.

CATALOGS

www.buyersindex.com. Search engine for 20,000 Web shopping sites and hundreds of mail order catalogs.

www.Dir.Yahoo.com/Business_and_Economy/Shopping_and_Services/Retailer/directories/Catalogs. This site has an excellent search engine for mail order catalogs and online retailers.

catalogs.google.com, www.homeshoppingguide.com, and www.shopathome .com. Great web sites to find lists of mail order catalogs.

CREATIVITY

www.creativityatwork.com. Site contains a newsletter about creating new products in the workplace, but many of the articles are useful to individual inventors.

www.creativityforlife.com. Has an online newsletter for using brainstorming and other strategies for thinking outside the box.

www.inventors.com. Includes many intriguing stories about how people use their ingenuity to find or create innovative product ideas.

www.slyasafox.com. This site has a free download of a 90-page booklet on creativity as it relates to new-product ideas. Contains exercises and a creativity toolbox that helps people see different ways to look for new-product ideas.

DIRECT RESPONSE TV

www.responsemag.com. The web site of *Response* magazine, which is the leading magazine for electronic direct marketing professionals. It covers the infomercial and short, one- to three-minute ad formats and home shopping networks.

Companies that license products that can be sold on TV:

Hawthorne Direct, www.hawthornedirect.com

Retail Distribution, LLC, www.dtrtv.com

Telebrands, www.telebrands.com

TriStar Products, Inc. www.tristarpeoductsinc.com

FINANCING

Angel Investors: Matching Startup Funds with Startup Companies—A Guide for Entrepreneurs, Individual Investors and Venture Capitalists by Mark Van Osnabrugge and Robert J. Robinson (Jossey-Bass, 2000). Helps you understand some of the legal ramifications and approaches you can take with industry helpers as well as family and friend investors.

Attracting Capital from Angels: How Their Money and Experience Can Help You Build a Successful Company, by Brian Hill and Dee Power (John Wiley & Sons, 2002). Great book on attracting angel investments, but it also includes excellent advice on making presentations (which is also applicable for attracting investments, manufacturers, and distributor companies).

http://directory.google.com/Top/Business/Financial_Services/Venture _Capital/Resources_for_Entrepreneurs/Conferences/. Google keeps an excellent current directory of all the upcoming venture conferences with their web sites for registration. You should check it regularly to see whether any conferences are coming to your area.

Finding Money for Your Small Business: The One-Stop Guide to Raising All the Money Your Business Will Need by Max Fallet and Kris Solie-Johnson (American Institute of Small Business, 2003). Lists more than 50 sources of funding and the steps you need to take to access that funding.

How to Finance Your Invention of Great Idea by Jack Lander (Exponent Publishing Company, 2004). Book is especially targeted at raising the initial money inventors need to get started.

www.zeromillion.com/resources. Web site provides information on starting a company and raising money. Has an excellent list of resources regarding most aspects of business operations.

INTERNET SALES

101 Ways to Promote Your Web Site: Filled with Proven Marketing Tips, Tools, Techniques and Resources to Increase Your Web Site Traffic by Susan Sweeney (Maximum Press, 2003). Lots of tips on getting your web site noticed that work well for small, one-product companies.

Information on selling on eBay. www.Auctioninsights.com/auction.seelers .html, www.mistupid.com/tutorials/ebay and www.ebay.com/help/ sell/fees/html.

Mompreneurs Online: Using the Internet to Build Work@Home Success by Patricia Cole and Ellen Parlapiano (Berkley Publishing, 2001). Book explains lots of Web-building strategies that are ideal for an inventor just starting out.

Striking it Rich.com by Jaclyn Easton (McGraw Hill, 2000). Profiles of 23 successful web sites. Shows how to set up a web site that will really build traffic.

INVENTOR SITES

www.baylor.edu/entrpreneur. Web site from Baylor University's John F. Baugh Center for entrepreneurship offers another method of product evaluation.

www.invent.org. Web site of the National Inventors Hall of Fame in Akron, Ohio. Site includes a short online workshop on the patenting process. Offers inventors a good overview of the patenting process.

www.inventorsdigest.com. Web site for the bimonthly *Inventor's Digest* magazine. Site contains past articles, many of which deal with the subject of creativity and new-product idea evaluation. A good source for books, services, and software related to inventors.

www.patentcafe.com. Includes general patent advice, a directory of services, discussion groups, and a patent newsletter. The best site for keeping track of upcoming changes in patent law.

www.tenonline.org. Contains a list of potential partners, collaborators, and vendors that could help inventors put their product on the market. Also includes a listing of companies looking for new ideas.

www.uiausa.com. Web site for the United Inventors Association. Contains helpful articles and referral sources for inventors starting out. Also has a list of inventor clubs. Inventor clubs typically meet monthly and can be helpful to both new and experienced inventors.

web.mit.edu/invent. Web site features an online inventors' workbook that's useful for all inventors, no matter what their experience level.

LICENSING

License Your Invention: Sell Your Idea and Protect Your Rights with a Solid Contract by Richard Stim (Nolo Press, 2004). This book covers the process of licensing once you have an interested licensee. Includes a CD with several licensing forms and contracts you can use in your own negotiations.

www.usa-canada-les.org. Web site of the Licensing Executives Society of the United States and Canada, a group of leading licensing professionals. The site includes a calendar of events, list of local chapters, and educational materials. The Society also publishes a newsletter and magazine.

MANUFACTURING

www.jobshoptechnology.com. Web site for *Job Shop Technology* magazine. Job shops are firms that make small to midsize production runs for other companies and often specialize with design assistance for new products. Great source for finding a manufacturer, and articles are also useful to learn about manufacturing processes. *Job Shop Technology* also has frequent regional shows where manufacturers who are looking for new products run exhibits.

Manufacturing Processes Reference Guide (Industrial Press, ed. 1, May 1, 1994) by Robert H. Todd, Dell K. Allen, and Leo Alting. This guide offers brief descriptions of 130 manufacturing processes. Includes numerous tables and illustrations.

www.mfgquote.com, www.chinzbiz/com, www.outsourceking.com, www.ec21.com. Web sites that offer overseas product pricing information.

www.morganindustries.com. Morgan Industries produces small prototype and short-run injection molding machines.

www.thomasregister.com. *The Thomas Register of American Manufacturers* is the most comprehensive directory of its kind. This multivolume set of large green books is found in the reference section of most libraries.

MARKET RESEARCH

www.prodcutscan.com. Web site of Market Intelligence Service. Tracks most new consumer-packaged products and yearly announces its pick of the 10 most innovative products on the market. Newsletters online plus announcements regarding new products.

MARKETING HELP

www.accudat.com. ACCU Data, 4210 Metro Parkway, Suite 300, Fort Meyers, FL 33916. Source of mailing lists.

www.plma.com. Private Label Manufacturers Association site.

www.privatelabelbuyer.com. Web site for *PL Buyer* magazine, a leading source information on the private label business.

www.profuturists.com. Site of the Association of Professional Futurists, who provide insight into future market trends long before they develop. Good site to visit to help you think about trends that might offer market opportunities.

www.tsnn.com. Web site with comprehensive lists of trade shows for most industries. I've found the site as helpful as some of the larger trade show directories that reside in the reference section of larger libraries.

info@us-council.org, www.uc-council.org. Uniform Code, Council, Inc., Princeton Pike Corporate Center, 7887 Washington Village Drive Suite 300, Dayton, OH 454459, phone 937-435-3870, fax 937-435-7317.

www.wholesaledistributorsnet.com. Listings of manufacturers, wholesalers, and distributors for many leading consumer markets.

NETWORKING

How to Work a Room: The Ultimate Guide to Savvy Socializing in Person and Online by Susan RoAne. This is the book for you if you have trouble starting a conversation at an industry event or with a new contact. Shows you how to sell yourself to people you meet who might be able to help you.

Nonstop Networking: How to Improve Your Life, Luck and Career by Andrea R. Nierenberg (Capital Books, 2002). You never stop networking for contacts once you enter the inventor's world, and this is a good book for making contacts and building relationships that allow you to keep going back to your contacts for help.

OVERSEAS SOURCES

www.mfgquote.com, www.chinzbiz/com, www.outsourceking.com, www.ec21.com. Web sites that offer overseas product pricing information.

www.hometwon.aol.com/egtgolbaltrading.com, www.acessasia.com. www
.deltechusa.com, and www.opsaamerica.com. Overseas sourcing agents.

www.mfgquote.com, www.chinabiz.com, www.ooutsourceking.com, www
.ec21.com, www.chinafacturing.com, and www.rockleighindustries.com.
Overseas manufacturing sourcing web sites.

PATENTS AND TRADEMARKS

How to Make Patent Drawings Yourself, by Jack Lo and David Pressman (Nolo
Press, 1999). You might save money doing the patent drawings yourself, even if you use a patent attorney or agent. Doing the drawings
yourself also helps you better understand your product concept.
Doing your own drawings is especially useful if you do a provisional
patent yourself.

www.cleansweepsupply.com and www.eurekalabook.com. Sources for inventor's notebooks, the best way to document your invention and its
progress. Usually accepted as evidence in patent disputes regarding
invention dates.

Patent It Yourself: Everything You Need to Create a Successful Patent Application,
ed. 10, by David Pressman (Nolo Press, 2004). This book by a patent
attorney has had 10 editions over a period of 20 years and is the most
widely used reference book on do-it-yourself patent applications. Available at most larger libraries.

The Patent Process: A Guide Intellectual Property for the Information Age by Craig
Hovey (John Wiley & Sons, 2002). This book offers an overview of the
world of intellectual property and explains the practical use of patents
as a resource for your business.

The Trademark Registration Kit: Register Your Trademark without a Lawyer by
Patricia Gima and Stephen Elias (Nolo Press, 1999). Trademarks are easier to do on your own than a patent, and this book shows you how to do
each step.

www.upsto.gov. Web site of the UP Patent Office. Has links to the Office for
the Independent Inventor, which is loaded with good resources to
understand the patent process. Patent Office also has a wide selection of
low-cost pamphlets explaining the patents and trademarks.

www.uspto.gov/web/offices/pacdisdo.html. Web site for the U.S. Patent
Office's low-cost Document Disclosure Program, which is designed to
help inventors document the date they invented their idea.

wsj.nameprotect.com. A service of the *Wall Street Journal* that allows inventors
to do a trademark search for any of their potential product names. A useful service to avoid starting out with a product name that has been
trademarked by someone else.

PRESENTATIONS

www.impactengine.com, www.infommersion.com, www.speaksmart.com.
Three Web pages that offer software and/or advice on how to make

effective presentations. Highly recommended if you haven't made presentations previously.

PRODUCT DESIGN

Design Secrets: Products: 50 Real Life Product Design Projects by the Industrial Designers Society of America (Rockport Publishers, 2001), www.rockpub .com. A good background book in how to give products a look that makes them appear special. The book is written more for company engineers, but I think it is useful for anyone in the invention game.

www.idsa.com. Web site of the Industrial Designer Society of America. Industrial designers create new product looks and new product functions for many big and medium-size company products. The Innovation Online newsletter on this site has tips on how to make your benefits obvious to your target customers, as well as the newest design trends that help give products a high-tech or modern appearance.

PRODUCT EVALUATIONS

www.dondebelak.com. This inventor help web site offers a product evaluation service that recommends the best invention introduction approach based on the inventor's capabilities and the product idea itself.

www.evaluation.patentcafe.com. Web site devoted to inventors, especially patent information for inventors. Includes an evaluation service targeted at inventors looking to license their product to a big company.

www.innovation-institute.com. Web site for the Wal-Mart Innovation Center, which evaluates products based on more than 30 criteria. Products that score well are eligible for presentation to Wal-Mart.

Other inventor evaluation sites: www.cbe.wsu.edu, Washington State University evaluation site; www.innovationcentre.ca, web site of the Canadian Innovation Center; and academics.uww.edu/BUSINESS/innovate/ innovate.htm, the web site of the University of Wisconsin Whitewater innovation center.

PROTOTYPES

www.dremel.com. Dremel, Division of Emerson Electric, 4915 21st Street, Racine, WI 53406. Source of miniature power tools that are handy for prototypes.

www.edsci.com. Edmond Scientific Company. Great catalog and web site for small motors, optical parts, and otherwise hard-to-find parts.

www.finecale.com. Web site of the *FineScale Modeler* magazine, which contains numerous ads for small parts and small-scale modeling equipment.

www.hysol.com. Hysol Electronic Chemicals. Supplier of casting and laminating compounds that are ideal for an inventor.

www.inventorhelp.com. Site of Jack Lander, who writes a column on prototyping for *Inventors' Digest* magazine (www.inventorsdigest.com). His site sells inexpensive reports, including *How to Cast Your Own Plastic Parts at Room Temperature Without Expensive Equipment* and *How to Make Drawings for Purchasing Prototypes.*

www.mcmastercarr.com. McMaster-Carr Supply Company. This is one of the largest national suppliers of a wide variety of industrial products, with offices in most midsize and large cities.

www.micromart.com. Web site of Micromart, a company with a wide range of modeling tools.

www.polytek.com. Polytek Development Corporation. Provides polymers for plastic molding. The catalog is well worth its $10 price because it includes a minicourse on plastic molding.

www.processregister.com/cadillac_plastic_and_chemical/supplies/sid109 .htm. Cadillac Plastics. The company has retail stores in most large cities throughout the country. Free catalog. Cadillac fabricates as well as supplies stock plastics. Phone 800-274-1000.

www.reproduce100s.com. Source of information on making silicone molds. The site is for the video/workbook combination *Reproduce Almost Anything,* an excellent book and video by Ben Ridge.

SALES AGENTS

www.douglaspublication.com. Lists of distributors, rack jobbers, and manufacturer's representatives for many different industries. The books are expensive, $220 to $400, but they are available in resource sections of large libraries.

www.manaonline.org. Web site of the Manufacturers' Agents National Association (MANA), includes a list of manufacturer's sales agents, also called manufacturer's representatives.

www.vmwininc.com/repsourcehome.html. Listing of manufacturer's representatives by region and product line.

TOYS

www.playthings.com. Web site for *Playthings* magazine, the leading toy industry trade magazine. Publishes an annual buyer's guide each December.

The Toy and Game Inventor's Handbook: Everything You Need to Know to Pitch, License and Cash In on Your Ideas by Richard Levy and Ronald Weingartner (Alpha, 2003). This book is written by the developer of the Furby and former vice president of product acquisition at Hasbro. Highly recommended for toy inventors.

www.toysandgamesinventors.com. Web site of the Toy and Game Inventors of America, an organization committed to helping toy and game inventors put their products on the market.

www.toybok.com. Another leading toy industry magazine.

www.toy-tma.com. Web site of the Toy Manufacturers of America. Contains plenty of helpful tips and resources for inventors.

TV SHOPPING NETWORKS

www.HSN.com. Home Shopping Network site has vendor information button you can click on to watch a demo on how to get started. Site also has an information page on how to get your product onto HSN.

www.shopnbc.com. ShopNBC uses vendor fairs rather than formal submissions. Check the web site often to see what products ShopNBC is looking for and for the locations of its vendor fairs.

www.QVC.com. QVC web site. Check this one frequently. QVC travels around the country looking for inventor products to sell. It also has days when you can present ideas at company headquarters, which is outside of Philadelphia.

INDEX